WORDPLAY

WORDPLAY
A CURIOUS DICTIONARY
OF LANGUAGE ODDITIES

Chris Cole

Illustrated by Patrick Khan
Introduction by Will Shortz

Sterling Publishing Co., Inc.
New York

Library of Congress Cataloging-in-Publication Data

Cole, Chris.
    Wordplay : a curious dictionary of language oddities / Chris Cole ; illustrated
by Patrick Khan ; introduction by Will Shortz.
      p.   cm.
    Includes index.
    ISBN 0-8069-1797-0
    1. English language—Lexicology—Miscellanea. 2. English language—
Glossaries, vocabularies, etc. 3. Word games—Miscellanea   I. Title
PE1574.C594   1999
423'.028—dc21   99–22459
                                                          CIP

2 4 6 8 10 9 7 5 3 1

Published by Sterling Publishing Company, Inc.
387 Park Avenue South, New York, N.Y. 10016
© 1999 by Chris Cole
Distributed in Canada by Sterling Publishing
⅝ Canadian Manda Group, One Atlantic Avenue, Suite 105
Toronto, Ontario, Canada M6K 3E7
Distributed in Great Britain and Europe by Chris Lloyd
463 Ashley Road, Parkstone, Poole, Dorset, BH14 0AX, England
Distributed in Australia by Capricorn Link (Australia) Pty Ltd.
P.O. Box 6651, Baulkham Hills, Business Centre, NSW 2153, Australia

Sterling ISBN 0-8069-1797-0

CONTENTS

INTRODUCTION
By Will Shortz

It has been said that every word in the English language is interesting from some aspect of wordplay.

For example, take WRONGED. This is the longest word, without repeating letters, whose letters appear in reverse alphabetical order.

Or SEQUOIA. It is the shortest common word that contains all five vowels.

PARAPROFESSIONALS is the longest common word that can be written entirely as the symbols of chemical elements (PaRaPrOFeSSiONAlS).

PLUNDER is the longest word that becomes another word when said in pig Latin (UNDERPLAY).

Even something that's seemingly as unremarkable as MOTTO is interesting: It is the longest common word that, when written in Morse code, consists entirely of dashes (10 of them, to be precise).

Dmitri Borgmann, the founder of modern logology—the study of wordplay—used to claim that he could find something interesting to say about every English word.

Frankly, I'm a little dubious of this claim. As the English language contains upwards of 2 million words, I find it hard to believe that something truly interesting can be found in every one of them.

Surely, though, the person who would know is my friend Chris Cole. A professional software entrepreneur, he has worked in the field of linguistics and artificial intelligence for many years, electronically compiling (along the way) what he believes is the most complete list of English words ever assembled. He is a longtime member of the National Puzzlers' League, the archive director for the online forum rec.puzzles, and an avid reader/collector of recreational linguistics. He has devoted years to amassing distinctive examples of wordplay and testing their uniqueness via his computer database.

What you're holding is probably the ultimate browser's book on language oddities. Up front you'll find a list of wordplay records arranged by category (for example, longest common word containing only four consonants), with the known record holder in each one (in this case, ONOMATOPOEIA). In the back of the book you'll find the same information in the reverse order—the record-holding words, listed alphabetically, with an explanation of why each one is remarkable. Also scattered through the book you'll find articles and charts on various kinds of wordplay—palindromes, transposals, crashing words, and many more.

As a professional puzzlemaker, who specializes in wordplay myself, I wish that Chris Cole had given this book just to me and not shared it with anyone else. Then I would have had years' worth of fascinating, private material to spin puzzles from.

Unfortunately for me (and fortunately for you), he insists on sharing his discoveries with everyone. Oh well.

Happy browsing!

—Will Shortz

PREFACE

What Is Wordplay?

If you place a monkey in front of a machine that will dispense food two times out of three when a light blinks and a red button is pushed, and one time out of three when a green button is pushed, the monkey will try to figure out the pattern. A pigeon will not, and quickly will learn just to press the red button. It is interesting to note that if there is no pattern, that is, if the red button dispenses food a random two-thirds of the time, then the monkey will not win as often as the pigeon. However, if there is a pattern, say, the green button is active every third push, then the monkey will soon be winning every time.

Evolution has endowed the monkey with a pattern matching ability that the pigeon lacks. It is a common observation that pattern matching is one of the hallmarks of intelligence. It is at the root of science and art, and much of what passes for thinking is really finding the underlying pattern. But evolution cannot proceed without some mechanism for reinforcing adaptive behavior. The monkey must get a reinforcement for trying to figure out the pattern in the lights. Similarly, human beings get a feeling of pleasure when they perceive underlying patterns, but this feeling is largely unconscious and not easily noticed.

To see that this search for patterns occurs at the unconscious level, we need look no further than poetry. Why is poetry enjoyable? Clement Wood stated that "rhyming is a brain stimulant." When we read a poem, our minds unconsciously notice the pattern of rhyme or meter, and we feel a sensation of pleasure. Perceiving patterns is pleasing. This may also account for why it is addictive to watch random processes like waves breaking on a beach or flames licking in a fireplace; the brain is unconsciously absorbed with trying to perceive a pattern, and the eyes cannot look away.

What does this have to do with wordplay? Wordplay, like poetry, is the perception of patterns where none were expected. Consider the word "deified." Did you immediately notice that it is spelled the same forward and backward? Or consider the word "abscond." Do you feel there is something odd about the word? Four of its seven letters are the first four letters of the alphabet. These patterns have nothing to do with the meaning of the words; they are free morsels of pattern floating on the sea of random spelling. Noticing them is like getting a free lunch.

It is therefore not surprising to learn that wordplay is as old as language, and that its origins are lost in the mists of time. We do know that the few snippets of Greek comedy that have survived the conflagrations of history are rife with wordplay. Aristophanes was fond of coining long words, for example, and *The Ecclesiazusae* contains a 185-letter word for hash. The Romans constructed the palindromic word square:

S A T O R
A R E P O
T E N E T
O P E R A
R O T A S

Historically, wordplay has as many forms as there are patterns in a random sequence, which is to say, a very large number. The challenge becomes how to organize all of the ways that words can be fascinating.

What Is in This Book?

This is a new kind of book, a dictionary not of word meanings but of wordplay. This book contains thousands of words that have unusual properties. Some of these words are spelled with surprising patterns; some are pronounced in unusual ways; some have interesting origins; some have unusual meanings;

some are members of groups of words which, taken together, have strange relationships.

The book is divided into four sections. The first section contains a glossary of wordplay terms. You'll need to familiarize yourself with these terms to fully appreciate this book.

The second section contains a taxonomy of wordplay. Here you can explore many of the forms of wordplay and how they are related to one another. If you are interested in palindromes, for example, you might like to discover tautonyms, which follow palindromes in the taxonomy.

The third section contains a collection of Selected Lists. These lists contain alphabetical or numerical lists of words that are particularly fascinating pieces of wordplay. Usually the area of wordplay involved has historically been so popular that wordplay experts have come up with one word for each letter of the alphabet, or for each number of letters, and so forth.

The fourth section contains an alphabetical list of words, much as in a dictionary, except that where you would find a definition in a dictionary, here you will find what is unusual about the word. If the word is an uncommon word, you will also find a definition in italics (unless it is the plural of another entry). Scattered throughout this section are articles on various aspects of wordplay, such as "Longest Word," "Words Ending in -Gry," "Misspelled Words," and "Pangrams."

The book has an index at the end, in which you can look up your favorite form of wordplay and find where it is mentioned.

Since this is a printed book we are limited in space, and we have to make some hard decisions about the types of wordplay we can include. In the main we will be playing with individual words with unusual properties. Alas, we do not have space to play with all the ways that words can work together to have fun; for example, word pairs that exchange parts like MAIDS, RAPTURE → MATURE, RAPIDS. Our coverage of this vast area will be spotty; we do discuss lists of crashing words (which are words that have the same letters in some position—see the article "Crashing Word Lists"), but we do not discuss word squares (which are crossword puzzles with no black squares). We will also be unable to include sentence, paragraph, and even book-length wordplay (such as the book *A Void* by Georges Perec, written entirely without the letter "e"). These are all entertaining forms of wordplay, but space prevents us from including them. Look for these in the references given in the Ackowledgments.

What Is a Word?

Deciding what is a word is an emotionally charged issue. Language is the universal heritage of all mankind, and who is to say what is a word and what is not a word? This cuts across the egalitarian grain. Nonetheless, if we are going to have a book on wordplay, we need to decide which words we will include.

The Scrabble community needed to decide an even more emotionally charged issue: what is a playable word in Scrabble? Since this is a similar need to ours, let us examine their solution. The National Scrabble Association relies upon the accumulated wisdom and resources (and sweat) of the professional lexicographers. *The Official Scrabble Players Dictionary, Second Edition*, includes any non-capitalized word without apostrophes or hyphens that is not designated as foreign, and that occurs in one of ten editions of five college-level dictionaries: *Funk & Wagnalls Standard College Dictionary* (1973 printing), *American Heritage Dictionary of the English Language* (First and Second College Editions), *Merriam-Webster's New Collegiate Dictionary* (Eighth through Tenth Editions), *Webster's New World Dictionary* (Second and Third College Editions), *Random House College Dictionary* (Original Edition and Revised Edition).

We said above that the Scrabble community's need was similar to ours, implying that it was not identical. Their decision is partially based upon the desire to make the game playable for the average person, which is not a concern for us. Here are the ways in which we will modify their decision:

    1. We will accept words from the larger, unabridged versions of the above dictionaries. We will also accept words from the major British dictionaries (except that in the case of the *Oxford English Dictionary*, which is a historical dictionary, we will only accept words with recent citations). We

will accept all main entries, all inflected forms that are explicitly indicated, and all inflected forms that can reasonably be inferred from similar words. We will accept words that are capitalized, as long as they are not in the biography or geography sections of these dictionaries. We will accept words that contain apostrophes and hyphens. We will accept words marked as foreign, dialectical, etc. We will even accept phrases.

2. We will accept words that occur in the latest edition of these unabridged dictionaries. If the editors have omitted a word from the latest edition, then it is returned to the pile of possible words that will be adjudicated according to rule 3 below. This is because we cannot tell whether the word was excluded due to lack of space or because the editors decided that it is not a word after all.

3. We will accept words that are not in one of these dictionaries if it can be shown that the word clearly exists. For example, the words "airflow," "airhole," and "airstream" occur in one or more of these dictionaries, but the word "airvent" occurs in none of them. Yet a citation analysis of Internet usage of this word shows that it is as valid as the other three. The reason it is excluded is that its meaning is easier to deduce than the other three, and the editors are always constrained for space. Nonetheless, it is a perfectly good word.

4. One last caveat: there is a temptation to coin words just to create a record-holding word. This occurs in particular with the longest word (see the "Longest Word" article, page 106). It also occurs in a few other cases. For example, the word "redivider" has many citations on the Internet, but a careful reading of the citations shows that all either discuss it as an example of a palindrome, or as the name of a rock group that clearly was chosen because it was a palindrome (the last "r" in the logo is reversed). A word will not be accepted unless it has "innocent" citations.

What Is a Common Word?

A common word is a word that will be recognized by most reasonably well-educated speakers of the English language. In preparing this book, we counted the number of times a word was used over a period of several years in articles posted to news groups on the Internet. These news groups cover several thousand topics, and represent a reasonably wide sample of English language discourse.

We then had to decide where the cutoff was between common words and uncommon words. This we did by selecting a sample of words, some of which we knew to be common, some uncommon, and some in between. We then asked several well-educated English speakers to rank each word as common or uncommon. Averaging these results, we arrived at a cutoff for the common/uncommon boundary in the Internet word sample. The common word list contains about 60,000 words.

One argument that is frequently heard in wordplay circles is that if one word is common, then another related word must be common also. This reasoning is akin to that employed to arrive at the Paradox of the Heap, which goes like this: A heap of sand contains a large number of grains of sand. If you remove one grain of sand, then you still have a heap left. Therefore, you can remove all the grains except one, and the single grain left must be a heap also.

This argument is obviously silly, and relies for its paradoxical effect on the difficulty in drawing a line where several nearby lines seem equally good. Is a heap 100 grains, or 90, or 110? Nonetheless, "heapness" decreases as the number of grains decrease, until the odds of calling something a heap become negligible.

In the same way, a common word may have an uncommon related word. For example, based upon our survey, the word "helmeted" is a common English word, whereas the word "helmeting" is not. This creates a feeling much like that experienced when contemplating the Paradox of the Heap, but after due consideration, it is the only sensible alternative.

How Do We Know We Have a Record?

How do we know that these words are record holders? It is impossible to prove that something does not exist, so it is possible that any one of these words is not the best in its category. In fact, the reader is challenged to try to find better words that satisfy the constraints listed above under "What Is a Word?"

This is not to say that we think that it will be easy to discover better words. On the contrary, we think that it will be quite difficult to find any words that beat these records. The reason we are this confident is that these records have been compared to decades of effort by wordplay experts, listed below in the Acknowledgments. Thus if you are able to beat any of these records, you have accomplished something to be proud of. In the unlikely event that you succeed, please e-mail your new record to me at wordplay@questrel.com.

Acknowledgments

All puzzle fans everywhere owe their undying gratitude to the premier puzzlist of our times: Martin Gardner. Aside from providing countless hours of enjoyment over the decades with his Mathematical Games section in *Scientific American*, Gardner edited reprint editions of classic wordplay books by Lewis Carroll, H.E. Dudeney, and C.C. Bombaugh. The extensive references to the literature contained in these reprints have kept the current century aware of the amazing efforts of the wordplay experts of the last. It was Gardner who also suggested to Greenwood Periodicals that they have Dmitri Borgmann edit *Word Ways, the Journal of Recreational Linguistics*.

Word Ways, which was edited in 1968 by Borgmann and in 1969 by Howard Bergerson, has been edited since 1970 by A. Ross Eckler. There is no significant topic in wordplay that has not been covered definitively in *Word Ways*. Eckler has recently published an extract of material from *Word Ways* called *Making the Alphabet Dance* (St. Martin's Press, 1996), which is the virtual bible of wordplay.

Eckler's book is the only book that can be compared to the two seminal books by Borgmann: *Language on Vacation* and *Beyond Language*. Both of these books are out of print, but look for them in your local library or used bookstore. They are classics of wordplay, and many of the wordplay forms in these books appear in the *Enigma*, the monthly newsletter of the National Puzzlers' League.

The National Puzzlers' League is the world's oldest wordplay organization. The author owes much to its members and in particular to Joe and Judy Adamski, Eric Albert, Philip Cohen, and Murray Pearce. Aside from publishing the *Enigma*, the League has a Web site (www.puzzlers.org) and holds annual conventions. The puzzlemaster of these conventions since 1976 has been Will Shortz.

Shortz is also the former editor of *Games Magazine*, the current editor of the *New York Times* crossword puzzle, the puzzlemaster of National Public Radio's Weekend Edition, the author of countless puzzle books, and the person most likely to inherit the mantle of premier puzzlist of our times from Martin Gardner. Incidentally, Shortz is the person who suggested the author to the editor of this book for Sterling Publishing, Peter Gordon.

Gordon has been instrumental in all aspects of this book, of course, but one feature is entirely Gordon's suggestion, namely, the listing of common words for each record. Without these common word records, this book would be much diminished, and the author wants to thank Gordon publicly for pushing him to research and produce them.

Since 1970, the author has been an active participant in the Internet, and many of the wordplay forms contained in this book were first suggested in the Internet puzzle news group rec.puzzles. The author is the editor of the rec.puzzles archive; puzzle fans are encouraged to seek it out.

It is traditional in the final paragraph of acknowledgments to thanks one's wife and family for their undying support, tolerance, and patience. I fear that here I am no less in need of thankfulness than other authors, and indeed more needy than most. Thank you: Chloe, Wyatt, and Joan.

GLOSSARY OF WORDPLAY TERMS

Any area of concerted human effort develops its own jargon, and as you might expect, wordplay generates more than its fair share. This is a glossary of the wordplay terms that we use in this book. Each term is both defined and illustrated by an example in brackets that follows the definition. As you read the sections that follow, you may want to refer back to this section frequently until these terms become familiar.

affix-clipping—word that is formed by moving a letter to or from a frequent companion word [a napple → an apple]

alternade—word made from two words that are interlaced every other letter [ballooned: blond & aloe]

alternating terminal elision—alternate between deleting first and last letters to form a word list [craters → crater → rater → rate → ate → at → t]

backswitch—change last letter and reverse the rest to form another word [ellipse & spilled]

balanced letter sum—average position of letters in alphabet equal to 13.5 [by: (2 + 25)/2 = 13.5]

beheadment—delete first letter in a word to form another word [that → hat]

binade—same as "alternade"

capitonyms—words that change pronunciation when capitalized [polish, Polish]

catoptron—word that remains the same when it is written in uppercase and reflected in a mirror [TOOT]

changeover—change one letter and move it to form another word [determinations & exterminations]

changing offset shift pair—shift letters by a changing offset to form another word [fracas & oblong: f + 9 = o; r + 10 = b; a + 11 = l; c + 12 = o; a + 13 = n; s + 14 = g]

charade—concatenate words to form another word [therein: the & rein]

charitable—delete any letter to form other words [coops: oops & cops & cops & coos & coop]

colliding plurals—words with homographic plurals [axe & axis → axes]

complete cyclic transposal—same as "complete letter rotation"

complete garble group—same as "onalosi"

complete letter rotation—all possible rotations of letters form other words [ate & tea & eat]

contranyms—homographic antonym [cleave: separate & join]

crash list—word list with matching letters in some positions

curtailment—delete last letter in a word to form another word [hate → hat]

descender—lowercase letter that dips below the line [g, j, p, q, y]

difference pair—subtracting adjacent letters forms another word [lint → cut: l (12) – i (9) = c (3); etc.]

digital charade pair—digital words are the same ignoring separations between numbers [clover (3, 12, 14, 22, 5, 18) & clobber (3, 12, 14, 2, 2, 5, 18)]

digital word—letters replaced by their alphabetical positions as decimal numbers [the → 20, 8, 5]

dismembered—delete either first or last letters to form words [preparations: reparations & preparation]

double-duty antonyms—antonyms of two or more words [lose: win & find & gain]

embedded word—word embedded inside another [phenomenal: anemone]

equidistant word—nth letter same distance from A as nth letter from end is from Z [wizard]

exchange—same as "metathesis"

false antonym—same as "pseudantonym"

Fibonacci sequence—letters whose positions in the alphabet are numbers in the Fibonacci sequence (1, 1, 2, 3, 5, 8, 13, 21, ...) [a, b, c, e, h, m, u]

fixed offset shift pair—shift letters by a fixed offset to form another word [fusion & layout: f (6) + 6 = l (12); u (21) + 6 = a (1); s (19) + 6 = y (25); etc.]

folk etymology—same as "affix-clipping"

fossil—word that occurs only in idioms ["kith" from "kith and kin"]

four-cadence—letter repeated every four [the i in distribution]

full symmetry letter—uppercase letter that has left-right and top-bottom symmetry [H, I, O, X]

gramograms—words that sound like sequences of letters [envy sounds like "NV"]

head 'n' tail word—identical string of letters surrounds a center letter [hotshot]

head-to-tail shift—move first letter from front of word to end to form another word [devolve → evolved]

homographs—words spelled the same but pronounced differently [lead (metal) & lead (guide the way)]

homophones—words spelled differently but pronounced the same [bear & bare]

horizontal symmetry letter—uppercase letter that has top-bottom symmetry [B, C, D, E, H, I, K, O, X]

hospitable—insert letter anywhere to form another word [lens: glens & liens & leans & lends & lense]

hostile—word in which a letter cannot be inserted anywhere to form word [ahem]

hydration—more than one way to add letter to front to form another word [enunciation: denunciation & renunciation]

iskot pair—reverse dots and dashes and ignore pauses in Morse code to form another word [at & tee → · − − & − · ·]

isogram—every letter appears only once in the word [ambidextrously]

isolano—word that cannot have a letter changed anywhere to form another word (opposite of onalosi) [upon]

isomorph—words that repeat letters in the same places [discriminative & simplification: both repeat letters in the 2nd, 6th, 8th, and 12th positions]

isomorse pair—same Morse code words if pauses are ignored [he & is → ·····]

isotel pair—word spells out same telephone number as another word [comprising & conspiring: both are 2667747464 on a phone]

length five linkade—word made from 5-letter overlapping words [pasterns: paste & aster & stern & terns]

length four linkade—word made from 4-letter overlapping words [amends: amen & mend & ends]

length three linkade—word made from 3-letter overlapping words [tapered: tap & ape & per & ere & red]

letter product—multiply together positions of letters in alphabet [hello = 8 × 5 × 12 × 12 × 15 = 86,400]

letter-shift pair—shift letters to new letters in the alphabet to form another word [green & terra: g (7) + 13 = t (20); r (18) + 13 = e (5); e (5) + 13 = r (18); e (5) + 13 = r (18); n (14) + 13 = a (1)]

letter subtraction—delete all copies of letter in a word to form another word [worldliness → wordiness: l's are removed]

letter sums—add together positions of letters in alphabet [hello = 8 + 5 + 12 + 12 + 15 = 52]

linkade—overlap words to form another word [tapered: tap & ape & per & ere & red]

lipogram—word missing certain letters ["by hook or by crook" has no e's]

matching letter pattern—same as "isomorph"

metanalysis—same as "affix-clipping"

metathesis—exchange two letters in a word to form another word [certification → rectification]

Morse code reversal pair—reversed Morse code words if pauses are ignored [time & wit → − · · − − · & · − − · · −]

multiplicative offset shift pair—shift letters by a multiplicative factor through alphabet to form another word [birds & fable: b (2) × 3 = f (6); i (9) × 3 = a (1); etc.]

numberdrome—digital word palindrome [is: 9, 19 → 919, which is a palindrome]

onalosi—word that can have a letter changed anywhere to form another word (opposite of isolano) [grass: brass & glass & gross & grabs & grasp]

pair isogram—each letter occurs two times [intestines]

palindrome—same word when letters are reversed [deified]

pangram—list of words containing all the letters of the alphabet [waqf & jynx & speltz & vugh & mockbird]

polygram—each letter occurs more than once [intensities]

portmanteau word—word formed by mixing two other words [brunch: breakfast, lunch]

primes—letters whose positions in the alphabet are prime numbers [b, c, e, g, k, m, q, s, w]

progressive charitable—all contiguous and non-contiguous subsequences are words [bye: bye & be & by & ye]

pseudantonyms—synonyms that appear to be antonyms [flammable & inflammable]

pyramid word—one letter occurs once; one letter occurs twice; etc. [sleeveless]

refractory rhyme—word with no common rhyme [orange, month, silver]

reversal pair—reverse the letters in a word to form another word [desserts & stressed]

reverse snowball—concatenate words decreasing in length to form another word [interventionist: inter & vent & ion & is & t]

reverse tetrahedron word—one letter occurs four times; two letters occur three times; etc. [argillaceocalcareous: one letter (a) occurs four times, two letters (c and l) occur three times, three letters (e, o, and r) occur two times, and four letters (g, i, s, and u) occur one time]

rhopalic—same as "snowball"

roller-coaster—word with letters that alternate between going forward and backward in alphabet [general: start at g, backward to e, forward to n, backward to e, forward to r, backward to a, forward to l]

rot-13 pair—shift letters by half the alphabet to form another word [green & terra]

sesquipedalian word—very long word [antidisestablishmentarianism]

short lowercase letter—lowercase letter that doesn't have an ascender or descender [a, c, e, m, n, o, r, s, u, v, w, x, z]

shiftgram pair—shift letters through alphabet and transpose to form another word [bad & fig: bad, shifted 5 positions, is gfi, which rearranges to fig]

shift pair—shift letters through alphabet to form another word [steeds + 1 → tuffet]

snowball—concatenate words increasing in length to form another word [temperamentally: t & em & per & amen & tally]

squares—letters whose positions in the alphabet are perfect squares [a, d, i, p, y]

stingy—cannot delete any letter to form another word

subtransposition—words with same letter product [bade & tab: both have letter products of 40 (bade = $2 \times 1 \times 4 \times 5$; tab = $20 \times 1 \times 2$)]

sum pair—adding adjacent letters forms another word [brief → tank: b (2) + r (18) = t (20), etc.]

switchback—change first letter and reverse the rest to form another word [regatta & wattage]

tall lowercase letter—lowercase letter that has an ascender or descender [b, d, f, g, h, i, j, k, l, p, q, t, y]

tautonym—word formed by repeating a sequence of letters [hotshots]

terminal elision—delete first and last letters to form another word [revolutionists → evolutionist]

tetrad isogram—each letter occurs four times [kukukuku]

tetrahedron word—one letter occurs once; two letters occur twice; etc. [oppositionists: one letter (n) occurs once, two letters (p and t) occur twice, three letters (i, o, and s) occur three times)]

three-cadence—letter repeated every three [the n in inconveniencing]

transaddition—add one letter and rearrange to form another word; see "transdeletion"

transdeletion—delete one letter and rearrange to form another word [people → elope]

transposition—rearrange letters to form another word [sheet & these]

transubstitution—substitute one letter and rearrange to form another word [sheet → there (the s becomes an r)]

trio isogram—each letter occurs three times [deeded]

two-cadence—letter repeated every two [the i in divisibility]

upside-down word—word that remains the same when it is turned upside down [dollop]

vertical symmetry letter—uppercase letter that has left-right symmetry [A, H, I, M, O, T, U, V, W, X, Y]

word torture—word in which all contiguous subsequences are words [fads: ads & fad & ad & ds & fa]

TAXONOMY
OF WORDPLAY

This is a hierarchy of types of wordplay. The top level of the hierarchy comprises "Spelling," "Pronunciation," "Etymology," and "Meaning," and there are up to five levels below the top level. For example, the longest word that can be typed on the top row of the typewriter is listed under "Spelling," "Structure," "Typewriter Order," "Entire Word," "all letters from typewriter top row, longest."

Under each wordplay category, there is a list of words, phrases, or word groups that are the best known example of that form of wordplay. These record holders have been divided into these classes:

common words

uncommon words

hyphenated words

phrases

hyphenated phrases

The Introduction explains how we determined that a word is common. Phrases is a catch-all class that in addition to phrases proper includes contractions, initialisms, words like "86ed" that contain digits, and other oddities such as "and/or."

A record for a lower class (e.g., uncommon words) is only listed if it is better than the record for a higher class (e.g., common words). For example, if there are both common and uncommon palindromes with eight letters, then only the common one is listed; an uncommon palindrome would need at least nine letters to be listed.

The class of a word group is the lowest class of any word in it. Thus if a group contains an uncommon word and nothing from a lower class, i.e., no hyphenated words or phrases, then it is listed in the uncommon word class.

The score, if applicable, associated with a record-holding word or word group follows it and is enclosed in parentheses. This is usually the number of letters in the word, but depending upon the particular record, it may be the number of syllables, the number of vowels, the ratio of selected letters to length, etc.

If there is a tie for the record, the score is followed by "-t," and the most common words or groups that tie for each record are listed. The commonality of a word group is the commonality of the least common word in it. Tying words or phrases are separated by commas; tying groups are listed on separate lines. Up to six common words or groups are listed; if there are more than six, five are listed with a count of additional words. Up to three uncommon words or groups are listed and up to two for the other classes. If one form of a word is listed (e.g., "barbarian"), the other related forms (e.g., "barbarians," "barbaric," "barbarism," etc.) are omitted. Thus, less than six common words will be listed if all the other words are forms of the already listed words.

Many word groups are termed "well-mixed." Well-mixed word groups contain words that do not share any string of four letters. This is done because there may be larger groups that contain many forms of the same word, or many identical prefixes or suffixes, etc. Such answers are not listed since the space could better be used listing more interesting words.

Spelling

I. Structure
A. Entire Word
1. sesquipedalian word, longest (long word)
    uncommon words: antidisestablishmentarianism, floccinaucinihilipilification, honorificabilitudinitatibus, supercalifragilisticexpialidocious, pneumonoultramicroscopicsilicovolcanoconiosis [see "Longest Word" article, page 106]
2. palindrome (same word when letters are reversed)
    a. longest
        common words: rotator, deified (7-t)
        uncommon word: kinnikinnik (11)
    b. beginning with each letter
        see page 51
    c. centered on each letter
        see page 52
3. tautonym (word formed by repeating a sequence of letters)
    a. longest
        common word: hotshots (8)
        uncommon words: chiquichiqui, tangantangan (12-t)
        hyphenated words: bumpety-bumpety, bumpity-bumpity (14-t)
        phrase: per second per second (18)
    b. beginning with each letter
        see page 53
4. head 'n' tail word (beginning and ending letters of word are identical)
    a. longest
        common word: hotshot (7)
        uncommon words: einsteins, galengale, ... and 8 others (9-t)
        hyphenated words: eensie-weensie, convexo-convex (13-t)
        phrase: gentleman's gentleman (19)
    b. centered on each letter
        see page 54
5. number of different letters
    a. isogram, longest (all letters different)
        common word: ambidextrously (14)
        uncommon words: uncopyrightable, dermatoglyphics (15-t)
    b. pair isogram, longest (each letter occurs two times)
        common word: intestines (10)
        uncommon word: scintillescent (14)
    c. trio isogram, longest (each letter occurs three times)
        common word: deeded (6)
        uncommon word: sestettes (9)
        hyphenated word: blah-blah-blah (12)
    d. tetrad isogram, longest (each letter occurs four times)
        uncommon word: kukukuku (8)
    e. polygram, longest (each letter occurs more than once)
        common word: intensities (11)
        uncommon word: unprosperousnesses (18)
        phrase: intestinal calculuses (20)
    f. geometric shapes

i. pyramid word, longest (one letter occurs once; one letter occurs twice; etc.)
>   common word: sleeveless (10)
>   hyphenated word: dead-endednesses (15)

ii. tetrahedron word, longest (one letter occurs once; two letters occur twice; etc.)
>   uncommon words: instantiations, oppositionists, ... and 3 others (14-t)

iii. reverse tetrahedron word, longest (one letter occurs four times; two letters occur three times; etc.)
>   uncommon words: argillaceocalcareous, autosuggestibilities, ... and 8 others (20-t)

g. ratio length to letters, highest
>   common word: senselessness (3.25)
>   uncommon word: kukukuku (4)
>   hyphenated word: tat-tat-tat (4.5)

h. ratio length to letters, highest non-tautonym
>   common word: senselessness (3.25)
>   uncommon word: senselessnesses (3.75)
>   hyphenated word: tat-tat-tat (4.5)

i. ratio length to letters, lowest for each length
>   see page 55

j. different letters, most
>   common words: incomprehensibility, comprehensibility, microencapsulated, ambidextrously (14-t)
>   uncommon words: blepharoconjunctivitis, pseudolamellibranchiata, ... and 13 others (16-t)
>   phrases: computerized axial tomography scanner, rocky mountain flowering raspberry (19-t)

6. isomorph (words that repeat letters in the same places)

a. longest well-mixed
>   common words: comprehensible & counterexample (14-t)
>   common words: discriminative & simplification (14-t)
>   common words: breathtakingly & chlorpromazine (14-t)
>   common words: demilitarizing & municipalities (14-t)
>   uncommon words: hygroexpansivity & hypermasculinity (16-t)
>   uncommon words: neurochemistries & postchlorination (16-t)
>   phrases: breakdown voltages & granulocytopenias (17-t)
>   phrases: knights commanders & meadow spittlebugs (17-t)

B. Subset of Word

1. identical letters

a. pairs

i. consecutive doubled letters, most
>   common word: bookkeeper (3)

ii. doubled letters, most
>   common words: successfully, committee, unsuccessfully, subcommittee, aggressiveness, ... and 22 others (3-t)
>   uncommon words: possessionlessness, successlessness, ... and 2 others (4-t)

b. starts and ends with the same letter

i. longest
>   common word: straightforwardness (19)
>   uncommon word: supercalifragilisticexpialidocious (34)

ii. for each letter, longest
>   see page 56

iii. for each letter, shortest
>> see page 57

c. tripled letter, shortest
>> uncommon word: brrr (4)
>> phrase: SSs (3)

d. most of any one letter (see also page 60)
>> common words: possessiveness, senselessness (6-t)
>> uncommon words: floccinaucinihilipilification, humuhumunukunukuapuaa, ... and 2 others (9-t)
>> phrase: between the devil and the deep blue sea (10)

2. repeated letters, most
> common word: electroencephalography (8)
> uncommon words: supercalifragilisticexpialidocious, dichlorodiphenyltrichloroethane, ... and 3 others (10-t)
> phrase: a bird in the hand is worth two in the bush (12)

3. alternating
> a. two-cadence, longest (letter repeated every two)
>> common words: divisibility, visibilities (5-t)
>> uncommon word: humuhumunukunukuapuaa (8)
> b. three-cadence, longest (letter repeated every three)
>> common words: inconveniencing, effervescence (5-t)
>> hyphenated word: swelled-headednesses (6)
> c. four-cadence, longest (letter repeated every four)
>> common words: distribution, treatment, discussions, imagination, institution, ... and many others (3-t)
>> uncommon words: inevitabilities, alveolopalatal, ... and 25 others (4-t)
>> phrase: binomial distribution, ... and 2 others (5)

4. repeated prefix, longest
> common words: barbaric, assassin, murmured, ... and 14 others (6-t)
> uncommon word: countercountermeasure (14)
> hyphenated word: testament-testamentar (18)

5. internal structure
> a. nontrivial internal palindrome, longest
>> common words: interpret, recognizing, exploitation, misinterpret, selfless, ... and 37 others (7-t)
>> uncommon words: sensuousness, kinnikinniks (11-t)
> b. nontrivial internal tautonym, longest
>> common words: bringing, singing, ringing, swinging, possessed, ... and 59 others (6-t)
>> uncommon word: countercountermeasure (14)
>> hyphenated word: testament-testamentar (18)
> c. nontrivial internal head 'n' tail, longest
>> common words: hodgepodge, fractionation, grandstands, handstands (9-t)
>> uncommon word: intestinointestinal (17)

6. unusual spelling
> a. to spell, most difficult
>> common word: dumbbell [see "Misspelled Words" article, page 125]
>> uncommon word: desiccate [see "Misspelled Words" article, page 125]
> b. exceptions to I before E
>> see page 67
> c. American word ending "our" but pronounced like "or," multisyllabic

common words: glamour, troubadour

d. variant spellings of a non-foreign word, most

uncommon words: catercorner: cater-corner & cater-cornered & catacorner & cata-cornered & catty-corner & catty-cornered & kitty-corner & kitty-cornered (9)

7. ending -gry, example

common words: angry, hungry [see "Words Ending in -Gry" article, page 96]

uncommon words: gry, aggry [see "Words Ending in -Gry" article, page 96]

II. Vowels

A. Entire Word

1. all vowels, longest

common words: a, e, i, o, u (1-t)

uncommon words: euouae, aiaiai (6-t)

B. Subset of Word

1. each once

a. each vowel once, longest

common words: subcontinental, countermanding (14-t)

uncommon words: entwicklungsroman, subpostmastership (17-t)

phrases: bucking transformers, disjunct tetrachords (19-t)

b. each vowel including y once, longest

common word: uncomplimentary (15)

uncommon word: hydrometallurgists (18)

phrase: florist's chrysanthemums (22)

c. each vowel once, shortest

common word: sequoia (7)

uncommon word: eunoia (6)

d. each vowel including y once, shortest

common word: eukaryotic (10)

uncommon words: oxyuridae, oxygeusia (9-t)

2. each once in order

a. each vowel once in order, longest

common word: facetious (9)

uncommon word: abstentious (11)

hyphenated word: gathering-ground (15)

b. each vowel including y once in order, longest

common word: facetiously (11)

uncommon word: abstemiously (12)

c. each vowel once in order, shortest

common word: facetious (9)

uncommon word: caesious (8)

d. each vowel including y once in order, shortest

common word: facetiously (11)

e. each vowel once in reverse order, longest

common word: subcontinental (14)

f. each vowel including y once in reverse order, longest

phrase: syrup of ipecac (13)

g. each vowel once in reverse order, shortest

common word: subcontinental (14)

uncommon word: muroidea (8)

h. each vowel including y once in reverse order, shortest

phrase: syrup of ipecac (13)

3. vowel string, longest
    common word: queueing (5)
    uncommon words: aiaiais, euouaes (6-t)
4. restricted numbers of vowels
    a. containing one vowel, longest
        common word: strengths (9)
    b. containing two vowels, longest
        common words: transcripts, strengthens, transplants, flashlights, strongholds, ... and
            12 others (11-t)
        uncommon words: promptscripts, schwartzbrots (13-t)
    c. containing three vowels, longest
        common word: forthrightness (14)
        uncommon word: strengthlessness (16)
        phrase: bursting strengths, ... and 3 others (17)
5. restricted vowel types
    a. univocalic or containing one type of vowel
        i. longest, for each vowel
            see page 58
    b. containing two types of vowels, longest
        common word: spectrophotometers (18)
        uncommon words: humuhumunukunukuapuaas, thermophosphorescences (22-t)
        phrase: there's no love lost between them (27)
    c. containing three types of vowels, longest
        common word: electroencephalogram (20)
        uncommon word: antidisestablishmentarianism (28)
        phrases: cut the ground from under someone's feet, intermediate range ballistic
            missile (33-t)

III. Consonants

A. Entire Word
1. all consonants, longest
    common words: nth, qts (3-t)
    uncommon word: tsktsks (7)
B. Subset of Word
1. consonant string, longest
    common words: postscript, worthwhile, offspring, downstream, witchcraft, ... and 38 others
        (5-t)
    uncommon words: catchphrase, festschrift, ... and 33 others (6-t)
    phrase: hirschsprung's disease (7)
2. containing one consonant, longest
    common words: audio, queue, eerie, adieu, aerie (5-t)
    uncommon words: aiaiais, euouaes, ouabaio (7-t)
3. containing two consonants, longest
    common words: nouveau, sequoia, aqueous, anaemia, aurorae (7-t)
    uncommon words: aizoaceae, epieikeia (9-t)
4. containing three consonants, longest
    common words: audacious, beauteous (9-t)
    uncommon words: ouagadougou, paeoniaceae (11-t)
5. containing four consonants, longest
    common word: onomatopoeia (12)
    uncommon word: fouquieriaceae (14)
6. containing five consonants, longest

common words: inauguration, inequalities, equalization, questionaire, inadequacies, ... and 12
      others (12-t)
   uncommon word: auriculariaceae (15)
7. monoconsonant or containing one type of consonant
    a. one type of consonant for each consonant, longest
       see page 58
8. containing two types of consonants, longest
    common words: attenuation, inattention (11-t)
    uncommon words: nauseousnesses, sensuousnesses (14-t)
9. containing three types of consonants, longest
    common words: unconsciousness, consciousnesses (15-t)
    uncommon word: unostentatiousnesses (20)
10. containing four types of consonants, longest
    common word: conscientiousness (17)
    uncommon word: unconscientiousnesses (21)
    phrase: not to put too fine a point on it (25)
11. containing five types of consonants, longest
    common words: internationalization, institutionalization (20-t)
    uncommon words: argillaceocalcareouses, counterreconnaissances (22-t)
    hyphenated word: pleasantness-unpleasantnesses (28)

IV. Vowel-Consonant Patterns

A. Entire Word

1. well-mixed words with the same consonants, longest
    common words: predicts & periodicities (13)
    uncommon words: sephardics & sphaerioidaceaes (16-t)
    uncommon words: subternatural & isobutyronitrile (16-t)
2. consonants minus vowels, highest
    common word: straightforwardness (9)
    uncommon words: handcraftsmanships, strengthlessness (10-t)
    phrase: go from strength to strength (14)
3. ratio consonants to vowels, highest
    common word: strengths (8)
4. vowels minus consonants, highest
    common word: onomatopoeia (4)
    uncommon words: euouae, aiaiai, fouquieriaceae (6-t)
    phrase: ua mau ke ea o ka aina i ka pono (9)
5. ratio vowels to consonants, highest
    common words: audio, queue, eerie, adieu, aerie (4-t)
    uncommon words: aiaiais, euouaes, ouabaio (6-t)
6. alternating vowels and consonants
    a. longest
       common words: verisimilitude, rehabilitative (14-t)
       uncommon words: diketopiperazines, reticulatoramoses, reticulatovenoses (17-t)
       phrases: morituri te salutamus, political executives (19-t)
    b. longest including y
       common words: verisimilitude, rehabilitative, supererogatory (14-t)
       uncommon word: honorificabilitudinity (22)
7. no matching vowel pattern, shortest
    common words: nouveau, aliquot (7-t)

V. Alphabetical Order

A. Entire Word

1. letters in alphabetical order
    a. longest
        common words: almost, begins, chimps, biopsy, chinos, chintz (6-t)
        uncommon word: aegilops (8)
    b. longest with possible repeat
        common word: billowy (7)
        uncommon word: aegilops (8)
2. letters in reverse alphabetical order
    a. longest
        common word: wronged (7)
    b. longest with possible repeat
        common words: spooled, wronged, sniffed, spooked, spoofed, ... and 2 others (7-t)
        uncommon words: spoonfed, trollied (8-t)
        hyphenated word: spoon-feed (9)
3. lipogram (word missing certain letters)
    a. containing letters from first half of alphabet, longest
        common words: blackmailed, blackballed (11-t)
        uncommon word: hamamelidaceae (14)
        phrase: a face like a fiddle (16)
        hyphenated phrase: black-backed jackal (17)
    b. containing letters from last half of alphabet, longest
        common word: torturous (9)
        uncommon words: nonsupports, nontortuous (11-t)
        hyphenated word: tootsy-wootsy (12)
    c. containing hexadecimal letters, longest
        common words: defaced, acceded, effaced (7-t)
        uncommon word: fabaceae (8)
        hyphenated word: face-bedded (10)
4. letter-shift pair (shift letters to new letters in the alphabet to form another word)
    a. rot-13 pair (shift letters by half the alphabet to form another word)
        i. longest
            common words: green & terra (5-t)
            common words: creel & perry (5-t)
            uncommon words: abjurer & nowhere (7-t)
            uncommon words: chechen & purpura (7-t)
        ii. longest reversed
            common words: ravine & ravine (6)
            uncommon words: tavering & tavering (8)
    b. fixed offset shift pair (shift letters by a fixed offset to form another word)
        i. longest
            common words: fusion & layout [shift of 6] (6-t)
            common words: steeds & tuffet [shift of 1] (6-t)
            uncommon words: corocoro & wiliwili [shift of 20] (8)
        ii. longest reversed
            common words: ravine & ravine [shift of 13] (6-t)
            common words: lethal & shoals [shift of 19] (6-t)
            common words: hitter & napped [shift of 22] (6-t)
            uncommon words: tavering & tavering [shift of 13] (8)
    c. changing offset shift pair, longest (shift letters by a changing offset to form another word)
    e.g., EMU → FOX: E + 1 → F, M + 2 → O, U + 3 → X
        common words: fracas & oblong [shift of 9] (6)

uncommon words: kahikateas & nemoricole [shift of 3] (10)

d. multiplicative offset shift pair, longest (shift letters by a multiplicative factor through alphabet to form another word)

e.g., ONE → WRY: O × 5 → W, N × 5 → R, E × 5 → Y

common words: birds & fable [factor of 3] (5-t)

common words: baron & punch [factor of 21] (5-t)

common words: didst & rural [factor of 11] (5-t)

common words: dough & twain [factor of 5] (5-t)

common words: divas & lance [factor of 3] (5-t)

... and 12 others

uncommon words: cereals & kanauri [factor of 21] (7-t)

uncommon words: martels & mundari [factor of 21] (7-t)

uncommon words: forebay & pavings [factor of 7] (7-t)

e. shiftgram pair, longest (shift letters through alphabet and transpose to form another word)

common words: preserving & refractive [shift of 13] (10)

uncommon words: pentadactyle & precipitants [shift of 15] (12)

phrases: harlequin opal & presumptively [shift of 4] (13-t)

phrases: doppler effect & tertius gaudet [shift of 11] (13-t)

5. roller-coaster, longest (word with letters that alternate between going forward and backward in alphabet)

common words: generalizations, decontamination, systematization, capitalizations (15-t)

uncommon word: multilateralization (19)

phrase: freshman compositions (20)

hyphenated phrase: through-and-through coal (21)

6. letter sums (add together positions of letters in alphabet)

a. highest, for each length

see page 59

b. lowest, for each length

see page 59

c. words with same letter sum, longest well-mixed

common words: extraterrestrials & electroencephalography (22)

uncommon words: strongylocentrotus & floccinaucinihilipilification (29)

hyphenated words: hystero-salpingo-oophorectomies & supercalifragilisticexpialidocious (34)

phrases: transmission electron microscopes & nicotinamide adenine dinucleotide phosphate (40)

d. balanced letter sum, longest (average position of letters in alphabet equal to 13.5)

common words: vasoconstriction, unconventionally (16-t)

uncommon words: noninstitutionalized, autotransplantations, ... and 9 others (20-t)

phrase: duchenne's muscular dystrophy (26)

e. letter sum divisible by each letter, longest

e.g., CAB = C(3) + A(1) + B(2) = 6, which can be evenly divided by 3, 1, and 2

common word: barbaric (8)

hyphenated word: teeter-tottered (14)

7. letter product (multiply together positions of letters in alphabet)

a. subtransposition, longest well-mixed (words with same letter product)

common words: procrastination & anachronistically (17)

uncommon words: reithrodontomyses & pseudosaccharomycetaceae (24)

phrases: creatine phosphokinases & as different as chalk and cheese (27-t)

b. closest to one million

common word: curing (1000188)

uncommon words: teaette, typey (1000000-t)

    c. closest to two million

        common words: raining, curbing, ingrain, cuffing (2000376-t)

        uncommon word: teethy (2000000)

    d. closest to three million

        common word: peyote (3000000)

    e. closest to four million

        common words: ruling, luring, girding (4000752-t)

    f. closest to five million

        common word: coining (5000940)

8. digital word (letters replaced by their alphabetical positions as decimal numbers)

    a. numberdrome, longest (digital word palindrome)

    e.g., HAIR = (8, 1, 9, 18)

        common word: deified (7)

        uncommon words: insulins, dehaired (8-t)

        hyphenated word: abba-dabba (9)

    b. digital charade pair, longest well-mixed (digital words the same ignoring separations

        between numbers)

    e.g., ABOVE = (1, 2, 15, 22, 5), LOVE = (12, 15, 22, 5)

        common words: clovers & clobbers (8-t)

        common words: parlays & parables (8-t)

        common words: staving & stabbing (8-t)

        common words: craving & crabbing (8-t)

    c. digital reversal pair, longest

    e.g., ABULIA = (1, 2, 21, 12, 9, 1), SULU = (19, 21, 12, 21)

        common words: hovel & bobber (6-t)

        common words: daimon & domain (6-t)

        common words: debug & gabbed (6-t)

        uncommon words: jararaca & maharaja (8)

9. sum pair (adding adjacent letters forms another word)

    a. longest

        common words: brief → tank (5-t)

        common words: fatty → guns (5-t)

        common words: canal → doom (5-t)

        common words: circa → laud (5-t)

        common words: dotty → sins (5-t)

        ... and 22 others

        uncommon words: canfuls → dotage (7-t)

        uncommon words: charpoy → kishen (7-t)

        ... and 7 others

    b. longest progressive

        common words: cane → dos → sh → a (4-t)

        common words: sank → toy → in → w (4-t)

        common words: trio → lax → my → l (4-t)

        common words: show → awl → xi → g (4-t)

        common words: aloe → mat → nu → i (4-t)

        uncommon words: sande → tori → iga → ph → x (5-t)

        uncommon words: cymba → bloc → nar → os → h (5-t)

        ... and 2 others

10. difference pair (subtracting adjacent letters forms another word)

    a. longest
        common words: eldest → shyly (6-t)
        common words: coffer → nizam (6-t)
        uncommon words: bonniest → mazedly (8)
    b. longest progressive
        common words: onto → ate → go → r (4-t)
        common words: lint → cut → ha → g (4-t)
        common words: barn → aid → re → m (4-t)
        common words: ohms → gut → la → k (4-t)
        common words: gong → rag → qt → w (4-t)
        ... and 6 others
        uncommon words: spoon → caza → bay → ab → y (5-t)
        uncommon words: oriel → wids → nek → it → o (5-t)
        uncommon words: dowts → orca → wob → hm → u (5-t)

11. letters restricted to mathematical sequences
    a. all letters restricted to squares = adipy, longest
        common words: papaya, payday (6-t)
        hyphenated word: yada-yada-yada (12)
    b. all letters restricted to primes = bcegkmqsw, longest
        common words: messes, emcees (6-t)
        uncommon word: sweeswees (9)
    c. all letters restricted to Fibonacci sequence = abcehmu, longest
        common words: became, hubbub (6-t)
        uncommon word: macacahuba (10)

12. equidistant word, longest (nth letter same distance from A as nth letter from end is from Z)
    common words: wizard, hovels (6-t)
    hyphenated word: klop-klop (8)

B. Subset of Word

1. contains consecutive letters in alphabet
    a. most
        common words: disenfranchising, goldfinches (7-t)
        uncommon words: perquisition, propinquities, ... and 25 others (8-t)
        hyphenated word: quasi-complimentary (10)
        phrases: knight of st. john of jerusalem (11)
    b. most, for each letter
        see page 64
    c. consecutive alphabetic letters in left-to-right order
        i. most
            common word: absconded (5)
        ii. most, for each letter
        see page 66
    d. consecutive alphabetic letters in order consecutively, most
        common words: understudy, overstuffed (4-t)
    e. consecutive runs of consecutive alphabetic letters, most
        common words: damndest, sophist, catastrophist, hiders (3-t)
        uncommon word: echinoders (4)
    f. ratio of consecutive alphabetic letters to length, highest
        common words: backed, squirt, quarts, braced, cabled (0.83-t)
        uncommon word: klompen (0.85)
    g. consecutive alphabetic letters in reverse order consecutively, most

common words: response, outside, environment, respond, responsible, ... and many others (3-t)

hyphenated word: bouts-rimes, ... and 3 others (4)

2. letters in alphabetical place or alphabet crashes
    a. letters in alphabetical place without shifting alphabet, most
        common words: leadership, readership, abide, abode, astonishingly, ... and 11 others (4-t)
        uncommon words: archetypical, abudefduf, ... and 11 others (5-t)
        phrase: archegonial chambers (6)
    b. letters in alphabetical place with shifting alphabet, most
        common words: inoperative, cooperatively (6-t)
        phrase: adenosine monophosphate, ... and 7 others (7)

3. last letter next in alphabet after first letter
    a. shortest, for each letter
        see page 57

VI. Typewriter Order

A. Entire Word

1. all letters from typewriter top row, longest
    common words: typewriter, repertoire, proprietor, perpetuity (10-t)
    uncommon word: teetertotter (12)
    hyphenated word: pretty-prettier (14)

2. all letters from typewriter middle row, longest
    common word: alfalfa (7)
    uncommon word: shakalshas (10)
    hyphenated word: algal-algals (11)

3. all letters from typewriter bottom row, longest
    common words: b, c, m, n, v, x, z (1-t)
    uncommon words: mm, bb (2-t)
    phrase: MNC (3)

4. all letters from typewriter in order, longest
    common words: weigh, quips, quash, quaff, quill, ... and 2 others (5-t)
    uncommon words: wettish, qwertys (7-t)

5. all letters from typewriter in reverse order, longest
    common words: soiree, sirree (6-t)
    uncommon word: boottree (8)

6. all letters from typewriter left hand, longest
    common words: aftereffects, stewardesses, reverberated, desegregated (12-t)
    uncommon words: sweaterdresses, tesseradecades (14-t)
    phrase: great crested grebes (18)

7. all letters from typewriter right hand, longest
    common words: polyphony, homophony (9-t)
    uncommon words: kinnikinnik, hypolimnion (11-t)
    hyphenated word: johnny-jump-up, ... and 2 others (12-t)

8. all letters from typewriter alternating hands, longest
    common word: dismantlement (13)
    uncommon words: antiskepticism, leucocytozoans (14-t)
    phrases: laugh and lay down, protocorm theory (15-t)

9. all letters from typewriter one finger, longest
    common word: deeded (6)
    uncommon word: deedeed (7)

10. all letters from typewriter adjacent keys, longest

common words: assessed, reseeded (8-t)

uncommon words: assertress, desertress (10-t)

VII. Frequency Order

A. Entire Word

1. lipogram

    a. without E, longest

        common word: institutionalization (20)

        uncommon word: floccinaucinihilipilification (29)

        phrase: you scratch my back and I'll scratch yours (34)

    b. without ET, longest

        common word: chlorofluorocarbons (19)

        uncommon word: hydrochlorofluorocarbon (23)

        phrase: anhydrous hydrofluoric acids (26)

    c. without ETA, longest

        common word: uncompromisingly (16)

        uncommon words: glycosphingolipids, coccidioidomycosis, diiodohydroxyquins

            (18-t)

        phrase: moldy corn poisonings (19)

    d. without ETAI, longest

        common word: unscrupulously (14)

        uncommon word: phyllospondylous (16)

        phrase: synchronous clocks (17)

    e. without ETAIN, longest

        common word: scrupulously (12)

        uncommon words: chylophyllously, hydrosulphurous, hypophosphorous (15-t)

        phrase: old world scops owl (16)

    f. without ETAINS, longest

        common word: chlorophyll (11)

        uncommon words: promorphology, rhombporphyry (13-t)

        phrase: by hook or by crook (15)

2. sumword (word converted to the sum of the frequency of its letters per thousand words in normal text)

    a. most infrequently used letters, for each length

        see page 62

    b. most frequently used letters, for each length

        see page 62

VIII. Miscellaneous

A. Entire Word

1. spelled with chemical symbols, longest

    common word: paraprofessionals (17)

    uncommon word: hypothalamicohypophyseals (25)

    phrases: infectious necrotic hepatitises, pneumocystis carinii pneumonias (29-t)

2. spelled with two-letter U.S. postal codes, longest

    common words: mainland, memorial, victoria, mandarin, armorial, ... and 5 others (8-t)

    uncommon word: convallarias (12)

3. spelled with piano notes, longest

    common words: baggage, cabbage, defaced, acceded, effaced (7-t)

    uncommon words: debagged, cabbaged, ... and 2 others (8-t)

    hyphenated word: face-bedded (10)

4. Morse code

    a. specific patterns of dots and dashes

    i. Morse code is entirely dots, longest
        common word: sissies (7)
    ii. Morse code is entirely dashes, longest
        common word: motto (5)
        uncommon word: motmot (6)
    iii. Morse code is entirely dot-dashes, longest
        common word: entente (7)
    iv. Morse code is entirely dash-dots, longest
        common word: tartar (6)
b. sequence of repeated dots in Morse code, longest
    common words: obsessive, possessive, possessiveness (18-t)
    uncommon words: bakhsheeshes, bakhshishes (24-t)
c. sequence of repeated dashes in Morse code, longest
    common word: servomotor (13)
    uncommon word: myomotomy (17)
d. Morse code for each letter is 1 symbol, longest
    common word: tee (3)
    uncommon word: teetee (6)
e. Morse code for each letter is 2 symbols, longest
    common words: minima, manana (6-t)
    uncommon words: anamnia, miamian (7-t)
f. Morse code for each letter is 3 symbols, longest
    common words: woodwork, dogwoods (8-t)
    uncommon words: woodworks, kukukukus, ... and 2 others (9-t)
    phrase: sour gourds (10)
g. Morse code for each letter is 4 symbols, longest
    common word: flyby (5)
h. palindrome in Morse code, longest
    common word: intransigence (13)
i. isomorse pair (same Morse code words if pauses are ignored)
    i. longest well-mixed
        common words: artefacts & entailments (11)
        uncommon words: balminess & bennettiteses (13-t)
        uncommon words: disspreading & bessemerizing (13-t)
        ... and 4 others
        phrases: plant houses & plate batteries (14-t)
        phrases: hand gallops & signature loans (14-t)
    ii. longest measured in number of dots and dashes
        common words: rakishly & aimlessly (25)
        uncommon words: disspreading & bessemerizing (31-t)
        uncommon words: highbinders & hephthalites (31-t)
        uncommon words: buckishly & thanklessly (31-t)
        phrases: hand gallops & signature loans (34)
j. Morse code reversal pair (reversed Morse code words if pauses are ignored)
    i. longest
        common words: urgently & maintenance (11-t)
        common words: fracture & intertwined (11-t)
        common words: identical & internecine (11-t)
        common words: preempted & intemperate (11-t)
        uncommon words: shiverings & settlednesses (13)
    ii. longest measured in number of dots and dashes

common words: specials & halftimes (23)

uncommon words: funiculars & secularized (30)

phrases: half islands & superhelices (33)

k. iskot pair (reverse dots and dashes and ignore pauses in Morse code to form another word)

i. longest

common words: nostalgia & lamentation (11)

uncommon words: coxalgia & alimentation (12)

phrases: second banana & once upon a time (13)

ii. longest measured in number of dots and dashes

common words: nostalgia & lamentation (22)

uncommon words: alarmedly & cornrowed (25-t)

uncommon words: goatsbeard & infamatory (25-t)

phrases: second banana & once upon a time (30)

5. Telephone keypad

a. isotel pair (word spells out same telephone number as another word)

i. longest well-mixed

common words: comprising & conspiring (10)

uncommon words: compurgator & constrictor (11-t)

uncommon words: reimbursing & reincurring (11-t)

uncommon words: ungossiping & uninspiring (11-t)

ii. isotel pair with no letters in common, longest

common words: amounts & contour (7-t)

common words: astride & brushed (7-t)

common words: astride & crushed (7-t)

common words: hotbeds & invader (7-t)

uncommon words: amoebids & bondager (8-t)

uncommon words: acacetin & cacafugo (8-t)

uncommon words: jingling & khoikhoi (8-t)

b. consecutive letters on adjacent keys, longest for each letter

see page 63

IX. Letter Appearance

A. Entire Word

1. spelled with short lowercase letters = acemnorsuvwxz, longest

common words: reassurances, necromancers (12-t)

uncommon word: curvaceousnesses (16)

phrase: arcanum arcanorums (17)

2. spelled with tall lowercase letters = bdfghijklpqty, longest

common words: highlight, hillbilly (9-t)

uncommon words: lighttight, lillypilly (10-t)

hyphenated word: highty-tighty (12)

3. spelled with letters with descenders = gjpqy, longest

common word: gyp (3)

uncommon word: gyppy (5)

4. rotation or reflection symmetry

a. spelled with vertical symmetry letters = AHIMOTUVWXY, longest

common word: automata (8)

uncommon words: homotaxia, myomotomy, thymomata (9-t)

hyphenated word: mouth-to-mouth (12)

b. spelled with horizontal symmetry letters = BCDEHIKOX, longest

common word: checkbook (9)

uncommon word: coccidiocide (12)

hyphenated word: hoochie-coochie (14)

c. spelled with full symmetry letters = HIOX, longest

 common word: ooh (3)

 uncommon word: ohio (4)

 hyphenated word: hoo-oo (5)

d. catoptron, longest (word which remains the same when it is reflected in a mirror)

 i. vertical catoptron, longest

  common word: toot (4)

  uncommon words: aitia, aiaia, imami (5-t)

  hyphenated word: tat-tat-tat (9)

e. upside-down word (word that remains the same when it is turned upside down)

 i. longest lowercase

  common words: passed, dollop (6-t)

  uncommon word: sooloos (7)

 ii. longest uppercase

  common word: swims (5)

f. upside-down word pair

 i. longest lowercase

  common words: dooms & swoop (5)

  uncommon words: salades & sapeles (7-t)

  uncommon words: pappous & snodded (7-t)

 ii. longest uppercase

  common words: nos & son (3-t)

  common words: mom & wow (3-t)

  common words: ohm & who (3-t)

  uncommon words: nonis & sinon (5)

B. Subset of Word

1. ratio dotted to undotted letters, highest

 common words: jig, jib (0.67-t)

 uncommon words: fiji, iiwi, jibi (0.75-t)

X. Relations to Other Words

A. Word Lists

1. pangram (list of words containing all the letters of the alphabet)

 a. fewest letters

  uncommon words: waqf & jynx & speltz & vugh & mockbird [see "Pangrams" article, page 142]

 b. fewest words

  uncommon words: qwerty & flax & buckjumping & vozhds [see "Pangrams" article, page 142]

 c. containing most different letters, two words

  uncommon words: poldavy & thumbscrewing (20-t)

  uncommon words: blacksmith & gunpowdery (20-t)

 d. containing most different letters, three words

  uncommon words: jumbling & frowzy & sketchpad (23-t)

  uncommon words: browzing & kvetchy & mudflaps (23-t)

2. overlapping words

 a. crash list (word list with matching letters in some positions)

  i. longest symmetric

   see "Crashing Word Lists" article, page 176

B. Entire Word

1. reversal pair, longest (reverse the letters in a word to form another word)

common words: desserts & stressed (8)

2. deletion

    a. beheadment (delete first letter in a word to form another word)

        i. longest

            common words: preconditioning → reconditioning (15)

            uncommon words: preacknowledgements → reacknowledgements (19-t)

            uncommon words: prestandardizations → restandardizations (19-t)

            phrases: asynchronous transmission → synchronous transmission (24)

        ii. longest progressive

            common words: flashes → lashes → ashes → shes → hes → es → s (7-t)

            common words: slashes → lashes → ashes → shes → hes → es → s (7-t)

            common words: crashes → rashes → ashes → shes → hes → es → s (7-t)

            common words: clashes → lashes → ashes → shes → hes → es → s (7-t)

            common words: smashes → mashes → ashes → shes → hes → es → s (7-t)

            ... and 2 others

            uncommon words: prestates → restates → estates → states → tates → ates → tes → es → s (9)

        iii. longest double progressive

            common words: immigrants → migrants → grants → ants → ts (10-t)

            common words: fireplaces → replaces → places → aces → es (10-t)

            common words: detractors → tractors → actors → tors → rs (10-t)

            common words: extractors → tractors → actors → tors → rs (10-t)

            common words: immigrates → migrates → grates → ates → es (10-t)

            uncommon words: reafforesting → afforesting → foresting → resting → sting → ing → g (13-t)

            uncommon words: rewarehousing → warehousing → rehousing → housing → using → ing → g (13-t)

            uncommon words: unimmigrating → immigrating → migrating → grating → ating → ing → g (13-t)

    b. curtailment (delete last letter in a word to form another word)

        i. longest progressive

            common words: matters → matter → matte → matt → mat → ma → m (7-t)

            common words: singers → singer → singe → sing → sin → si → s (7-t)

            common words: pastels → pastel → paste → past → pas → pa → p (7-t)

            common words: passers → passer → passe → pass → pas → pa → p (7-t)

            common words: parsecs → parsec → parse → pars → par → pa → p (7-t)

            common words: parsers → parser → parse → pars → par → pa → p (7-t)

            uncommon words: romanisers → romaniser → romanise → romanis → romani → roman → roma → rom → ro → r (10)

        ii. longest double progressive

            common words: mythically → mythical → mythic → myth → my (10-t)

            common words: informally → informal → inform → info → in (10-t)

            uncommon words: prosodiacally → prosodiacal → prosodiac → prosodi → proso → pro → p (13-t)

            uncommon words: reversionally → reversional → reversion → reversi → rever → rev → r (13-t)

            ... and 2 others

    c. delete letter from any position to form another word

i. longest progressive

    common words: thrashes → trashes → rashes → ashes → shes → hes → es → s (8-t)

    common words: ashtrays → ashtray → astray → stray → tray → ray → ay → y (8-t)

    uncommon words: cantharidates → cantharidaes → cantharides → cantharids → cantharis → canthari → cathari → cathar → athar → thar → har → ar → r (13)

ii. longest nontrivial

    common words: acknowledgements → acknowledgments (16)

    uncommon words: hydroxydesoxycorticosterones → hydroxydeoxycorticosterones (28)

    phrases: transmission electron microscopies → transmission electron microscopes (32)

d. alternating terminal elision (alternate between deleting first and last letters to form a word list)

common words: craters → crater → rater → rate → ate → at → t (7-t)

common words: stoners → stoner → toner → tone → one → on → n (7-t)

common words: laments → lament → ament → amen → men → me → e (7-t)

uncommon words: carousers → carouser → arouser → arouse → rouse → rous → ous → ou → u (9-t)

uncommon words: ketamines → etamines → etamine → tamine → tamin → amin → ami → mi → m (9-t)

uncommon words: upraisers → upraiser → praiser → praise → raise → rais → ais → ai → i (9-t)

e. terminal elision (delete first and last letters to form another word)

i. longest

    common words: revolutionists → evolutionist (14-t)

    common words: gratifications → ratification (14-t)

    uncommon words: prestandardizations → restandardization (19-t)

    uncommon words: preacknowledgements → reacknowledgement (19-t)

    phrases: asexual reproductions → sexual reproduction (20)

ii. longest progressive

    common words: ashamed → shame → ham → a (7-t)

    common words: beaters → eater → ate → t (7-t)

    common words: bracers → racer → ace → c (7-t)

    common words: blowers → lower → owe → w (7-t)

    common words: craters → rater → ate → t (7-t)

    ... and 44 others

    uncommon words: charoseth → haroset → arose → ros → o (9-t)

    uncommon words: carousers → arouser → rouse → ous → u (9-t)

    ... and 22 others

    phrase: strainings → training → rain in → aini → in (10)

f. dismembered (delete either first or last letters to form words)

i. longest

    common words: preparations: reparations & preparation (12-t)

    common words: particulates: articulates & particulate (12-t)

    common words: prepositions: repositions & preposition (12-t)

    uncommon words: preacknowledgements: reacknowledgements & preacknowledgement (19-t) uncommon words: prestandardizations: restandardizations & prestandardization (19-t)

    ii. word torture, longest (word all of whose contiguous subsequences are words)

common words: fads: ads & fad & ad & ds & fa (4-t)

common words: byes: bye & yes & by & es & ye (4-t)

common words: bels: bel & els & be & el & ls (4-t)

common words: ayes: aye & yes & ay & es & ye (4-t)

common words: emus: emu & mus & em & mu & us (4-t)

... and 24 others

uncommon words: amides: amide & mides & amid & ides & mide & ami & des & ide & mid & am & de & es & id & mi (6-t)

uncommon words: alares: alare & lares & alar & ares & lare & ala & are & lar & res & al & ar & es & la & re (6-t)

... and 25 others

phrases: blowers: blower & lowers & blowe & lower & owers & blow & lowe & ower & wers & blo & ers & low & owe & wer & BL & er & lo & ow & rs & we (7-t)

phrases: amusers: amuser & musers & amuse & muser & users & amus & muse & sers & user & amu & ers & mus & ser & use & 'se & am & er & mu & rs & us (7-t)

    iii. word with no contiguous subsequence that is a word, longest

common word: crazily (7)

uncommon word: quiaquia (8)

    iv. word with no subsequence that is a word, longest

common words: tuck (4-t)

common words: razz (4-t)

hyphenated word: cui-ui (5)

g. delete consecutively repeated letters to form a word, longest

common words: adventuress → adventure (11)

uncommon words: multimillionairess → multimillionaire (18)

h. letter subtraction (delete all copies of letter in a word to form another word)

    i. longest

common words: worldliness → wordiness (11-t)

common words: adventuress → adventure (11-t)

common words: smatterings → mattering (11-t)

uncommon words: multimillionairess → multimillionaire (18)

phrases: chenodesoxycholic acids → chenodeoxycholic acid (22)

... and 3 others

    ii. longest progressive

common words: estates → stats → tat → a (7-t)

common words: erasers → eases → ass → a (7-t)

common words: titbits → ibis → bs (7-t)

uncommon words: restarters → estates → stats → tat → a (10-t)

uncommon words: sputterers → putterer → puerer → purr → pu (10-t)

uncommon words: tetrasters → erasers → eases → ass → a (10-t)

hyphenated words: passe-passes → paepae → papa → aa (11)

i. charitable (delete any letter to form another word)

    i. longest

common words: boats: oats & bats & bots & boas & boat (5-t)

common words: shoot: hoot & soot & shot & shot & shoo (5-t)

common words: coops: oops & cops & cops & coos & coop (5-t)

common words: moats: oats & mats & mots & moas & moat (5-t)

common words: seats: eats & sats & sets & seas & seat (5-t)

uncommon words: dearns: earns & darns & derns & deans & dears & dearn (6-t)

uncommon words: hairns: airns & hirns & harns & hains & hairs & hairn (6-t)

... and 12 others

ii. progressive charitable, longest (all contiguous and non-contiguous subsequences are words)

common words: bye: bye & be & by & ye (3-t)

common words: ash: ash & ah & as & sh (3-t)

common words: dos: dos & do & ds & os (3-t)

common words: ads: ads & ad & as & ds (3-t)

common words: els: els & el & es & ls (3-t)

... and 24 others

uncommon words: beens: beens & been & bees & bens & eens & bee & ben & bes & een & ees & ens & be & bs & ee & en & es & ns (5-t)

uncommon words: aides: aides & ades & aide & aids & aies & ides & ade & ads & aes & aid & aie & ais & des & ide & ids & ies & ad & ae & ai & as & de & ds & es & id & ie & is (5-t)

... and 40 others

j. stingy, shortest (cannot delete any letter to form another word)

common words: few (3-t)

common words: dry (3-t)

common words: cry (3-t)

common words: egg (3-t)

common words: fez (3-t)

... and 25 others

k. delete-reverse

i. longest

common words: demander → renamed (8-t)

common words: delivery → reviled (8-t)

common words: delivers → reviled (8-t)

common words: animates → stamina (8-t)

common words: assuaged → degauss (8-t)

... and 11 others

uncommon words: kinnikinnick → kinnikinnik (12-t)

uncommon words: kinnikinniks → kinnikinnik (12-t)

ii. longest progressive

common words: spacers → recaps → space → caps → spa → as → s (7-t)

common words: despots → stoped → depot → tope → pot → to → o (7-t)

common words: deports → stoped → depot → tope → pot → to → o (7-t)

uncommon words: animates → stamina → animas → samia → aims → sma → am → m (8-t)

uncommon words: cinerins → sirenic → ineris → siren → neri → ire → er → r (8-t)

... and 35 others

phrase: snap traps → spartans → satraps → sparts → strap → part → tap
→ pa → a (9-t)

phrase: stop order → redroots → to order → red rot → order → redo →
ode → ed → d (9-t)

3. insertion

a. hydration, longest (more than one way to add letter to front to form another word)

common words: enunciation: denunciation & renunciation (0.11)

uncommon words: evolutionists: devolutionists & revolutionists (0.13-t)

uncommon words: athematically: mathematically & pathematically (0.13-t)

uncommon words: irelessnesses: tirelessnesses & wirelessnesses (0.13-t)

b. hospitable, longest (insert letter anywhere to form another word)

common words: lens: glens & liens & leans & lends & lense (4)

uncommon words: cares: scares & chares & cadres & caries & carers & caress (5-t)

uncommon words: curie: ecurie & courie & cuirie & curnie & curiae & curies (5-t)

... and 6 others

c. hostile, shortest length > 3 (cannot insert letter anywhere to form word)

common words: ahem (4-t)

common words: anew (4-t)

common words: apex (4-t)

common words: achy (4-t)

common words: ahoy (4-t)

... and 43 others

4. deletion and insertion

a. charitable and hospitable, longest

uncommon words: abas: bas & aas & abs & aba & babas & abbas & abbas & abacs
& abase (4-t)

uncommon words: amas: mas & aas & ams & ama & camas & agmas & amaas &
amaas & amass (4-t)

... and 12 others

b. stingy and hostile, shortest

common words: ugly (4-t)

common words: idly (4-t)

common words: foci (4-t)

common words: razz (4-t)

5. substitution

a. onalosi, longest (word that can have a letter changed anywhere to form another word)

common words: grass: brass & glass & gross & grabs & grasp (5-t)

common words: clink: blink & chink & clank & click & cline (5-t)

common words: cline: aline & chine & clone & clime & cling (5-t)

common words: tents: bents & tints & teats & tends & tenth (5-t)

common words: boots: coots & blots & boats & boobs & booth (5-t)

... and 4 others

uncommon words: classes: glasses & chasses & clesses & clauses & clashes &
classis & classed (7-t)

uncommon words: delater: relater & dilater & debater & deleter & delayer & delator
& delated (7-t)

... and 2 others

b. isolano, shortest (word that cannot have a letter changed anywhere to form another word)

common words: upon (4-t)

        common words: evil (4-t)

        common words: envy (4-t)

        common words: epee (4-t)

        common words: ankh (4-t)

        common words: imam (4-t)

c. word ladders

    i. full vowel substitution, longest

        common words: patting & petting & pitting & potting & putting (7)

        uncommon words: chacking & checking & chicking & chocking & chucking (8-t)

        uncommon words: clacking & clecking & clicking & clocking & clucking (8-t)

        ... and 4 others

    ii. full vowel including y substitution, longest

        uncommon words: happed & hepped & hipped & hopped & hupped & hypped (6)

    iii. full vowel including y substitution, shortest > 1

        uncommon words: as & es & is & os & us & ys (2-t)

        uncommon words: ma & me & mi & mo & mu & my (2-t)

        uncommon words: ba & be & bi & bo & bu & by (2-t)

6. movement

a. head-to-tail shift (move letters from front of word to end to form another word)

    i. longest nontrivial one letter

        common words: devolve → evolved (7-t)

        common words: emanate → manatee (7-t)

        common words: griffin → riffing (7-t)

        uncommon words: denunciate → enunciated (10)

        phrases: dactinomycin → actinomycin D (12)

    ii. longest two letter

        common words: allocation → locational (10)

b. complete letter rotation, longest (all possible rotations of letters form other words)

        common words: ate & tea & eat (3-t)

        common words: asp & spa & pas (3-t)

        uncommon words: aras & rasa & asar & sara (4)

c. metathesis, longest (exchange two letters in a word to form another word)

        common words: certification → rectification (13-t)

        common words: accouterments → accoutrements (13-t)

        uncommon words: microspectrophotometers → microspectrophotometres (23)

7. transposition (rearrange letters to form another word)

a. well-mixed, longest

        common words: antiparticles & paternalistic (13)

        uncommon words: cinematographers & megachiropterans (16-t)

        uncommon words: antiferromagnets & refragmentations (16-t)

b. most

        common words: apres & pares & parse & pears & rapes & reaps & spare & spear (8)

        uncommon words: atles & laets & lates & least & leats & salet & setal & slate & stale & steal & stela & taels & tales & teals & tesla (15-t)

        uncommon words: anestri & antsier & nastier & neritas & ranties & ratines & resiant & restain & retains & retinas & retsina & stainer & starnie & stearin & taniers (15-t)

... and 2 others
>   phrases: angriest & angrites & astringe & gairtens & ganister & gantries & granites
>   & inert gas & ingrates & rangiest & reasting & seat ring & stearing &
>   tangiers & tasering & tea rings & tearings (17-t)

>   phrases: anestri & antsier & in tears & nastier & neritas & ranties & ratines &
>   resiant & restain & retains & retinas & retsina & stainer & starnie & stearin
>   & taniers & tin ears (17-t)

8. transdeletion (delete one letter and rearrange to form another word)
>   a. longest well-mixed
>>   common words: astrophysicist → psychiatrists (14-t)
>>   common words: discontinuance → denunciations (14-t)
>>   uncommon words: hypsistenocephalism → panmyelophthisises (19)
>>   phrases: atmospheric inversion → comprehensivisation (20-t)
>>   phrases: cutter classification → facilities contracts (20-t)
>   b. longest progressive
>>   common words: sweltering → wrestling → wresting → winters → strewn → wrest
>>   → west → wet → we → w (10-t)
>>   common words: amplifiers → imperials → imperils → simpler → primes → prism
>>   → rips → sir → rs → s (10-t)
>>   uncommon words: coadministrations → coadministration → romanticisation →
>>   ratiocinations → narcotisation → notarisation → nitrosation → intortions
>>   → sortition → tortonis → risotto → stroot → trots → tots → tot → to → t
>>   (17-t)
>>   uncommon words: internationalised → internationalise → interlineations →
>>   renointestinal → intenerations → internations → trentonians → stentorian
>>   → tontiners → trentons → rottens → otters → trots → tots → tot → to → t
>>   (17-t)
>   ... and 3 others

9. transaddition (add one letter and rearrange to form another word)
>   a. cannot add a letter and transpose to form word, shortest
>>   common words: hazy (4-t)
>>   common words: crux (4-t)
>>   common words: waxy (4-t)
>>   common words: razz (4-t)
>>   common words: jews (4-t)
>>   ... and 4 others

10. transubstitution (substitute one letter and rearrange to form another word)
>   a. longest well-mixed
>>   common words: transliterations → gastrointestinal (16)
>>   uncommon words: centrifugalisation → intercartilaginous (18-t)
>>   uncommon words: internationalities → tetranitroanilines (18-t)
>>   ... and 4 others
>>   phrases: adenosine monophosphate → put an ape in someone's hood (22)
>   b. changeover, longest (change one letter and move it to form another word)
>>   common words: determinations & exterminations (14-t)
>>   common words: expressiveness & repressiveness (14-t)
>>   uncommon words: attitudinarianisms & latitudinarianisms (18-t)
>>   uncommon words: preacknowledgement & reacknowledgements (18-t)
>>   ... and 2 others
>>   phrases: eastern diamondback rattlesnake & western diamondback rattlesnake (29)

c. switchback, longest (change first letter and reverse the rest to form another word)

e.g., SPOT → ATOP

    common words: regatta & wattage (7-t)

    common words: assuage & degauss (7-t)

    common words: dresser & presser (7-t)

    uncommon words: metallics & oscillate (9)

d. backswitch, longest (change last letter and reverse the rest to form another word)

e.g., AREA → ERAS

    common words: ellipse & spilled (7-t)

    common words: animals & laminar (7-t)

    common words: redrawn & warders (7-t)

    common words: nailers & reliant (7-t)

    common words: animals & laminae (7-t)

    uncommon words: levitators & rotatively (10)

11. words within words

    a. charade (concatenate words to form another word)

        i. snowball, longest (concatenate words increasing in length to form another word)

            common words: temperamentally: t & em & per & amen & tally (15)

            uncommon words: hexachlorocyclohexane: h & ex & ach & loro & cyclo & hexane (21)

        ii. reverse snowball, longest (concatenate words decreasing in length to form another word)

            common words: interventionist: inter & vent & ion & is & t (15-t)

            common words: interventionism: inter & vent & ion & is & m (15-t)

            uncommon words: heterotransplantation: hetero & trans & plan & tat & io & n (21-t)

            uncommon words: stereophotogrammetric: stereo & photo & gram & met & ri & c (21-t)

    b. linkade (overlap words to form another word)

        i. length three linkade, longest (word made from 3-letter overlapping words)

            common words: tapered: tap & ape & per & ere & red (7-t)

            common words: panther: pan & ant & nth & the & her (7-t)

            common words: anthems: ant & nth & the & hem & ems (7-t)

            common words: papered: pap & ape & per & ere & red (7-t)

            uncommon words: thanatopsides: tha & han & ana & nat & ato & top & ops & psi & sid & ide & des (13)

        ii. length four linkade, longest (word made from 4-letter overlapping words)

            common words: amends: amen & mend & ends (6-t)

            common words: honest: hone & ones & nest (6-t)

            common words: forest: fore & ores & rest (6-t)

            common words: irises: iris & rise & ises (6-t)

            common words: cramps: cram & ramp & amps (6-t)

            ... and 17 others

            uncommon words: demitasse: demi & emit & mita & itas & tass & asse (9-t)

            uncommon words: galanases: gala & alan & lana & anas & nase & ases (9-t)

            ... and 2 others

        iii. length five linkade, longest (word made from 5-letter overlapping words)

            common words: pasterns: paste & aster & stern & terns (8)

uncommon words: supranasal: supra & upran & prana & ranas & anasa & nasal (10)

c. alternade, longest (word made from two words that are interlaced every other letter)

common words: ballooned: blond & aloe (9-t)

common words: calliopes: clips & aloe (9-t)

common words: broadness: bodes & rans (9-t)

uncommon words: carpetweeds: crewes & apted (11-t)

uncommon words: curtainless: cranes & utils (11-t)

... and 2 others

d. embedded word (word embedded inside another word)

i. longest reversed

common words: phenomenal: anemone (7-t)

common words: phenomenally: anemone (7-t)

uncommon words: listerelloses: sollerets (9-t)

uncommon words: listerellosis: sollerets (9-t)

C. Subset of Word

1. games

a. Hangman, best words to play

see "Hangman" article, page 116

b. Jotto

see "Crashing Word Lists" article, page 176

d. Scrabble

i. highest single word score

common word: psychoanalyzing (1427)

uncommon word: oxyphenbutazone (1508)

Pronunciation

I. Syllables

A. Entire Word

1. longest

a. for each number of syllables

i. one syllable, for each letter

see page 68

ii. two syllables, for each letter

see page 68

2. shortest, for each number of syllables

see page 68

3. add one letter to add two syllables, shortest

common words: are → area (3-t)

common words: ide → idea (3-t)

4. no known pronunciation, shortest

uncommon word: balge (5)

5. change one letter to radically change pronunciation, longest

common words: encourage → entourage (9-t)

common words: telephone → telephony (9-t)

II. Rhyme

A. Entire Word

1. refractory rhyme, example of (word with no common rhyme)

see "Rhymes" article, page 158

III. Homophones (words spelled differently but pronounced the same)

A. longest

       uncommon words: uncomplementarinesses → uncomplimentarinesses (21)

B. homophones with no removable prefix or suffix, longest

       uncommon words: corespondent → correspondent (25)

C. most letters in list with no removable prefix or suffix

       uncommon words: scissel & scissile & sicel & sisal & sisel & sissle & syssel (42)

D. longest phrase with no removable prefix or suffix

       phrases: Grothendieck K-theory → growth-and-decay theory

E. most

       uncommon words: aer & air & are & ayer & ayr & e'er & ere & err & eyre & heir & ur (11)

F. longest with few letters in common

       uncommon words: shofar → chauffeur (3 out of 15)

       uncommon words: ceresin → Saracen (2 out of 14)

       uncommon words: cotter → Kadir (1 out of 11)

       uncommon words: cough → Kaf (0 out of 8)

G. longest transposal

       uncommon words: discreteness → discreetness (12)

H. confusing code words

e.g. G as in GNU, K as in KNOT

       see page 69

IV. Homographs (words spelled the same but pronounced differently)

A. different pronunciations, most

       uncommon word: as (like; Roman coin; Persian card game; plural of a; Norse Aesir god) (5)

B. capitonyms (words that change pronunciation when capitalized)

       see page 71

V. Miscellaneous

A. Entire Word

1. gramograms (words that sound like sequences of letters)

       a. longest

           common word: elementarily (LMNTRLE) (12)

           uncommon word: eosinophilous (ESNFLS) (13)

       b. for each letter sound

           see page 71

2. phonetic spellings identical with regular spelling, longest

       common word: spendthrifts (12)

       uncommon word: transformists (13)

3. pig Latin words that also are words, longest

       common words: plunder → underplay (7)

B. Subset of Word

1. silent letters

       a. longest sequence

           uncommon word: brougham (4, ugha)

       b. for each letter

           see page 70

       c. homophones, for each letter

           see page 69

2. ghost letters, for each letter

       see "Ghosts" article, page 84

3. suffix, most variable pronunciation

       common words: borough, thorough, tough, hiccough, nought, bough, trough, though, ought, cough, through [see "Pronunciation Variants" article, page 135]

Etymology

I. Initialisms, acronyms, portmanteaus
A. acronym that has become an uncapitalized word
1. longest
> wysiwyg (What You See Is What You Get) (7)

2. for each letter
> see page 72

B. portmanteau word (word formed by mixing two other words)
1. oldest
> parsec (PARallax SECond, 1913)

2. for each letter
> see page 73

II. Words with unusual origins
A. fossil (word that occurs only in idioms)
1. for each letter
> see page 72

B. affix clipping (words formed by moving a letter to or from a frequent companion word)
1. for each letter
> see page 73

Meaning

I. Ambiguity
A. different meanings or senses, most
> common word: break (245)

B. different parts of speech, most
> common word: like (8)

II. Synonyms and Antonyms
A. double synonyms or words with two different synonymous meanings, shortest
> common words: list & roll: set of names; tilt (4)

B. synonymic and antonymic reversals and transposals
1. synonymous reversal, longest
> common words: pat → tap (3)

2. synonymous transposal, longest
> common words: angered → enraged (7)
> uncommon words: adulation → laudation (9-t)
> uncommon words: amatorian → inamorata (9-t)
> uncommon words: listerize → sterilize (9-t)

C. contranyms (homographic antonym)
1. for each letter
> see page 74

2. contranyms, homophonic
> common words: aural & oral: heard & spoken
> common words: fiancé & fiancée: female betrothed & male betrothed
> common words: raise & raze: erect & tear down
> common words: succor & sucker: aid & hoodwink
> common words: enumerable & innumerable: countable & uncountable
> uncommon words: erupt & irrupt: burst out & burst in

uncommon words: eradicate & irradicate: pull up by the roots & root deeply

uncommon words: petalless & petalous: lacking petals & having petals

uncommon words: reckless & wreckless: careless & careful

D. double-duty antonyms (antonyms of two or more words)

1. antonyms, most

common word: lose: win & find & gain (3)

2. for each letter

see page 74

E. pseudantonyms (synonyms that appear to be antonyms)

see page 75

III. Plurals

A. Unusual

1. ending, for each letter

see page 75

2. drop s to make a plural

a. shortest

common words: assess → asses (6-t)

common words: caress → cares (6-t)

uncommon words: cess → ces (4-t)

uncommon words: dess → des (4-t)

... and 4 others

b. longest

common words: adventuress → adventures (11)

uncommon words: multimillionairess → multimillionaires (18)

c. makes its own plural

uncommon words: necropolis → necropoli

3. switching first two letters to make plural, example of

uncommon words: falaj → aflaj

4. add letters to beginning to make plural, example of

uncommon words: loti → maloti

uncommon words: sente → lisente

uncommon words: xhosa → amaxhosa

5. no letters in common with plural, longest

uncommon words: cow → kine (3/4)

6. colliding plurals, example of (words with homographic plurals)

common words: axe & axis → axes

common words: base & basis → bases

common words: ellipse & ellipsis → ellipses

IV. Pronouns

A. word containing most pronouns, shortest

common word: ushers: us & she & he & her & hers (5)

V. Miscellaneous

A. Sentences

1. repeated words, most

see "Repeated Words in a Sentence" article, page 166

SELECTED LISTS

Longest Palindrome Beginning with Each Letter	
a common word: anna (4) uncommon word: adinida (7) hyphenated word: abba-dabba (9)	p common words: poop, peep (4-t) uncommon word: peeweep (7)
b common word: boob (4)	q common word: q (1) uncommon word: qazaq (5)
c common word: civic (5)	r common word: rotator (7) uncommon word: rotavator (9)
d common word: deified (7)	s common words: stats, sexes, solos, sagas (5-t) uncommon words: sawbwas, seedees, ... and 4 others (7-t) phrase: stent nets (9)
e common words: eye, eve, ere, ewe (3-t) uncommon words: esse, ecce (4-t)	
f common word: f (1) phrase: FF (2)	
g common words: gig, gag (3-t) uncommon word: goog (4)	t common word: tenet (5) uncommon words: tippit, terret, ... and 3 others (6-t) hyphenated word: tat-tat-tat (9)
h common words: huh, hah (3-t) uncommon words: hagigah, halalah (7-t)	
i common word: i (1) uncommon words: imami, igigi (5-t)	u common word: u (1) uncommon word: ululu (5)
j common word: j (1)	v common word: v (1) uncommon word: vav (3)
k common word: kayak (5) uncommon word: kinnikinnik (11)	w common word: wow (3) hyphenated word: wow-wow (6)
l common word: level (5)	x common word: x (1)
m common words: madam, minim (5-t) uncommon word: malayalam (9)	y common word: y (1) uncommon word: yaray (5)
n common word: noon (4) uncommon word: nauruan (7)	z common word: z (1) uncommon words: zuz, ziz (3-t)
o common word: o (1) uncommon words: otto, oppo (4-t)	

Longest Palindrome Centered on Each Letter

a	common word: rotator (7) hyphenated word: tat-tat-tat (9)
b	common word: b (1) uncommon word: sawbwas (7)
c	common word: c (1) uncommon words: soccos, succus (6-t)
d	common word: redder (6) uncommon words: deedeed, murdrum, seedees (7-t) hyphenated word: abba-dabba (9)
e	common words: sees, deed, peep (4-t) uncommon words: racecar, sememes (7-t)
f	common word: deified (7)
g	common word: sagas (5) uncommon word: degged (6)
h	common word: aha (3)
i	common words: did, gig, bib, sis, tit, pip (3-t) uncommon words: reviver, hagigah (7-t)
j	common word: j (1) uncommon word: kajak (5)
k	common word: k (1) uncommon word: kinnikinnik (11)
l	common word: solos (5) uncommon word: sooloos (7)
m	common word: m (1) uncommon words: sammas (6)
n	common words: tenet, minim (5-t) uncommon word: adinida (7)

o	common words: noon, poop, boob, toot, kook (4-t) uncommon word: devoved (7)
p	common word: p (1) uncommon word: tippit (6)
q	common word: q (1)
r	common word: ere (3) uncommon word: nauruan (7)
s	common word: s (1) uncommon word: seesees (7)
t	common word: rotor (5) uncommon word: seities (7) phrase: stent nets (9)
u	common words: huh, nun, tut, pup, mum, dud (3-t) uncommon words: ululu, alula, ... and 2 others (5-t)
v	common words: level, civic (5-t) uncommon word: rotavator (9)
w	common word: ewe (3) uncommon word: peeweep (7)
x	common word: sexes (5)
y	common word: kayak (5) uncommon word: malayalam (9)
z	common word: z (1) uncommon words: kazak, qazaq (5-t)

Longest Tautonym Beginning with Each Letter	
a — uncommon words: atlatl, akeake (6-t) hyphenated word: agar-agar (8) hyphenated word: alang-alang, ... and 2 others (10)	**l** — uncommon words: lapulapu, lavalava, lomilomi (8-t) hyphenated word: links-links (10)
b — common word: bulbul (6) uncommon words: bellabella, bunyabunya (10-t) hyphenated words: bumpety-bumpety, bumpity-bumpity (14-t)	**m** — common word: murmur (6) uncommon words: mahimahi, makomako, ... and 2 others (8-t)
c — common word: chichi (6) uncommon word: chiquichiqui (12)	**n** — uncommon word: nagnag (6) hyphenated word: never-never, ... and 4 others (10)
d — common word: dodo (4) uncommon word: dividivi (8) hyphenated word: devil-devil (10)	**o** — uncommon word: oo (2) hyphenated word: onga-onga (8)
e — uncommon word: eses (4)	**p** — common word: pawpaw (6) uncommon words: palapala, pioupiou, ... and 2 others (8-t) hyphenated word: pretty-pretty (12) phrase: per second per second (18)
f — uncommon word: froufrou (8) hyphenated word: fifty-fifty (10)	
g — common word: gaga (4) uncommon words: ganggang, greegree, ... and 2 others (8-t) hyphenated word: goody-goody (10)	**q** — uncommon word: quinaquina (10)
	r — uncommon words: riroriro, rewarewa (8-t)
	s — uncommon word: sweeswee (8) hyphenated word: softly-softly (12)
h — common word: hotshots (8) hyphenated words: housey-housey, housie-housie (12-t)	**t** — common words: tartar, testes, tsetse (6-t) uncommon word: tangantangan (12)
i — uncommon word: ipilipil (8) hyphenated word: ilang-ilang (10)	**u** — uncommon word: ulaula (6)
	v — uncommon words: valval, verver (6-t)
j — uncommon word: jigjig (6) hyphenated word: jacky-jacky (10)	**w** — uncommon word: wallawalla (10)
	y — uncommon word: yariyari (8) hyphenated word: yabber-yabber (12)
k — uncommon words: khuskhus, kukukuku, ... and 6 others (8-t)	**z** — uncommon word: zoozoo (6) hyphenated word: zero-zero (8)

Longest Head 'n' Tail Centered on Each Letter			
a	common words: dad, gag, hah, tat, pap (3-t) uncommon words: muckamuck, pungapung (9-t) hyphenated word: tetes-à-tetes (11) phrases: biblia abiblia, goutte à goutte (13-t)	m	common word: mamma (5)
		n	common word: sense (5) uncommon words: galengale, tarantara (9-t)
b	common word: b (1) uncommon words: obo, aba (3-t) hyphenated words: argie-bargie, argle-bargle (11-t)	o	common words: pop, mom, bob, wow, tot (3-t) uncommon words: ingoing, mesomes (7-t) hyphenated word: convexo-convex (13)
c	common word: c (1) uncommon words: outscouts, overcover (9-t)	p	common word: p (1) uncommon word: apa (3)
		q	common word: q (1)
d	common word: d (1) uncommon word: okeydokey (9) hyphenated word: river-driver (11)	r	common word: verve (5)
		s	common word: hotshot (7) phrase: gentleman's gentleman (19)
e	common word: pep (3) uncommon words: arear, caeca, peepe (5-t) hyphenated word: do-se-dos (7) phrase: malariae malaria (15)	t	common word: t (1) uncommon word: einsteins (9)
		u	common word: shush (5)
		v	common word: eve (3) hyphenated word: arsy-varsy (9)
f	common word: f (1) uncommon words: efe, ofo (3-t) hyphenated word: artsy-fartsy (11)	w	common word: ewe (3) uncommon word: abwab (5) hyphenated word: eensie-weensie (13)
g	common words: edged, magma, algal (5-t) hyphenated word: old-gold (7)	x	common word: x (1) uncommon word: manxman (7)
h	common word: aha (3) uncommon word: outshouts (9)	y	common word: eye (3) uncommon word: calycal (7) hyphenated words: eighty-eight, nighty-night (11-t)
i	common word: onion (5) uncommon word: trinitrin (9)		
j	common word: j (1) uncommon word: anjan (5)	z	common word: z (1) hyphenated word: aza- (3)
k	common word: k (1) uncommon word: arkar (5)		
l	common word: salsa (5) uncommon words: ingling, khalkha (7-t)		

Word with the Lowest Ratio Length to Number of Different Letters, for Each Length

16	common words: acknowledgements, incomprehensibly, overcompensating, extemporaneously (1.23-t) uncommon words: ventriculography, pulmobranchiates (1.06-t)	21	uncommon words: dimethyltubocurarines, superacknowledgements (1.31-t)
17	common words: comprehensibility, microencapsulated (1.21-t) uncommon words: entwicklungsroman, diacetylmorphines, ... and 3 others (1.13-t) phrases: buckthorn families, pitch nodule makers (1.06-t)	22	common words: counterrevolutionaries, electroencephalography (1.83-t) uncommon words: blepharoconjunctivitis, diphenylthiocarbazones (1.37-t) phrase: calcium hydrogen sulfite (1.29)
		23	uncommon words: pseudolamellibranchiata, pseudolamellibranchiate (1.43-t) phrase: calcium hydrogen sulfites, ... and 2 others (1.35)
18	common words: australopithecines, compartmentalizing (1.38-t) uncommon words: entwicklungsromane, carboxyhemoglobins, ... and 9 others (1.20-t) phrase: hydromagnetic waves (1.12)	24	uncommon words: blepharoconjunctivitises, pseudolamellibranchiatas (1.50-t) phrases: double wingback formations, public works and ways system (1.33-t)
19	common word: incomprehensibility (1.35) uncommon words: psychogalvanometric, superacknowledgment (1.18-t)	25	uncommon word: spectroheliokinematograph (1.66) hyphenated word: d-gluco-pentahydroxy-pentyls (1.56) phrase: public works and ways systems (1.38)
20	common word: tetrahydrocannabinol (1.53) uncommon words: carbomethoxyglycines, mandibulopharyngeals, ... and 3 others (1.25-t)		

Longest Word That Starts and Ends with Each Letter

a	common words: agoraphobia, anaesthesia, abracadabra (11-t) uncommon word: abetalipoproteinemia (20) hyphenated word: alpha-naphthylthiourea (21)
b	common words: bathtub, brewpub (7-t) uncommon word: breadcrumb (10)
c	common words: crystallographic, chemotherapeutic (16-t) uncommon word: cineangiocardiographic (22)
d	common words: disenfranchised, discombobulated (15-t) uncommon word: deinstitutionalized (19)
e	common word: extraordinaire (14) uncommon word: ethylenediaminetetraacetate (27)
f	common word: flameproof (10) uncommon word: feedingstuff (12)
g	common word: gerrymandering (14) uncommon words: governmentalising, governmentalizing (17-t)
h	common word: horseradish (11) uncommon word: hygrothermograph (16)
i	common word: incubi (6) uncommon words: ichthyocephali, improvisatrici (14-t)
k	common words: kickback, knapsack, kinsfolk (8-t) uncommon word: killickinnick (13)
l	common word: lexicographical (15) uncommon word: litiscontestational (19)
m	common word: multiculturalism (16) uncommon word: magnetoencephalogram (20)
n	common words: nationalization, nonintervention (15-t) uncommon word: nonindustrialization (20) hyphenated phrase: Niceno-Constantinopolitan (24)
o	common word: obbligato (9) uncommon word: overbravado (11)
p	common word: proprietorship (14) uncommon word: primogenitureship (17)
q	uncommon word: qaraqalpaq (10)
r	common words: refrigerator, restaurateur (12-t) uncommon words: radiobroadcaster, reindustrializer (16-t) hyphenated word: refrigerator-freezer (19)
s	common word: straightforwardness (19) uncommon word: supercalifragilisticexpialidocious (34)
t	common word: traditionalist (14) uncommon word: transubstantiationalist (23)
u	uncommon word: ushabtiu (8)
v	uncommon word: vav (3)
w	common word: wheelbarrow (11) hyphenated word: winter-fallow (12)
x	common word: xerox (5)
y	common word: yesterday (9) uncommon word: yieldability (12)
z	uncommon word: zizz (4)

Shortest Word That Starts and Ends with Each Letter

a	common word: aha (3) uncommon word: aa (2)	m	common words: mom, mum (3-t) uncommon word: mm (2)
b	common words: bob, bib (3-t) uncommon word: bb (2)	n	common word: nun (3)
c	common word: chic (4) phrase: CFC (3)	o	common words: onto, oleo, olio (4-t) uncommon word: oo (2)
d	common words: did, dad, dud (3-t) phrase: DD (2)	p	common words: pop, pup, pap, pip, pep (3-t)
e	common words: eye, eve, ere, ewe (3-t) uncommon word: ee (2)	q	uncommon word: qazaq (5)
f	common word: fief (4) phrase: FF (2)	r	common words: rear, roar (4-t)
g	common words: gig, gag (3-t)	s	common word: sis (3) uncommon word: ss (2)
h	common words: huh, hah (3-t)	t	common words: tot, tut, tat, tit (3-t)
i	common word: incubi (6) uncommon word: ihi (3)	u	uncommon words: utu, ulu, uku (3-t)
k	common words: kick, kink, kirk, kook (4-t)	v	uncommon word: vav (3)
l	common words: lull, loll (4-t) phrase: LDL (3)	w	common word: wow (3)
		x	common word: xerox (5)
		y	common word: yummy (5) uncommon word: yay (3)
		z	uncommon words: zuz, ziz (3-t)

Shortest Word with Last Letter Next in Alphabet After First, for Each Letter

a	common word: alb (3) uncommon word: ab (2)	m	common words: man, men (3-t)
b	common word: bloc (4) phrases: BSc, BHC (3-t)	n	common word: no (2)
c	common words: cod, cad, cud (3-t) phrases: CD (2)	o	common words: overlap, outcrop, overtop (7-t) uncommon word: op (2)
d	common words: die, due, dye, doe (3-t) uncommon word: de (2)	p	uncommon word: pdq (3)
e	common word: elf (3) uncommon word: ef (2)	q	common word: queer (5)
f	common words: fog, fig, fag (3-t)	r	common word: rs (2)
g	common words: gosh, gash, gush (4-t)	s	common words: set, sit, sat, sot (3-t) uncommon word: st (2)
h	common word: hi (2)	t	common word: tau (3)
j	common words: junk, jack, jerk, jock (4-t) uncommon word: jak (3)	v	common word: vow (3)
k	common words: kill, keel, kohl (4-t) uncommon word: kol (3)	w	common word: wax (3)
l	common words: loom, loam (4-t) uncommon words: lam, lum, lym (3-t) phrase: LM (2)	x	common word: xerography (10) uncommon word: xylary (6) hyphenated word: x-ray (4)
		y	uncommon word: yez (3)
		z	common word: zeta (4) uncommon words: zia, zea, zoa (3-t)

Longest Word Containing One Type of Vowel, for Each Vowel

a	common words: transplants, grandstands, crankshafts, abracadabra (11-t) uncommon word: tathagatagarbhas (16) hyphenated phrase: macassar agar-agars (17)	o	common words: strongholds, schoolbooks, schoolrooms (11-t) uncommon word: loxolophodonts (14) phrase: worst of both worlds (17)
e	common word: speechlessness (14) uncommon word: strengthlessnesses (18)	u	common words: untruthful, numbskulls (10-t) uncommon word: struldbrugs (11) phrases: thrush fungus, turn up trumps (12-t)
i	common words: highlighting, disciplining, philistinism (12-t) uncommon word: instinctivistic (15) phrases: filling knittings, pitching niblicks (16-t) hyphenated phrase: bright-light districts (20)	y	common word: rhythms (7)

Longest Word Containing One Type of Consonant, for Each Consonant

b	common words: babe, beau, oboe, boob, abbe (4-t) uncommon word: ouabaio (7)	n	common words: union, onion, inane, ennui, anion (5-t) uncommon words: nonunion, anianiau (8-t)
c	common word: acacia (6) uncommon word: coccaceae (9)	p	common word: pupae (5) uncommon words: epopoeia, papiopio, pioupiou (8-t)
d	common words: iodide, deeded, doodad (6-t) uncommon words: diiodide (8)	q	common word: queue (5) uncommon word: quiaquia (8)
f	common words: fife, fief (4-t) uncommon word: feoffee (7)	r	common word: aurorae (7) uncommon word: riroriro (8)
g	common words: gauge, gouge, aggie (5-t) hyphenated words: goo-goo, gee-gee (6-t) phrase: OO gauge (7)	s	common word: assesses (8) uncommon word: assessees (9) hyphenated word: sous-souses (10)
h	common words: huh, hoe, hah, hue, ooh, ... and 2 others (3-t) uncommon word: heiau (5) hyphenated words: hee-hee, hoo-hah (6-t)	t	common word: tattoo (6) uncommon word: autoette (8) hyphenated word: tete-à-tete, ... and 2 others (9)
j	common word: j (1) uncommon word: ouija (5)	v	common word: viva (4) uncommon word: evovae (6)
k	common word: kook (4) uncommon word: kukukuku (8)	w	common words: owe, wow, wee, awe, woo, ... and 2 others (3-t) uncommon words: weewee, waiwai (6-t)
l	common word: allele (6) uncommon words: alleluia, lulliloo (8-t)	x	common word: axe (3) uncommon words: euxoa, oxeae (5-t)
m	common words: momma, mamma (5-t) uncommon words: mommie, mammie, ... and 11 others (6-t)	z	common word: ooze (4) uncommon words: zooeae, zoozoo (6-t)

Word with Highest Letter Sum, for Each Length

2	common word: zs (45) uncommon word: wy (48)	10	common word: tumultuous (183) uncommon word: puttyroots (189) hyphenated word: tuzzy-muzzy (229)
3	common word: wry (66) uncommon word: zuz (73)	11	common word: trustworthy (207)
4	common word: yurt (84) uncommon word: tuzz (93) hyphenated word: zu-zu (94)	12	common word: synonymously (217) uncommon word: tumultuously (220) hyphenated word: tuzzy-muzzies (237)
5	common word: tizzy (106) uncommon word: muzzy (111) hyphenated word: zu-zus (113)	13	common word: sportswriters (219) uncommon word: untrustworthy (242)
6	common word: trusty (123) uncommon word: xystus (128)	14	common word: presumptuously (241) uncommon word: topsyturviness (242) hyphenated word: topsy-turvydoms (252) phrase: statutory trust (257)
7	common word: tryouts (138) uncommon word: zyzzyva (151)	15	common words: trustworthiness, superstitiously (248-t) uncommon word: untrustworthily (263) phrase: statutory trusts (276)
8	common word: synonymy (150) uncommon word: zyzzyvas (170)		
9	common word: torturous (167) uncommon word: zorotypus (175)		

Word with Lowest Letter Sum, for Each Length

2	common word: ad (5) uncommon word: aa (2)	11	common word: abracadabra (52) uncommon word: cabbagehead (39)
3	common word: baa (4)	12	common word: academicians (82) uncommon word: cabbageheads (58) hyphenated word: bibble-babble (56)
4	common words: babe, abbe (10-t) uncommon words: baba, abba (6-t)	13	common word: decaffeinated (83) uncommon word: anacardiaceae (66) phrase: bag and baggage (59)
5	common word: abaci (16) uncommon words: abaca, caaba (8-t)	14	common word: megalomaniacal (107) uncommon word: hamamelidaceae (81) phrase: heading cabbage (69)
6	common words: dabbed, acacia (18-t) uncommon word: bacaba (10)	15	common word: lackadaisically (123) uncommon word: lardizabalaceae (101) phrase: heading cabbages (88) hyphenated phrase: bald-headed eagle (76)
7	common word: cabbage (21) uncommon word: cachaca (20)		
8	common words: beheaded, backache (34-t) uncommon word: fabaceae (24)		
9	common word: beachhead (37) uncommon word: beccaccia (30) hyphenated word: abba-dabba (16)		
10	common words: backhanded, bareheaded (53-t) uncommon words: deadheaded, chachalaca (41-t) hyphenated word: face-bedded (39)		

Word Containing the Most Repeats of Each Letter

a	common word: abracadabra (5) uncommon words: taramasalata, astragalocalcaneal, ... and 7 others (6-t) phrase: anathema maranatha, ... and 6 others (7)
b	common words: bubble, babble, bubbly, bobby, blubber, ... and 31 others (3-t) uncommon words: flibbertigibbet, beblubbered, ... and 6 others (4-t) hyphenated word: bibble-babble (6)
c	common words: accuracy, acceptance, characteristic, conscience, coincidence, ... and many others (3-t) uncommon words: chroococcaceae, chroococcaceous, ... and 5 others (5-t)
d	common word: muddleheaded (4) uncommon word: dunderheadededness (5) hyphenated word: diddle-daddled (7)
e	common words: interdependence, interdependencies, beekeeper, representativeness, enfeeblement, ... and 2 others (5-t) uncommon word: ethylenediaminetetraacetate (7) phrase: between the devil and the deep blue sea (10)
f	common word: riffraff (4) hyphenated word: fluffy-ruffle (5)
g	common words: giggling, gagging, gigging, aggregating, goggling, zigzagging (4-t) uncommon word: huggermuggering (5) hyphenated word: wagger-pagger-bagger (6)
h	common words: highlight, hashish, hitchhike, photolithography, ... and 6 others (3-t) uncommon words: dichlorodiphenyltrichloroethane, dinaphthothiophene, ... and 12 others (4-t) phrases: hold with the hare and run with the hounds, run with the hare and hunt with the hounds (7-t)
i	common words: initialization, incompatibilities, initializing, invisibility, individualistic, ... and 12 others (5-t) uncommon word: floccinaucinihilipilification (9)
j	common words: jujutsu, jejune, jujitsu (2-t)
k	common word: kickback (3) uncommon words: kukukuku, kakkak, ... and 10 others (4-t)
l	common words: volleyball, illegally, intellectually, willfully, skillfully, ... and 10 others (4-t) uncommon words: allochlorophyll, alloplastically, ... and 7 others (5-t) phrases: all hell is let loose, all's well that ends well (6-t)
m	common words: minimum, maximum, commitment, momentum, communism, ... and 45 others (3-t) uncommon words: mammogram, immunocompromised, ... and 28 others (4-t) phrase: maximum and minimum thermometer (8)

### Word Containing the Most Repeats of Each Letter (continued)	

n	common words: inconveniencing, nondenominational, nonintervention (5-t) hyphenated words: nonny-nonny (6) phrase: noncondensing engine (7)	t	common words: intermittent, constitutionality, institutionalization, scuttlebutt, statuette, ... and 8 others (4-t) uncommon words: anticonstitutionalist, ethylenediaminetetraacetate, ... and 15 others (5-t) hyphenated word: tittle-tattle (6) phrase: pentaerythritol tetranitrate, ... and 3 others (7)
o	common word: chlorofluorocarbon (5) uncommon words: hydrochlorofluorocarbon, monogonoporous, pseudomonocotyledonous (6-t) phrase: don't halloo till you're out of the wood (8)		
		u	common words: unscrupulous, tumultuous (4-t) uncommon word: humuhumunukunukuapuaa (9)
p	common word: whippersnapper (4) hyphenated word: pepper-upper (5) phrase: philadelphia pepper pot (6)	v	common words: survive, conservative, involve, survival, involvement, ... and many others (2-t) uncommon words: ovoviviparous, overconservative, ... and 14 others (3-t)
q	common words: question, quite, quality, request, sequence, ... and many others (1-t) uncommon word: qaraqalpaq (3)	w	common word: powwow (3) hyphenated word: wow-wow (6)
r	common words: refrigerator, extraterrestrial, extracurricular, extraterritorial, extraterritoriality, ... and 2 others (4-t) uncommon words: ferriprotoporphyrin, ferroprotoporphyrin, ... and 2 others (5-t) hyphenated words: refrigerator-freezer, strawberry-raspberry (6-t) hyphenated phrase: reverse-current circuit breaker (7)	x	common word: xerox (2) uncommon word: hexahydroxycyclohexane (3)
		y	common words: polygyny, synonymously, polydactyly, synonymy (3-t) uncommon words: polyhydroxybutyrate, hyperpolysyllabically (4-t)
		z	common words: jazz, pizza, fuzzy, puzzle, buzz, ... and many others (2-t) uncommon words: pizzazz, razzamatazz, ... and 9 others (4-t)
s	common words: possessiveness, senselessness (6-t) uncommon word: possessionlessnesses (9)		

Word with the Most Infrequently Used Letters, for Each Length

2	common word: by (37) uncommon word: ky (29) phrase: BZ (18)
3	common word: jug (54) uncommon word: zuz (33)
4	common word: buzz (50)
5	common word: fuzzy (73) uncommon word: buzzy (70)
6	common word: dybbuk (128) uncommon word: kumbuk (125) hyphenated word: jug-jug (108)
7	common word: mugwump (181) uncommon word: zyzzyva (134)
8	common word: mugwumps (247) uncommon word: kukukuku (160)
9	common word: piggyback (296) uncommon word: kukukukus (226)
10	common words: blackjacks, zigzagging (374-t) uncommon word: xyloglyphy (319) hyphenated word: fuddy-duddy (292) hyphenated word: fuzzy-wuzzy (145)
11	common word: quizzically (396) uncommon word: bumfuzzling (331)
12	common word: skullduggery (493) uncommon word: zygophyllums (421) hyphenated word: wibbly-wobbly (380)
13	common word: swashbuckling (573) uncommon word: brachyphyllum (496) hyphenated word: high-mucky-muck (414)
14	common word: unscrupulously (624) uncommon word: brachyphyllums (562) hyphenated word: high-muck-a-mucks (540) phrase: milky way galaxy (536)
15	common word: psychologically (701) uncommon word: chylophyllously (637) hyphenated word: high-muckety-muck (623) phrase: roxbury waxworks (605)

Word with the Most Frequently Used Letters, for Each Length

2	common word: en (186) uncommon word: ee (236)
3	common word: tee (327)
4	common word: teen (395) uncommon word: tete (418)
5	common words: eerie, tenet (486-t) uncommon word: teene (513)
6	common word: settee (602) uncommon word: teetee (654)
7	common word: entente (672) uncommon word: entêtée (722)
8	common word: teetered (748) uncommon word: teaettes (773)
9	common word: reiterate (808) uncommon word: theetsees (835) hyphenated word: tete-à-tete (916)
10	common word: entreaties (882) uncommon word: teentsiest (899) hyphenated word: tete-à-tetes (982)
11	common word: teetotalers (953) uncommon word: tennesseean (979) hyphenated word: tetes-à-tetes (1048)
12	common word: testosterone (1043) uncommon word: teetertotter (1125)
13	common word: entertainment (1071) uncommon word: tetraacetates (1118) hyphenated word: teeter-totters (1191)
14	common word: entertainments (1137) uncommon word: heteronereises (1200) hyphenated word: teeter-tottered (1277)
15	common word: interpenetrated (1211) uncommon word: heterogeneratae (1267) hyphenated word: teeter-tottering (1285)

Longest Word with Consecutive Letters Adjacent on Phone Keypad for Each Letter	
a common word: anticoagulants (14) uncommon word: antichristianly (15)	l common word: luxuriant (9) uncommon words: luxuriantly, lecithality (11-t) phrase: lots to blanks (12)
b common words: bluntly, biplane, blandly (7-t) uncommon word: bicentricity (12) phrase: block and block (13)	m common word: maladjustment (13) uncommon word: multicentricity (15)
c common word: councilman (10) uncommon word: christocentric (14)	n common word: nuptials (8) uncommon word: neothalamus (11)
d common words: download, downtown, docility (8-t) uncommon word: downthrusts (11)	o common word: obelisks (8) uncommon word: obliviality (11)
e common words: entitlements, enchantments (12-t) uncommon word: enchaicnements (14)	p common word: phlebitis (9) uncommon words: phleboliths, pilpulistic, ptolemaists (11-t)
f common words: flourish, flamenco, fourthly (8-t) uncommon word: flagsticks (10)	r common words: rundown, rupiahs, risible (7-t) uncommon word: rhadamanthus (12) phrase: rice christian (13)
g common word: gamecocks (9) uncommon word: gaelicists (10) phrase: game of chance (12)	s common word: shantytown (10) uncommon words: silicicolous, stylistician (12-t) phrase: silence cloths (13)
h common word: humanlike (9) uncommon word: hustlements (11) phrases: hail columbia, handle blanks (12-t) hyphenated phrase: half-Christian (13)	t common words: triviality, thumbnails (10-t) uncommon words: trivialists, thricecocks, tylenchulus (11-t) phrase: triple blocks (12)
i common words: island, iambic, iceman, icicle, icebox (6-t) uncommon word: ileocolitis (11)	u common word: unchristian (11) uncommon word: unchristianlike (15)
j common words: jealously, joviality (9-t) uncommon words: jovicentric, jumblements (11-t) phrase: justice courts (13)	v common words: visibility, virulently (10-t)
	w common words: would, wound, woken (5-t) uncommon word: wolvishly (9)
k common word: kilovolts (9) uncommon words: kamchadale, kamchadals (10-t) hyphenated word: kana-majiris (11)	x common word: x (1) uncommon word: xoana (5) phrase: x virus (6)
	y common word: yokels (6) uncommon word: yokelish (8)

Word Containing Most Consecutive Letters in the Alphabet After Each Letter

a	common words: feedback, fabricated, boldface, backfired, backfield, ... and 5 others (6-t) uncommon word: blackfigured (7) hyphenated word: right-about-faced (9)
b	common words: feedback, fabricated, boldface, backfired, backfield, ... and 5 others (5-t) uncommon words: fredericksburg, blackfigured (6-t) hyphenated word: right-about-faced (8)
c	common words: disenfranchising, goldfinches (7-t) phrase: floodlight projector (8)
d	common words: frightened, delightful, foreshadowing, figurehead, farsighted, ... and 8 others (6-t) phrase: floodlight projector (7)
e	common words: fighter, refreshing, freight, delightful, frighten, ... and 50 others (5-t) uncommon word: jetfighter (6) phrases: knight of st. john of jerusalem, knights of st. john of jerusalem (11-t)
f	common words: fight, flight, fishing, finishing, straightforward, ... and many others (4-t) uncommon word: jetfighter (5) hyphenated word: half-joking (7) phrases: knight of st. john of jerusalem, knights of st. john of jerusalem (10-t)
g	common words: hijacking, straightjacket (5-t) uncommon words: jacklight, kjeldahlizing, ... and 5 others (6-t) phrases: knight of st. john of jerusalem, knights of st. john of jerusalem (9-t)
h	common words: hijack, straightjacket, ... and 2 others (4-t) uncommon words: jacklight, jakhalsbessie, ... and 12 others (5-t) phrase: checkbook journalism, ... and 5 others (8)
i	common words: jokingly, jaywalking, jailbreak, jerkily, killjoy, kilojoules (4-t) uncommon word: jasminelike (6) hyphenated word: checkbook journalism, ... and 7 others (7)
j	common word: lumberjack (4) uncommon word: jasminelike (5) phrase: japanese hemlock (7)
k	common words: sportsmanlike, kleptomaniac (6-t)
l	common words: development, implementation, complain, employment, compilation, ... and many others (5-t) uncommon words: plasmoquin, plasmoquine, ... and 3 others (6-t) hyphenated word: quasi-complimentary (10)

Word Containing Most Consecutive Letters in the Alphabet After Each Letter (continued)		
m	common words: important, company, development, performance, programming, ... and many others (4-t) uncommon words: plasmoquin, plasmoquine, ... and 5 others (5-t) hyphenated words: quasi-complimentary, quasi-important (9-t)	s	common word: liverwurst (5)
		t	common words: overwrought, liverwurst (4-t)
		u	common words: purview, overwrought, unswerving, liverwurst (3-t)
		v	common words: however, whatever, view, review, whenever, ... and many others (2-t) hyphenated words: ex-servicewoman, grave-wax (3-t) phrase: downy false foxglove, ... and 4 others (4)
n	common words: quadraphonic, propinquity (5-t) uncommon words: perquisition, propinquities, ... and 22 others (8-t) phrase: equivalent evaporations, ... and 10 others (9)	w	common words: expressway, waxy (3-t) phrase: waxy maize (5)
		x	common words: exactly, extremely, approximately, syntax, explicitly, ... and many others (2-t) uncommon word: benzoxyacetanilide (8)
o	common words: quadraphonic, equiprobable, propinquity (4-t) uncommon words: perquisition, propinquities, ... and 40 others (7-t) hyphenated words: quasi-productive, quasi-provocative (8-t)	y	common words: recognizably, recognizability (5-t) uncommon word: brazenfacedly (8) hyphenated phrase: gazelle-faced wallaby (9)
		z	common words: cannibalized, carbonized (6-t) uncommon word: brazenfaced (7) phrase: exchange stabilization fund (10)
p	common words: prerequisite, picturesque, pratiques, perquisite, quadruplets, ... and 2 others (6-t) uncommon words: preacquisitive, superequivalent, superinquisitive (7-t) hyphenated phrase: quarter-wave plates (8)		
q	common word: ventriloquist (6) hyphenated word: quasi-interviewed (7)		
r	common word: liverwurst (6)		

Word Containing Most Consecutive Letters in Order After Each Letter

a	common word: absconded (5)	o	common words: opaque, opaqueness (3-t) uncommon word: opaquers (5)
b	common words: blockade, backside, backwardness, barricade, backhanded, ... and 11 others (4-t) hyphenated word: backside-front (5)	p	common words: prerequisite, opaque, politique, plaque, physique, ... and 20 others (2-t) uncommon words: pulquerias, opaquers, ... and 5 others (4-t)
c	common words: code, include, children, consider, candidate, ... and many others (3-t) uncommon words: schadenfreude, codefendant, ... and 11 others (4-t) phrase: code flag (5)	q	common word: aquarist (4)
		r	common words: restaurant, infrastructure, redistribute, prostitution, reconstruction, ... and 38 others (4-t) uncommon words: reconstructive, redistributive, ... and 5 others (5-t)
d	common words: defending, defining, identifying, defeating, deafening, ... and 23 others (4-t) hyphenated word: dead-freight (5)	s	common words: constructive, destructive, instructive, distributive, constitutive, ... and 6 others (4-t) phrase: distributive law (5)
e	common words: spaceflight, preflight, overflight (4-t) hyphenated word: self-naughting (5)	t	common words: constructive, destructive, intuitive, turnover, truelove, ... and 22 others (3-t) phrase: distributive law, ... and 4 others (4)
f	common word: flagship (4)	u	common word: purview (3)
g	common words: graphic, laughing, graphical, gathering, geographic, ... and 77 others (3-t) phrase: laughing jackass (5)	v	common words: view, review, interview, everywhere, viewpoint, ... and 95 others (2-t) hyphenated word: grave-wax (3)
h	common word: hijack (4)	w	common word: waxy (3) phrase: waxy maize (4)
i	common words: hijack, straitjacket, straightjacket, ... and 4 others (3-t) uncommon word: rijksdaalder (4)	x	common words: exactly, extremely, approximately, explicitly, homosexuality, ... and many others (2-t) uncommon word: oxygenizable (5)
j	common words: jokingly, jackal, jerkily (3-t) phrase: jack salmon (5)		
k	common word: kleptomaniac (4)	y	common words: synchronization, polymerization, stylization, symbolization, systemization (3-t) uncommon words: etymologizable, hydrolyzable, ... and 20 others (4-t)
l	common words: elimination, illumination, luminous, flamenco, culmination, ... and 18 others (4-t) uncommon words: aluminotype, alimentotherapy, ... and 28 others (5-t)		
		z	common words: recognizable, sizable, sizeable, customizable, mozambique, ... and 4 others (3-t) uncommon words: mozambican, mozarabic, ... and 2 others (4-t)
m	common words: minicomputer, menopause, immunosuppression, magnetosphere, acetaminophen, ... and 9 others (4-t) uncommon word: semnopitheque (5)		
n	common words: newsgroup, envelope, censorship, incomplete, incompatible, ... and many others (3-t) uncommon words: nonopaque, semnopitheque (4-t) phrase: animis opibusque parati, ... and 2 others (5)		

Word Spelled with E Before I, Beginning with Each Letter

a	albeit		n	neither
b	being		o	obeisance
c	counterfeit		p	protein
d	deity		q	quisqueite
e	either		r	reveille
f	feisty		s	seize
g	geiger		t	their
h	height		u	ureic
i	isocheim		v	verein
j	jangadeiro		w	weird
k	kaleidoscope		x	xylindein
l	leisure		y	yankeeism
m	murein		z	zeitgeist

Word Spelled with I Before E After C, Beginning with Each Letter

a	ancient		n	nescience
b	boccie		o	omniscient
c	concierge		p	proficient
d	deficient		q	quiescencies
e	efficient		r	rubefacient
f	financier		s	species
g	glacier		t	theocracies
h	hacienda		u	unscientific
i	inefficient		v	valenciennes
j	juicier		w	wardencies
k	kakistocracies		x	xylomancies
l	liquefacient		z	zincier
m	mutafacient			

Shortest Word for Each Number of Syllables

2	aa (2)	7	epidemiology (12)
3	w (1)	8	epizootiology (13)
4	ieie (4)	9	epizootiological (16)
5	oxyopia (7)	10	epizootiologically (18)
6	oniomania (9)	12	humuhumunukunukuapuaa (21)

Longest One-Syllable Word Beginning with Each Letter

a	arched (6)	n	naughts (7)
b	broughams (9)	o	oinked (6)
c	craunched (9)	p	preached (8)
d	draughts (8)	q	quenched (8)
e	earthed (7)	r	reached (7)
f	flinched (8)	s	squirrelled (11)
g	grouched (8)	t	thoughts (8)
h	haunched (8)	u	umphs (5)
i	itched (6)	v	vouched (7)
j	jounced (7)	w	wreathed (8)
k	knights (7)	x	xysts (5)
l	launched (8)	y	yearned (7)
m	mooched (7)	z	zouaves (7)

Longest Two-Syllable Word Beginning with Each Letter

a	archfiends (10)	n	nightclothes (12)
b	breakthroughs (13)	o	outstretched (12)
c	clotheshorse (12)	p	ploughwrights (13)
d	draughtboards (13)	q	quickthorns (11)
e	earthtongues (12)	r	roughstrings (12)
f	flameproofed (12)	s	scratchbrushed (14)
g	groundsheets (12)	t	throatstraps (12)
h	hairsbreadths (13)	u	unstretched (11)
i	inthralled (10)	v	versesmiths (11)
j	juneteenths (11)	w	wherethrough (12)
k	knickknacks (11)	x	xanthines (9)
l	lightweights (12)	y	yourselves (10)
m	moosetongues (12)	z	zeitgeists (10)

Homophones Differing by One Letter, for Each Differing Letter

a	oar & or		n	damn & dam
b	lamb & lam		o	callous & callus
c	scent & sent		p	psalter & salter
d	add & ad		r	carries & caries
e	bye & by		s	scent & cent
f	waff & waf		t	butt & but
g	reign & rein		u	buy & by
h	hour & our		v	civvies & civies
i	waive & wave		w	two & to
j	hajji & haji		x	beaux & beau
k	knot & not		y	rey & re
l	halve & have		z	bizz & biz
m	primmer & primer			

Word That Is a Confusing Code Word for Each Letter

a	aisle (isle)		m	mnemic (nemic)
b	bdell- (dell)		o	oued (wed)
c	ctene (teen)		p	psi (sigh)
d	djin (gin)		q	Qatar (gutter)
e	ewe (you)		s	Saar (czar)
f	frays (phrase)		t	tsine (sign)
g	gnu (new)		u	uang (wang)
h	heir (air)		v	vrow (fro)
i	ius (use)		w	wrap (rap)
j	juca (yuca)		x	xurel (jurel)
k	knot (not)		y	ye (the)
l	llareta (yareta)		z	zabra (sabra)

Word That Begins with Each Silent Letter

a	aisle	k	know
b	bdellium	m	mnemonic
c	czar	n	Ngo
d	djinni	o	oedipal
e	eider	p	psyche
g	gnaw	r	Rzeszow
h	hour	t	tsunami
i	ius	w	write
j	justitiae	y	yean

Word That Contains Each Silent Letter

a	liar	n	monsieur
b	debt	o	people
c	indict	p	sapphire
d	handsome	q	cinq-cents
e	twitched	r	forecastle
f	halfpenny	s	viscount
g	phlegm	t	apostle
h	ghost	u	plaque
i	business	v	fivepence
j	rijsttafel	w	two
k	blackguard	x	fauxbourg
l	talk	y	prayer
m	panmnesia	z	rendezvous

Word That Ends with Each Silent Letter

a	parmigiana	l	fauteuil
b	comb	n	autumn
c	en banc	p	coup
d	sangfroid	r	foyer
e	borne	s	apropos
f	roman à clef	t	rapport
g	bourg	u	nunchaku
h	myrrh	w	tow
i	hegari	x	doux
j	Bitolj	y	day
k	Perak	z	oyez

Word Pronounced Differently When Capitalized, Beginning with Each Letter

a	august (majestic, month)	m	mole (birthmark, Sudanese people)
b	begin (start, former Israeli leader)	n	nestles (snuggles, beverage maker)
c	concord (agree, New Hampshire capital)	o	our (belonging to us, river in Belgium)
d	degas (remove gas from, French artist)	p	polish (shine, of Poland)
e	ewe (female sheep, African language)	q	quiche (egg pie, department in Guatemala)
f	forest (area with trees, town in Belgium)	r	rainier (more rainy, U.S. mountain)
g	guy (male, Flemish ruler)	s	said (spoke, Middle Eastern port)
h	herb (plant, short for Herbert)	t	tangier (more tangy, city in Morocco)
i	ill (sick, river in Austria)	v	vital (essential, Palestinian author)
j	job (occupation, Bible character)	w	worms (invertebrates, German city)
k	kin (relatives, Manchu ancestors)	x	xi (Greek letter, river in China)
l	lima (bean, Peru city)	z	zemi (fetish, Naga people)

Word That Sounds Like Letters, Beginning with Each Letter Sound

a	apiarian (APREN)	n	anencephalous (NNCFLS)
b	beadier (BDR)	o	obediency (OBDNC)
c	cesium (CZM)	p	penial (PNEL)
d	devious (DVS)	q	curiosity (QRESET)
e	eosinophilous (ESNFLS)	r	arcadian (RKDN)
f	effeminacy (FMNSE)	s	aesculapian (SQLAPN)
g	gillotti (GLOT)	t	tedious (TDS)
h	echevarria (HAVREA)	u	european (UROPN)
i	Iberian (IBREN)	v	veneer (VNER)
j	jacuzzi (JQZ)	w	doubloon (WN)
k	caseous (KSES)	x	expediency (XPDNC)
l	elementarily (LMNTRLE)	y	wireless (YRLS)
m	eminency (MNNC)	z	xerophagy (ZRFAG)

Acronym That Has Become Uncapitalized, Beginning with Each Letter

a	asdic (Anti-Submarine Detection Investigation Committee)	n	nitinol (NIckel + TIn + Naval Ordinance Laboratory)
b	base (Building + Aerial + Span + Earthbound object)	o	obo (Oil Bulk Ore)
c	canola (CANada Oil + Low Acid)	p	parsec (PARallax SECond)
d	dopa (DihydrOxyPhenylAlanine)	q	quango (QUAsi-Non Governmental Organization)
e	elhi (ELementary school + HIgh school)	r	radar (RAdio Detection And Ranging)
f	fido (Freaks + Irregulars + Defects + Oddities)	s	scuba (Self-Contained Underwater Breathing Apparatus)
g	gox (Gaseous OXygen)		
h	hela (HEnrietta LAcks)	t	tepa (Tri-Ethylene Phosphor-Amide)
i	ibuprofen (Iso-BUtyl PROpionic PHENyl)	u	ursigram (Union Radiophonique Scientifique Internationale GRAM-)
j	jato (Jet-Assisted TakeOff)		
k	kip (KIlo- + Pound)	v	vidicon (VIDeo + ICONoscope)
l	laser (Light Amplification by Stimulated Emission of Radiation)	w	wysiwyg (What You See Is What You Get)
		y	yuppie (Young Urban Professional + -PIE)
m	maser (Microwave Amplification by Stimulated Emission of Radiation)	z	zip (Zone Improvement Plan)

Word That Exists Only in an Idiom, Beginning with Each Letter

a	agley (gang aft agley)	n	nip (nip and tuck)
b	bejeebers (scare the bejeebers out of)	o	offing (in the offing)
c	cockles (cockles of the heart)	p	petard (hoist by one's own petard)
d	druthers (if I had my druthers)	q	QT (on the QT)
e	escutcheon (blot on the escutcheon)	r	raring (raring to go)
f	fritz (on the fritz)	s	shebang (the whole shebang)
g	gird (gird one's loins)	t	tat (tit for tat)
h	haw (hem and haw)	u	umbrage (take umbrage at)
i	ish (ish kabibble)	v	vale (vale of tears)
j	jig (the jig is up)	w	welkin (make the welkin ring)
k	kith (kith and kin)	y	yen (have a yen for)
l	lam (on the lam)	z	zoot (zoot suit)
m	muchness (much of a muchness)		

Word Formed by Borrowing or Lending Letters to Frequent Companions, Beginning with Each Letter

a	common word: accomplice (a complice → accomplice) common word: adder (a naddre → an addre) common word: apple (a napple → an apple) common word: apron (a napron → an apron) common word: auger (a nauger → an auger) common word: aught (a naught → an aught) uncommon word: auncel (lancelle → l'auncelle) uncommon word: aventail (la ventaille → l'aventaille) hyphenated word: aitch-bone (a nachebon → an achebon)	i	common word: ingot (lingot → l'ingot)
		l	common word: lone (alone → a lone) uncommon word: lierre (l'ierre → lierre)
		n	common word: newt (an ewt → a newt) common word: nickname (an ekename → a nekename) uncommon word: nain (mine ain → my nain)
		o	common word: orange (a naranj → an aranj) common word: ouch (a nouche → an ouche)
		p	uncommon word: precle (l'aprecle → la precle)
		r	uncommon word: rouse (drink carouse → drink a rouse)
b	common word: broil (amb-ustulare → am-bustulare)	s	slope (aslope → a slope)
		t	common word: tone (thet on → the tone) uncommon word: tother (thet other → the tother)
c	uncommon word: cunette (lacunetta → la cunetta)		
d	uncommon word: dab (adept → a dab)		
e	uncommon word: emony (anemone → an emony) uncommon word: eyas (a neyas → an eyas)	u	common word: umpire (a noumpere → an oumpere)
g	uncommon word: guglia (l'aguglia → la guglia)	w	uncommon word: wis (iwis → i wis)
h	uncommon word: haberdine (labordean → l'abordean)	z	uncommon word: zamia (azaniae → a zaniae)

Portmanteau Beginning with Each Letter

a	anecdotage (anecdote, dotage)	n	nickelodeon (nickel, melodeon)
b	brunch (breakfast, lunch)	o	Oxbridge (Oxford, Cambridge)
c	chortle (chuckle, snort)	p	prissy (prim, sissy)
d	dramedy (drama, comedy)	q	quiddle (quiddity, fiddle)
e	edutainment (education, entertainment)	r	ruckus (ruction, rumpus)
f	flunk (flinch, funk)	s	smog (smoke, fog)
g	gerrymander (Gerry, salamander)	t	transceiver (transmitter, receiver)
h	hokum (hocus-pocus, bunkum)	u	umpteen (umpty, -teen)
i	immittance (impedance, admittance)	v	volumeter (volume, -meter)
j	jolt (joll, jot)	w	wistful (wistly, wishful)
k	knurl (knur, gnarl)	x	xeriscape (xeric, landscape)
l	lidar (light, radar)	y	Yinglish (Yiddish, English)
m	motel (motor, hotel)	z	zillionaire (zillion, millionaire)

Self-Antonym Beginning with Each Letter

a	aught (all, nothing)	o	overlook (inspect, ignore)
b	bull (edict, nonsense)	p	peruse (examine in detail, look over casually)
c	cleave (separate, join)	q	quiddity (an inessential feature, the essence)
d	dust (remove fine particles, cover with fine particles)	r	ravel (entangle, disentangle)
e	enjoin (direct or impose, prohibit or forbid)	s	seed (remove the seeds, distribute the seeds)
f	fast (rapid, unmoving)	t	temper (harden steel, soften justice)
g	garnish (add to food, subtract from wages)	u	unbending (rigid, relaxing)
h	hysterical (terrified, funny)	v	vernacular (nonstandard speech, standard speech)
i	into (divided into, multiplied by)	w	weather (withstand a storm, wear away)
j	jake (uncouth, fine)	x	x (select, deselect)
k	kick off (begin, die)	y	yuk (express pleasant surprise, express unpleasant surprise)
l	literally (actually, figuratively)	z	zing (improve, criticize)
m	moot (debatable, not worthy of debate)		
n	nervy (showing calm courage, excitable)		

Antonym of Two Different Words, Beginning with Each Letter

a	acute (blunt, obtuse, dull, grave)	n	noble (cheap, base, ignoble)
b	bare (covered, full)	o	obscure (bright, famous, lucid)
c	close (open, remote, aloof, liberal)	p	poor (wealthy, good)
d	dull (sharp, clear, interesting)	q	quicken (slacken, arrest, deaden)
e	establish (disprove, abolish, repeal, abrograte)	r	rise (fall, sit, retire)
f	free (costly, enslaved)	s	soft (loud, rough, harsh)
g	go (stop, come)	t	tough (soft, weak)
h	hard (soft, easy)	u	universal (parochial, particular)
i	ill (well, good)	v	various (uniform, many)
j	just (unfair, extremely)	w	well (ill, badly)
k	keep (release, break, neglect)	x	x (select, unselect)
l	little (big, great, important)	y	yield (keep, withstand)
m	mad (calm, sane)	z	zero (infinite, entity)

False Antonym Beginning with Each Letter

a	abuse & disabuse		m	merge & immerge
b	bar & debar		n	nude & denude
c	catenate & concatenate		o	ovoid & obovoid
d	dent & indent		p	passive & impassive
e	estimable & inestimable		q	quest & inquest
f	flammable & inflammable		r	ravel & unravel
g	genius & ingenious		s	scribe & inscribe
h	habited & inhabited		t	tend & intend
j	join & conjoin		v	valuable & invaluable
l	loosen & unloosen		w	weave & inweave

Plural That Ends with Each Letter

a	vasa		n	kronen
b	sleyb		o	derrings-do
c	calpullec		p	aides-de-camp
d	filid		q	qaraqalpaq
e	alae		r	kroner
f	ashraf		t	matzot
g	airig		u	haleru
h	liroth		v	tiv
i	bani		w	sons-in-law
j	khawarij		x	eaux
k	pulik		y	groszy
l	armsful		z	hertz
m	goyim			

LEXICON

A

a—longest common word containing all vowels (1-t)

aa—shortest two-syllable word (2)—uncommon word with lowest letter sum for length 2 (2)—shortest uncommon word that starts and ends with letter a (2)—see "passe-passes"—*lava that is filled with air holes*

aas—see "abas" and "amas"

ab—shortest uncommon word with last letter next in alphabet after first for letter a (2)—see "spoon"—*abdomen*

aba—longest uncommon head 'n' tail centered on letter b (3-t)—see "abas"—*Arabian sleeveless coat*

abaca—uncommon word with lowest letter sum for length 5 (8-t)—*Philippine banana*

abaci—common word with lowest letter sum for length 5 (16)

abacs—see "abas"—*graphs used to aid calculations*

abas—longest charitable and hospitable with an uncommon word [bas & aas & abs & aba & babas & abbas & abbas & abacs & abase] (4-t)

abba—uncommon word with lowest letter sum for length 4 (6-t)—*variant of aba*

abba-dabba—longest hyphenated palindrome beginning with letter a (9)—longest hyphenated palindrome centered on letter d (9)—longest hyphenated numberdrome (9)—hyphenated word with lowest letter sum for length 9 (16)—*something of little importance*

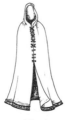

abba

abbas—see "abas"

abbe—common word with lowest letter sum for length 4 (10-t)—longest common word containing one type of consonant for consonant b (4-t)

abetalipoproteinemia—longest uncommon word that starts and ends with letter a (20)—*disease of fat metabolism*

abide—most letters in alphabetical place without shifting alphabet for a common word (4-t)

a bird in the hand is worth two in the bush—most repeated letters for a phrase (12)—*a certainty is twice as good as a slim chance*

abjurer—longest rot-13 pair with an uncommon word [nowhere] (7-t)—*one who abstains*

abode—most letters in alphabetical place without shifting alphabet for a common word (4-t)

abracadabra—common word containing the most repeats of letter a (5)—common word with lowest letter sum for length 11 (52)—longest common word containing one type of vowel for vowel a (11-t)—longest common word that starts and ends with letter a (11-t)

abs—see "abas"

absconded—common word containing most consecutive letters in order after letter a (5)—most consecutive alphabetic letters in left-to-right order for a common word (5)

abstemiously—longest uncommon word containing each vowel (including y) once in order (12)—*without overindulgence*

abstentious—longest uncommon word containing each vowel once in order (11)—*self-restrained*

abudefduf—most letters in alphabetical place without shifting alphabet for an uncommon word (5-t)—*damsel fish*

abuse—example of a false antonym beginning with letter a [disabuse]

abwab—longest uncommon head 'n' tail centered on letter w (5)—*Indian tax*

acacetin—longest uncommon isotel pair with no letters in common [cacafugo] (8-t)—*a chemical from the leaves of the common locust*

acacia—common word with lowest letter sum for length 6 (18-t)—longest common word containing one type of consonant for consonant c (6)

academicians—common word with lowest letter sum for length 12 (82)

acceded—longest common word spelled with hexadecimal letters (7-t)—longest common word spelled with piano notes (7-t)

accomplice—example of a common word formed by borrowing or lending letters to frequent companions, beginning with letter a [a complice → accomplice]

accouterments—longest metathesis with common words [accouterments → accoutrements] (13-t)

accoutrements—see "accouterments"

acetaminophen—common word containing most consecutive letters in order after letter m (4-t)

ach—see "hexachlorocyclohexane"—*expression of impatience*

achy—shortest hostile common word (4-t)

acknowledgements—common word with the lowest ratio length to number of different letters for length 16 (1.23-t)—longest common word that can nontrivially delete letter from any position to form another word [acknowledgements → acknowledgments] (16)

acknowledgments—see "acknowledgements"

actinomycin D—see "dactinomycin"

acute—example of an antonym of four different words, beginning with letter a [blunt, obtuse, dull, grave]

ad—common word with lowest letter sum for length 2 (5)—see "add"

add—example of homophones differing by letter d [ad]

adder—example of a common word formed by borrowing or lending letters to frequent companions, beginning with letter a [a naddre → an addre]

ade—see "aides"—*fruit drink*

adenosine monophosphate—longest well-mixed phrase transubstitution [adenosine monophosphate → put an ape in someone's hood] (22)—most letters in alphabetical place with shifting alphabet for a phrase (7)—*nucleotide found in muscle cells*

ades—see "aides"

adieu—highest ratio vowels to consonants for a common word (4-t)—longest common word containing one consonant (5-t)

adinida—longest uncommon palindrome beginning with letter a (7)—longest uncommon palindrome centered on letter n (7)—*a type of protozoan having two flagella*

ads—longest progressive charitable with common words [ads & ad & as & ds] (3-t)

adulation—longest synonymous transposal with common words [adulation → laudation] (9-t)

adventure—see "adventuress"

adventures—see "adventuress"

adventuress—longest common word in which deleting consecutively repeated letters forms a word [adventuress → adventure] (11)—longest common word in which dropping s makes a plural [adventuress → adventures] (11)—longest letter subtraction with common words [adventuress → adventure] (11-t)

aegilops—longest uncommon word with letters in alphabetical order (8)—*a type of grass that is an ancestor of wheat*

aegilops

aer—most homophones with an uncommon word [air & are & ayer & ayr & e'er & ere & err & eyre & heir & ur] (11)—*veil used in ceremonies of the Eastern Orthodox Church*

aerie—highest ratio vowels to consonants for a common word (4-t)—longest common word containing one consonant (5-t)

aes—see "aides"—*letter a's*

aesculapian—example of a word that sounds like letters, beginning with letter s sound [SQLAPN]—*staff with snake wrapped around it used as a symbol of medicine*

a face like a fiddle—longest phrase with letters from first half of alphabet (16)—*dour expression*

afforesting—see "reafforesting"—*converting into a forest*

aflaj—see "falaj"—*Arabian water channels*

aftereffects—longest common word with type-writer letters from left hand (12-t)

agar-agar—longest hyphenated tautonym beginning with letter a (8)—*jelling agent in foods*

aggie—longest common word containing one type of consonant for consonant g (5-t)

aggregating—common word containing the most repeats of letter g (4-t)

aggressiveness—most doubled letters for a common word (3-t)

aggry—example of an uncommon word ending -gry [see "Words Ending in -Gry" article, page 96]—*African multicolored glass*

agley—example of a word that exists only in an idiom, beginning with letter a [gang aft agley]—*Scottish word meaning awry*

agmas—see "amas"—*sounds or symbols of the sound of ng in Greek or Latin*

agoraphobia—longest common word that starts and ends with letter a (11-t)

aha—longest common head 'n' tail centered on letter h (3)—longest common palindrome centered on letter h (3)—shortest common word that starts and ends with letter a (3)

ahem—shortest hostile common word (4-t)

ahoy—shortest hostile common word (4-t)

ai—see "aides" and "upraisers"—*Japanese fish*

aiaia—longest vertical catoptron for an uncommon word (5-t)—*roseate spoonbill*

aiaiai—highest vowels minus consonants for an uncommon word (6-t)—longest uncommon word containing all vowels (6-t)—*variant of "aiaia"*

aiaiai

aiaiais—highest ratio vowels to consonants for an uncommon word (6-t)—longest uncommon word containing one consonant (7-t)—longest vowel string for an uncommon word (6-t)

aides—longest progressive charitable with an uncommon word [aides & ades & aide & aids & aies & ides & ade & ads & aes & aid & aie &

ais & des & ide & ids & ies & ad & ae & ai & as & de & ds & es & id & ie & is] (5-t)

aides-de-camp—example of a plural that ends with letter p—*military aides*

aie—see "aides"—*expression of grief*

aies—see "aides"

aimlessly—see "rakishly"

aini—see "strainings"—*native Peruvian custom of trading help*

air—see "aer"

airig—example of a plural that ends with letter g—*Irish noblemen*

airns—see "hairns"—*Scottish for irons*

ais—see "aides" and "upraisers"

aisle—example of a word that begins with silent letter a—example of a word that is a confusing code for letter a [isle]

aitch-bone—example of a hyphenated word formed by borrowing or lending letters to frequent companions, beginning with letter a [a nachebon → an achebon]—*rump bone or the cut of beef above it*

aitia—longest vertical catoptron for an uncommon word (5-t)—*stories that explain the origin of a ceremony*

aizoaceae—longest uncommon word containing two consonants (9-t)—*herbs or small shrubs in the order Caryophyllales commonly called carpetweed or fig marigold*

akeake—longest uncommon tautonym beginning with letter a (6-t)—*a small tropical tree*

al—see "alares"—*Indian mulberry*

alae—example of a plural that ends with letter e—*winglike parts*

alan—see "galanases"—*heraldic figure of a dog*

alang-alang—longest hyphenated tautonym beginning with letter a (10)—*Philippine grass*

alare—see "alares"—*outside point on the side of the nose*

alares—longest uncommon word torture [alare & lares & alar & ares & lare & ala & are & lar & res & al & ar & es & la & re] (6-t)

alarmedly—longest uncommon iskot pair measured in number of dots and dashes [corn-rowed] (25-t)—*in an alarmed or excited way*

alb—shortest common word with last letter next in alphabet after first for letter a (3)

albeit—example of a word spelled with e before i, beginning with letter a

alfalfa—longest common word with typewriter letters from middle row (7)

algal—longest common head 'n' tail centered on letter g (5-t)

algal-algals—longest hyphenated word with typewriter letters from middle row (11)—*Malaysian agars or extracts of algae*

alimentation—see "coxalgia"—*a source of nourishment*

alimentotherapy—uncommon word containing most consecutive letters in order after letter l (5-t)—*food therapy*

aliquot—shortest common word with no matching vowel pattern (7-t)

allele—longest common word containing one type of consonant for consonant l (6)

alleluia—longest uncommon word containing one type of consonant for consonant l (8-t)—*hallelujah*

all hell is let loose—phrase containing the most repeats of letter l (6-t)—*chaos*

allocation—longest common word with two letter head-to-tail shift [allocation → locational] (10)

allochlorophyll—uncommon word containing the most repeats of letter l (5-t)—*isomer of chlorophyll*

alloplastically—uncommon word containing the most repeats of letter l (5-t)—*in a way that is molded by external factors*

all's well that ends well—phrase containing the most repeats of letter l (6-t)

almost—longest common word with letters in alphabetical order (6-t)

aloe—longest common progressive sum pair [aloe → mat → nu → i] (4-t)

alpha-naphthylthiourea—longest hyphenated word that starts and ends with letter a (21)—*rat poison*

alula—longest uncommon palindrome centered on letter u (5-t)—*the part of the bird wing corresponding to the thumb*

aluminotype—uncommon word containing most consecutive letters in order after letter l (5-t)—*aluminum printing plate*

alveolopalatal—longest uncommon four-cadence (4-t)—*between the sounds of "ch" and "t"*

ama—see "amas"—*Japanese woman diver*

amaas—see "amas"—*non-lethal form of smallpox*

amas—longest charitable and hospitable with an uncommon word [mas & aas & ams & ama & camas & agmas & amaas & amaas & amass] (4-t)

ama

amatorian—longest synonymous transposal with an uncommon word [amatorian → inamorata] (9-t)—*pertaining to love*

amaxhosa—see "xhosa"—*Ngoni Banti-speaking people of Cape province*

ambidextrously—longest common isogram (14)—most different letters for a common word (14-t)

amends—longest length four linkade with common words [amen & mend & ends] (6-t)

ami—see "amides" and "ketamines"—*French for friend*

amides—longest uncommon word torture [amide & mides & amid & ides & mide & ami & des & ide & mid & am & de & es & id & mi] (6-t)

amin—see "ketamines"—*minor official in the Indian government*

amoebids—longest uncommon isotel pair with no letters in common [bondager] (8-t)—*single-*

celled animals that move by extending their cell wall

amounts—longest common isotel pair with no letters in common [contour] (7-t)

amplifiers—longest common progressive trans-deletion [amplifiers → imperials → imperils → simpler → simper → prism → rips → sir → rs → s] (10-t)

amps—see "cramps"—*units of electric current*

amu—see "amusers"—*unit of atomic mass*

amus—see "amusers"

amuser—see "amusers"—*one who amuses*

amusers—longest phrase word torture [amuser & musers & amuse & muser & users & amus & muse & sers & user & amu & ers & mus & ser & use & 'se & am & er & mu & rs & us] (7-t)

ana—see "thanatopsides"—*old monetary unit of India*

anacardiaceae—uncommon word with lowest letter sum for length 13 (66)—*type of shrub*

anachronistically—see "procrastination"

anaemia—longest common word containing two consonants (7-t)

anaesthesia—longest common word that starts and ends with letter a (11-t)

anamnia—longest uncommon word where each letter is two symbols in Morse code (7-t)—*vertebrates that develop no amnion, the fluid-filled sac in which the embryo develops*

anas—see "galanases"—*collections of anecdotes*

anasa—see "supranasal"—*type of bug*

anathema maranatha—phrase containing the most repeats of letter a (7)—*a supposed curse*

ancient—example of a word spelled with i before e after c, beginning with letter a

anecdotage—example of a portmanteau, beginning with letter a [anecdote, dotage]—*old age accompanied by a tendency to ramble*

anemone—see "phenomenal" and "phenomenally"

anencephalous—example of a word that sounds like letters, beginning with letter n sound [NNCFLS]—*without a brain*

anestri—most transpositions with an uncommon word [antsier & nastier & neritas & ranties & ratines & resiant & restain & retains & retinas & retsina & stainer & starnie & stearin & taniers] (15-t)—most transpositions for a phrase [uncommon word list above & in tears & tin ears] (17-t)—*periods between estruses or heats*

anew—shortest hostile common word (4-t)

angered—longest synonymous transposal with common words [angered → enraged] (7)

angriest—most transpositions for a phrase [angrites & astringe & gairtens & ganister & gantries & granites & inert gas & ingrates & rangiest & reasting & seat ring & stearing & tangiers & tasering & tea rings & tearings] (17-t)

angrites—see "angriest"—*meteorites containing titanium and not magnesium*

angry—example of a common word ending -gry [see "Words Ending in -Gry" article, page 96]

anhydrous hydrofluoric acids—longest phrase without ET (26)

anianiau—longest uncommon word containing one type of consonant for consonant n (8-t)—*Hawaiian honeycreeper*

animals—longest common backswitch [laminae, laminar] (7-t)

animas—see "animates"—*inner selves*

animates—longest common progressive delete-reverse [animates → stamina → animas → samia → aims → sma → am → m] (8-t)—longest delete-reverse with common words [animates → stamina] (8-t)—*makes an animated cartoon or brings to life*

animis opibusque parati—phrase containing most consecutive letters in order after letter n (5)—*motto of South Carolina "prepared in mind and resources"*

anion—longest common word containing one type of consonant for consonant n (5-t)

Ghosts

What words sound like they contain letters that they do not?

When we first learn to read, we are taught to pronounce words by "sounding out" their letters. This strategy works fairly well since most letters correspond to phonemes, and where they do not, many exceptions are easy to learn. However, Dmitri Borgmann compiled a list of words containing an Invisible Alphabet in *Beyond Language* (Scribner's, 1967, p. 250). His list contains one word for each letter in the alphabet, where each word contains the phoneme usually associated with its letter—but the letter itself is not in the word. We call such letters "ghost letters."

A list of words for each letter in the alphabet makes sense if each letter represents one phoneme, but this is the very assumption Borgmann is having fun with. Below is a similar list, which instead contains words for each phoneme—but the letter or letters that are usually pronounced as the phoneme are missing. We will call such missing letters "ghost phonemes."

My choice of phonemes is entirely subjective, but I have been guided somewhat by the International Phonetic Alphabet. In compiling the list, I preferred words in which no letter represents the phoneme (e.g., BURGH /bu-ro/, MBIRA /em-bir-a/), words that are common, and words not recently borrowed from a foreign language (if the word was recently borrowed, the language of origin is bracketed, except French). I do not consider proper names or acronyms (e.g., P.O.W. for a word containing the sound of L but not the letter L). I do allow mispronunciations that have become common enough to be listed in *Merriam-Webster's Collegiate Dictionary* without a substandard or dialect label (e.g., I do allow GOVERNMENT with the V pronounced like a B, but I do not allow OPERA pronounced like OPRY). Finally, I do not list words where it makes more sense to consider a letter as silent than it does to consider it as being pronounced unusually, e.g., PSALM.

Many people have seen the spelling GHOTI for FISH (GH sounded like F in LAUGH, O sounded like I in WOMEN, TI sounded like SH in NATION). From the list below we also have the spelling WAS for FISH (W sounded like F in TAW, A sounded like I in AGATE, S sounded like SH in SURE). What does CLOMP spell? (Answer at end of article.)

Phoneme	Usual	Example	Ghost	Example
schwa	various		–	CHASM
\a\	A	ADD	E	THRESH
			EI	CEINTURE
			ER	CHERT
			I	MERINGUE
			UI	GUIMPE
\A\	A	APE	OI	QUOIT
	EI	LEI	EE	GEEST [German]
	ER	FOYER	OE	ROEMER [German]
	EY	PREY	UI	UITLANDER [Afrikaans]
\à\	A	AH	I	LINGERIE
	E	ENTREE	U	FURTHEST
	O	COT		
\b\	B	BABY	P	MUNICIPAL
			V	GOVERNMENT
\ch\	CH	CHIN	SE	RINSE
	SI	TENSION	SH	WELSH
	TE	RIGHTEOUS	TH	POSTHUMOUS
	TI	QUESTION	CK	KOLACKY [Czech]

	T	NATURE	CZ	CZARDAS [Hungarian]
			KY	KYAT [Burmese]
			TT	AFFETTUOSO [Italian]
\d\	D	DO	T	TAO [Chinese]
			T	PARTNER
			TT	BUTTINSKY
			Z	INTERMEZZO [Italian]
\e\	E	ELF	–	MBIRA [Bantu]
	A	ANY	I	DOMINICK
	U	BURY	AOI	TAOISEACH [Irish]
\E\	E	EAT	A	BOLOGNA
	I	SKI	AY	QUAY
	Y	PRETTY	OIS	CHAMOIS
			J	FJORD
			AGH	SHILLELAGH [Irish]
\f\	F	FAN	V	LEV [Bulgarian]
	PH	PHASE	W	TAW [Hebrew]
	GH	LAUGH		
\g\	G	GO	C	ECZEMA
	X	EXAM	K	KIP [Lao]
\h\	H	HAT	–	THRESHOLD
	WH	WHO	G	GILA MONSTER [Spanish]
			J	JUNTA [Spanish]
			X	QUIXOTE [Spanish]
\hw\	WH	WHO	JU	MARIJUANA [Spanish]
			HU	AYAHUASCA [Spanish]
\i\	I	IS	A	AGATE
	E	AGED	O	WOMEN
	U	BUSY		
	Y	GYM		
\I\	AI	AISLE	AE	BRACCAE
	AY	AYE		
	EI	HEIST		
	EY	EYE		
	I	ICE		
	UY	BUY		
	Y	SLY		
\j\	J	JOB	CH	OSTRICH
	G	GEM	SI	TRANSIENT
	D	PROCEDURE		
\k\	K	KID	G	LENGTH
	C	CAB	GH	LOUGH [Irish]
	Q	QUEUE		
	X	FIX		
\kh\	GH	AUGHT	H	HAZAN [Hebrew]
	CH	OCH	TH	CLARSETH [Scottish]
			X	XAT [Haida]
\l\	L	LOW	–	KU KLUX KLAN
\m\	M	ME	ND	GRANDPA SANDWICH

			N	BOYSENBERRY
				DAVENPORT
\n\	N	NO	MP	COMPTROLLER
			M	MUSHROOM
\o\	O	OFF	U	CRITERIUM
	A	ALL		
	AU	HAUL		
	OU	FOUR		
\O\	O	OPEN	–	BURGH
	EAU	EAU	A	QUAHOG [Narraganset]
	EW	SEW		
	AU	HAUT		
\oe\	EU	BLEU	OE	OEILLADE
\oi\	OI	OIL	AW	LAWYER
	OY	BOY	AU	FRAULEIN [German]
			EU	KREUZER [German]
\ou\	OU	OUT	O	COMPT
	OW	NOW		
	AU	KRAUT		
\p\	P	PORT	–	HAMSTER
			F	CHAMFER
			GH	HICCOUGH
			B	ABLAUT [German]
\r\	R	RED	LO	COLONEL
			F	NEUFCHATEL
			U	MILIEU
			Y	BOGEYMAN
			J	JEN [Chinese]
			OE	LOESS [German]
\s\	S	SAY	Z	LOZENGE
	C	CELL	TH	HETH [Hebrew]
	X	WAX		
\sh\	SH	SHY	S	SURE
	TI	NATION	X	LUXURY
	CH	CHEF		
	CI	APPRECIATE		
\t\	T	TEA	Z	PALAZZO [Italian]
	D	WUNDERKIND	–	MARZIPAN
	ED	PASSED		
	–	ABUNDANCE		
	–	ANSWER		
\th\	TH	THIN	GH	TROUGH
			D	AMADAN [Irish]
			T	TAOISEACH [Irish]
\dh\	THE		D	CAID [Spanish]
			DD	EISTEDDFOD [Welsh]
\u\	U	UP	WO	TWOPENCE
	O	OF	OO	BLOOD
	A	WAS		
	E	THE		

	I	BIRD		
\U\	U	GNU	–	GEODUCK [Chinook]
	O	DO	W	CWM [Welsh]
	OO	OOZE	WO	TWO
	EW	EWE		
\ue\	UE	BIENVENUE	U	GUDE [Scottish]
\v\	V	VERY	B	HABDALAH [Hebrew]
			F	OF
			GH	TROUGHS
			PH	NEPHEW [British]
			W	WAGON-LIT
\w\	W	WAY	–	ONE
	U	QUA	O	COIF
			V	PECCAVI
			JU	MARIJUANA [Spanish]
\y\	Y	YARD	G	LASAGNA
	U	UNIT	J	HALLELUJAH [Hebrew]
	I	OPINION	J	JAEGER [German]
	EW	EWE	H	SENHOR [Portuguese]
	LL	BILLION		
\z\	Z	ZONE	TH	CLOTHES
	S	IS	G	PARMIGIANA
	X	XYLOPHONE		
\zh\	Z	AZURE	G	GENRE
	S	VISUAL	J	BIJOU
	SI	ASIA	X	LUXURY
	TI	EQUATION		

Answer: CLOMP spells GROAN (C sounds like G in ECZEMA, LO sounds like R in COLONEL, nothing sounds like OA in BURGH, and MP sounds like N in COMPTROLLER).

anjan—longest uncommon head 'n' tail centered on letter j (5)—*an Indian tree*

ankh—shortest common isolano (4-t)

anna—longest common palindrome beginning with letter a (4)

anthems—longest length three linkade with common words [ant & nth & the & hem & ems] (7-t)

antichristianly—longest uncommon word with consecutive letters adjacent on phone keypad beginning with letter a (15)—*acting in a way that is not befitting a Christian*

anticoagulants—longest common word with consecutive letters adjacent on phone keypad beginning with letter a (14)

anticonstitutionalist—uncommon word containing the most repeats of letter t (5-t)—*one opposed to a constitution*

antidisestablishmentarianism—longest uncommon word containing three types of vowels (28)—example of a sesquipedalian word [see "Longest Word" article, page 106]—*opposition to separation of church and state*

antiferromagnets—longest well-mixed transposal with an uncommon word [refragmentations] (16-t)—*resisting magnets*

antiparticles—longest well-mixed transposal with common words [paternalistic] (13)

antiskepticism—longest uncommon word with typewriter letters from alternating hands (14-t)—*opposition to skepticism*

antsier—see "anestri"—*more restless*

apa—longest uncommon head 'n' tail centered on letter p (3)—*South American lumber tree*

apex—shortest hostile common word (4-t)

apiarian—example of a word that sounds like letters, beginning with letter a sound [APREN]—*relating to bees*

apostle—example of a word that contains silent letter t

apple—example of a common word formed by borrowing or lending letters to frequent companions, beginning with letter a [a napple → an apple]

apres—most transpositions with common words [pares & parse & pears & rapes & reaps & spare & spear] (8)

apron—example of a common word formed by borrowing or lending letters to frequent companions, beginning with letter a [a napron → an apron]

apropos—example of a word that ends with silent letter s

apted—see "carpetweeds"—*made fitting and proper*

aquarist—common word containing most consecutive letters in order after letter q (4)

aqueous—longest common word containing two consonants (7-t)

ar—see "alares" and "cantharidates"—*letter r*

aras—longest complete letter rotation with an uncommon word [rasa & asar & sara] (4)—*Polynesian screw pines*

arcadian—example of a word that sounds like letters, beginning with letter r sound [RKDN]—*pastoral*

arcanum arcanorums—longest phrase spelled with short lowercase letters (17)

arched—longest one-syllable word beginning with letter a (6)—*curved*

archegonial chambers—most letters in alphabetical place without shifting alphabet for a phrase (6)—*curved cavities*

archetypical—most letters in alphabetical place without shifting alphabet for an uncommon word (5-t)—*the original after which others are copied*

archfiends—longest two-syllable word beginning with letter a (10)—*chief devils*

are—shortest common word in which adding one letter adds two syllables [are → area] (3-t)

area—see "are"

arear—longest uncommon head 'n' tail centered on letter e (5-t)—*rearward*

argie-bargie—longest hyphenated head 'n' tail centered on letter b (11-t)—*tedious argument*

argillaceocalcareous—longest uncommon reverse tetrahedron word (20-t)—*made of both clay and calcium*

argillaceocalcareouses—longest uncommon word containing five types of consonants (22-t)

argle-bargle—longest hyphenated head 'n' tail centered on letter b (11-t)—*tedious argument*

arkar—longest uncommon head 'n' tail centered on letter k (5)—*large Asian wild sheep*

armorial—longest common word spelled with two-letter U.S. postal codes (8-t)

armsful—example of a plural that ends with letter l

arouser—see "carousers"—*someone who wakes up or excites*

arsy-varsy—longest hyphenated head 'n' tail centered on letter v (9)—*head over heels*

artefacts—longest common well-mixed isomorse pair [entailments] (11)

articulates—see "particulates"

artsy-fartsy—longest hyphenated head 'n' tail centered on letter f (11)—*overly artistic or affected*

as—most different pronunciations for a common word [like; Roman coin; Persian card game; plural of a; Norse Aesir god] (5)—shortest full vowel (including y) substitution with multi-letter uncommon words [es & is & os & us & ys] (2-t)

asar—see "aras"—*combs or geological formations shaped like combs such as glacial ridges*

asdic—example of an acronym that has become uncapitalized, beginning with letter a [Anti-Submarine Detection Investigation Committee]—*sonar*

as different as chalk and cheese—see "creatine phosphokinases"

ases—see "galanases"—*Roman coins*

asexual reproductions—longest terminal elision for a phrase [asexual reproductions → sexual reproduction] (20)

ash—longest progressive charitable with common words [ash & ah & as & sh] (3-t)

ashamed—longest common progressive terminal elision [ashamed → shame → ham → a] (7-t)

ashraf—example of a plural that ends with letter f—*Islamic nobles*

ashtrays—longest common progressive delete letter from any position to form another word [ashtrays → ashtray → astray → stray → tray → ray → ay → y] (8-t)

asp—longest complete letter rotation with common words [spa & pas] (3-t)

assassin—longest repeated prefix for a common word (6-t)

asse—see "demitasse"—*African fox*

assertress—longest uncommon word with typewriter letters from adjacent keys (10-t)—*a female asserter*

asses—see "assess"

assess—shortest common word in which dropping s makes a plural [assess → asses] (6-t)

assessed—longest common word with typewriter letters from adjacent keys (8-t)

assessees—longest uncommon word containing one type of consonant for consonant s (9)—*payees*

assesses—longest common word containing one type of consonant for consonant s (8)

assuage—longest common switchback [degauss] (7-t)

assuaged—longest delete-reverse with common words [assuaged → degauss] (8-t)

astonishingly—common word with most letters in alphabetical place without shifting alphabet (4-t)

astragalocalcaneal—uncommon word containing the most repeats of letter a (6-t)—*of the ankle and heel bone*

astride—longest common isotel pair with no letters in common [brushed or crushed] (7-t)

astringe—see "angriest"—*draw tissue together*

astrophysicist—longest common well-mixed transdeletion [astrophysicist → psychiatrists] (14-t)

asynchronous transmission—longest beheadment for a phrase [asynchronous transmission → synchronous transmission] (24)—*transmission of information at a variable rate*

ate—longest complete letter rotation with common words [tea & eat] (3-t)

athar—see "cantharidates"—*perfume from flowers*

athematically—longest uncommon hydration [mathematically & pathematically] (0.13-t)—*without a theme*

atlatl—longest uncommon tautonym beginning with letter a (6-t)—*a notched stick serving as a spear thrower*

atles—most transpositions with an uncommon word [laets & lates & least & leats & salet & setal & slate & stale & steal & stela & taels & tales & teals & tesla] (15-t)—*Asian trees*

atlatl

atmospheric inversion—longest well-mixed transdeletion for a phrase [atmospheric inversion → comprehensivisation] (20-t)—*temperature rising with altitude*

ato—see "thanatopsides"—*governmental unit of native Philippine village*

attenuation—longest common word containing two types of consonants (11-t)

attitudinarianisms—longest uncommon change-over [latitudinarianisms] (18-t)—*posturings*

audacious—longest common word containing three consonants (9-t)

audio—highest ratio vowels to consonants for a common word (4-t)—longest common word containing one consonant (5-t)

auger—example of a common word formed by borrowing or lending letters to frequent companions, beginning with letter a [a nauger → an auger]

aught—example of a common word formed by borrowing or lending letters to frequent companions, beginning with letter a [a naught → an aught]—example of a self-antonym, beginning with letter a [all, nothing]

august—example of a word pronounced differently when capitalized, beginning with letter a [majestic, month]

auncel—example of an uncommon word formed by borrowing or lending letters to frequent companions, beginning with letter a [lancelle → l'auncelle]—*medieval English balance*

aural—example of common homophonic contranyms [aural: heard & oral: spoken]

auriculariaceae—longest uncommon word containing five consonants (15)—*fungi in the order Tremellales*

aurorae—longest common word containing one type of consonant for consonant r (7)—longest common word containing two consonants (7-t)

australopithecines—common word with the lowest ratio length to number of different letters for length 18 (1.38-t)

autoette—longest uncommon word containing one type of consonant for consonant t (8)—*a motored tricycle*

automata—longest common word spelled with vertical symmetry letters (8)

autosuggestibilities—longest uncommon reverse tetrahedron word (20-t)—*self-hypnoses*

autotransplantations—longest uncommon word with balanced letter sum (20-t)—*transplantations within one person*

autumn—example of a word that ends with silent letter n

aventail—example of an uncommon word formed by borrowing or lending letters to frequent companions, beginning with letter a [la ventaille → l'aventaille]—*medieval mail hood*

awe—longest common word containing one type of consonant for consonant w (3-t)

axe—longest common word containing one type of consonant for consonant x (3)

axes—example of a colliding plural [axe, axis]

ayer—see "aer"—*one who says "ay"*

ayes—longest common word torture [aye & yes & ay & es & ye] (4-t)

ayr—see "aer"—*from a Scottish port*

aza-—longest hyphenated head 'n' tail centered on letter z (3)—*containing nitrogen instead of carbon*

B

b—longest common head 'n' tail centered on letter b (1)—longest common palindrome centered on letter b (1)—longest common word with typewriter letters from bottom row (1-t)

ba—shortest full vowel (including y) substitution with multi-letter uncommon words [be & bi & bo & bu & by] (2-t)

baa—common word with lowest letter sum for length 3 (4)

baba—uncommon word with lowest letter sum for length 4 (6-t)—*small cake*

babas—see "abas"

babble—common word containing the most repeats of letter b (3-t)

babe—common word with lowest letter sum for length 4 (10-t)—longest common word containing one type of consonant for consonant b (4-t)

bacaba—uncommon word with lowest letter sum for length 6 (10)—*a palm in the genus Oenocarpus*

backache—common word with lowest letter sum for length 8 (34-t)

backed—highest ratio of consecutive alphabetic letters to length for a common word (0.83-t)

backfield—common word containing most consecutive letters in the alphabet after letter a (6-t)—common word containing most consecutive letters in the alphabet after letter b (5-t)

backfired—common word containing most consecutive letters in the alphabet after letter a (6-t)—common word containing most consecutive letters in the alphabet after letter b (5-t)

backhanded—common word containing most consecutive letters in order after letter b (4-t)—common word with lowest letter sum for length 10 (53-t)

backside—common word containing most consecutive letters in order after letter b (4-t)

backside-front—hyphenated word containing most consecutive letters in order after letter b (5)—*turned around*

backwardness—common word containing most consecutive letters in order after letter b (4-t)

bag and baggage—phrase with lowest letter sum for length 13 (59)—*completely*

baggage—longest common word spelled with piano notes (7-t)

bakhsheeshes—longest sequence of repeated dots in Morse code for an uncommon word (24-t)

bakhshishes—longest sequence of repeated dots in Morse code for an uncommon word (24-t)

bald-headed eagle—hyphenated phrase with lowest letter sum for length 15 (76)—*North American eagle*

balge—shortest uncommon word with no known pronunciation (5)—*bright yellow*

ballooned—longest common alternade [blond & aloe] (9-t)

balminess—longest uncommon well-mixed isomorse pair [bennettiteses] (13-t)—*warmness and wetness of the air*

bani—example of a plural that ends with letter i—*Romanian money*

bar—example of a false antonym beginning with letter b [debar]

barbaric—longest common word with a letter sum divisible by each letter (8)—longest repeated prefix for a common word (6-t)

bare—example of an antonym of two different words, beginning with letter b [covered, full]

bareheaded—common word with lowest letter sum for length 10 (53-t)

barn—longest common progressive difference pair [barn → aid → re → m] (4-t)

baron—longest common multiplicative offset shift pair [punch] [factor of 21] (5-t)

barricade—common word containing most consecutive letters in order after letter b (4-t)

base—example of an acronym that has become uncapitalized, beginning with letter b [Building + Aerial + Span + Earthbound object]

bases—example of a colliding plural [base, basis]

bathtub—longest common word that starts and ends with letter b (7-t)

bb—longest uncommon word with typewriter letters from bottom row (2-t)—shortest uncommon word that starts and ends with letter b (2)—*small metal ball*

bdell-—example of a word that is a confusing code for letter b [dell]—*leech-like*

bdellium—example of a word that begins with silent letter b—*aromatic gum resin*

be—see "ba"

beachhead—common word with lowest letter sum for length 9 (37)

beadier—example of a word that sounds like letters, beginning with letter b sound [BDR]—*more like a bead*

beaters—longest common progressive terminal elision [beaters → eater → ate → t] (7-t)

beau—longest common word containing one type of consonant for consonant b (4-t)—see "beaux"

beauteous—longest common word containing three consonants (9-t)

beaux—example of homophones differing by letter x [beau]

beblubbered—uncommon word containing the most repeats of letter b (4-t)—*crying uncontrollably*

became—longest common word containing all letters restricted to Fibonacci sequence (6-t)

beccaccia—uncommon word with lowest letter sum for length 9 (30)—*woodcock*

beekeeper—common word containing the most repeats of letter e (5-t)

beens—longest progressive charitable with an uncommon word [beens & been & bees & bens & eens & bee & ben & bes & een & ees & ens & be & bs & ee & en & es & ns] (5-t)

begin—example of a word pronounced differently when capitalized, beginning with letter b [start, former Israeli leader]

begins—longest common word with letters in alphabetical order (6-t)

beheaded—common word with lowest letter sum for length 8 (34-t)

being—example of a word spelled with e before i, beginning with letter b

bejeebers—example of a word that exists only in an idiom, beginning with letter b [scare the bejeebers out of]—*stuffing*

bellabella—longest uncommon tautonym beginning with letter b (10-t)—*native of western Canada*

bels—longest common word torture [bel & els & be & el & ls] (4-t)

ben—see "beens"—*Scottish for tall hill*

bennettiteses—see "balminess"

bens—see "beens"

benzoxyacetanilide—uncommon word containing most consecutive letters in the alphabet after letter x (8)—*pain reliever*

bes—see "beens"—*letter b's*

bessemerizing—see "disspreading"—*medical treatment involving a blast of air*

between the devil and the deep blue sea—phrase containing the most repeats of letter e (10)—phrase with the most repeats of any one letter [e] (10)—*presented with only bad options*

BHC—shortest phrase with last letter next in alphabet after first for letter b (3-t)—*insecticide benzene hexachloride*

bi—see "ba"—*bisexual*

bib—longest common palindrome centered on letter i (3-t)—shortest common word that starts and ends with letter b (3-t)

bibble-babble—hyphenated word containing the most repeats of letter b (6)—hyphenated word with lowest letter sum for length 12 (56)—*babble*

biblia abiblia—longest head 'n' tail phrase centered on letter a (13-t)—*worthless book*

bicentricity—longest uncommon word with consecutive letters adjacent on phone keypad· beginning with letter b (12)—*the condition of having two centers*

billowy—longest common word with letters in alphabetical order when allowing repeats (7)

binomial distribution—longest phrase four-cadence (5)—*bell curve*

biopsy—longest common word with letters in alphabetical order (6-t)

biplane—longest common word with consecutive letters adjacent on phone keypad beginning with letter b (7-t)

birds—longest common multiplicative offset shift pair [fable] [factor of 3] (5-t)

Bitolj—example of a word that ends with silent letter j—*from a city in Yugoslavia*

biz—see "bizz"—*business*

bizz—example of homophones differing by letter z [bizz]—*business*

BL—see "blowers"—*bachelor of laws*

black-backed jackal—longest hyphenated phrase with letters from first half of alphabet (17)—*South African jackal*

blackballed—longest common word with letters from first half of alphabet (11-t)

blackfigured—uncommon word containing most consecutive letters in the alphabet after letter a (7)—uncommon word containing most consecutive letters in the alphabet after letter b (6-t)—*Greek vase painting style*

blackguard—example of a word that contains silent letter k—*bad person*

blackjacks—common word with the most infrequently used letters for length 10 (374-t)

blackmailed—longest common word with letters from first half of alphabet (11-t)

blacksmith—one of two common words that together contain the most different letters [gunpowdery] (20)

blah-blah-blah—longest hyphenated trio isogram (12)—*babble*

blandly—longest common word with consecutive letters adjacent on phone keypad beginning with letter b (7-t)

blepharoconjunctivitis—uncommon word with the lowest ratio length to number of different letters for length 22 (1.37-t)—most different letters for an uncommon word (16-t)—*disease of the eyelid*

blepharoconjunctivitises—uncommon word with the lowest ratio length to number of different letters for length 24 (1.50-t)

blo—see "blowers"—*color that is mostly black with a little blue*

bloc—shortest common word with last letter next in alphabet after first for letter b (4)

blockade—common word containing most consecutive letters in order after letter b (4-t)

block and block—longest phrase with consecutive letters adjacent on phone keypad beginning with letter b (13)—*crowded*

blowe—see "blowers"—*spring forth*

blowers—longest common progressive terminal elision [blowers → lower → owe → w] (7-t)—longest phrase word torture [blower & lowers & blowe & lower & owers & blow & lowe & ower & wers & blo & ers & low & owe & wer & BL & er & lo & ow & rs & we] (7-t)

blubber—common word containing the most repeats of letter b (3-t)

bluntly—longest common word with consecutive letters adjacent on phone keypad beginning with letter b (7-t)

bo—see "ba"—*hobo*

boats—longest common charitable [oats & bats & bots & boas & boat] (5-t)

bob—longest common head 'n' tail centered on letter o (3-t)—shortest common word that starts and ends with letter b (3-t)

bobber—see "hovel"

bobby—common word containing the most repeats of letter b (3-t)

boccie—example of a word spelled with i before e after c, beginning with letter b—*Italian lawn bowling*

boccie

boldface—common word containing most consecutive letters in the alphabet after letter a (6-t)—common word containing most consecutive letters in the alphabet after letter b (5-t)

bondager—see "amoebids"—*indentured servant*

bonniest—longest difference pair with an uncommon word [bonniest → mazedly] (8)—*most fair*

boob—longest common palindrome beginning with letter b (4)—longest common palindrome centered on letter o (4-t)—longest common word containing one type of consonant for consonant b (4-t)

bookkeeper—most consecutive doubled letters for a common word (3)

boots—longest common onalosi [coots & blots & boats & boobs & booth] (5-t)

boottree—longest uncommon word containing letters in reverse order from typewriter (8)—*rack for storing boots*

borne—example of a word that ends with silent letter e

borough—example of a common word with the most variably pronounced suffix [see "Pronunciation Variants" article, page 135]

bough—example of a common word with the most variably pronounced suffix [see "Pronunciation Variants" article, page 135]

bourg—example of a word that ends with silent letter g—*town*

bouts-rimes—hyphenated word with most consecutive alphabetic letters in reverse order consecutively (4)—*rhyming words to work into a poem*

braced—highest ratio of consecutive alphabetic letters to length for a common word (0.83-t)

bracers—longest common progressive terminal elision [bracers → racer → ace → c] (7-t)

brachyphyllum—uncommon word with the most infrequently used letters for length 13 (496)—*fossil coniferous plants*

brachyphyllums—uncommon word with the most infrequently used letters for length 14 (562)—*fossil plants*

brazenfaced—uncommon word containing most consecutive letters in the alphabet after letter z (7)—*impudent*

brazenfacedly—uncommon word containing most consecutive letters in the alphabet after letter y (8)—*shamelessly*

breadcrumb—longest uncommon word that starts and ends with letter b (10)—*small piece of bread*

break—common word with most different meanings or senses (245)

breakdown voltages—longest well-mixed phrase isomorph [granulocytopenias] (17-t)—*voltages at which sparking occurs*

breakthroughs—longest two-syllable word beginning with letter b (13)

breathtakingly—longest common well-mixed isomorph [chlorpromazine] (14-t)

brewpub—longest common word that starts and ends with letter b (7-t)

brief—longest sum pair with common words [brief → tank] (5-t)

bright-light districts—longest hyphenated phrase containing one type of vowel for vowel i (20)—*urban areas with bright lights*

bringing—longest nontrivial internal tautonym for a common word (6-t)

broadness—longest common alternade [bodes & rans] (9-t)

broil—example of a common word formed by borrowing or lending letters to frequent companions, beginning with letter b [amb-ustulare → am-bustulare]

brougham—uncommon word with longest silent-letter sequence [4, ugha]—*light horse carriage*

broughams—longest one-syllable word beginning with letter b (9)

browzing—one of three uncommon words that together contain the most different letters [kvetchy & mudflaps] (23)—*skimming or grazing*

brrr—shortest uncommon word with a tripled letter (4)—*shiver*

brunch—example of a portmanteau, beginning with letter b [breakfast, lunch]

brushed—see "astride"

BSc—shortest phrase with last letter next in alphabet after first for letter b (3-t)—*bachelor of science*

bu—see "ba"—*old Japanese coin*

bubble—common word containing the most repeats of letter b (3-t)

bubbly—common word containing the most repeats of letter b (3-t)

bucking transformers—longest phrase containing each vowel once (19-t)—*transformers that oppose other transformers*

buckishly—longest uncommon isomorse pair, measured in number of dots and dashes [thanklessly] (31-t)—*foppishly*

buckjumping—see "qwerty"—*bucking*

buckthorn families—phrase with the lowest ratio length to number of different letters for length 17 (1.06-t)—*types of trees and shrubs*

bulbul—longest common tautonym beginning with letter b (6)

bull—example of a self-antonym, beginning with letter b [edict, nonsense]

bumfuzzling—uncommon word with the most infrequently used letters for length 11 (331)—*confusing*

bumpety-bumpety—longest hyphenated tautonym beginning with letter b (14-t)—longest tautonym for a hyphenated word (14-t)—*bumpy*

bumpity-bumpity—longest hyphenated tautonym beginning with letter b (14-t)—longest tautonym for a hyphenated word (14-t)—*bumpy*

bunyabunya—longest uncommon tautonym beginning with letter b (10-t)—*Australian pine tree*

bursting strengths—longest phrase containing three vowels (17)—*weights at which failure occurs*

business—example of a word that contains silent letter i

but—see "butt"

butt—example of homophones differing by letter t [but]

buy—example of homophones differing by letter u [by]

buzz—common word with the most infrequently used letters for length 4 (50)

buzzy—uncommon word with the most infrequently used letters for length 5 (70)—*buzzing or talkative*

by—common word with the most infrequently used letters for length 2 (37)—see "ba" and "buy" and "bye"

bye—example of homophones differing by letter e [by]—longest progressive charitable with common words [bye & be & by & ye] (3-t)

byes—longest common word torture [bye & yes & by & es & ye] (4-t)

by hook or by crook—longest phrase without ETAINS (15)—*by any means*

BZ—phrase with the most infrequently used letters for length 2 (18)—*poison gas*

Words Ending in -Gry

Find three completely different words ending in "-gry."

Aside from "angry" and "hungry" and words derived therefrom, there is no stand-alone word ending in "gry" that is in current usage. Both *Webster's Third New International Dictionary of the English Language, Unabridged* and the *Oxford English Dictionary, Second Edition* contain the phrase "aggry bead." To find a third word ending in "gry" that is not part of a phrase, you must turn to obsolete words or personal or place names. A list of 130 of these is given at the end of this article.

So, basically, this puzzle has no good answer. Why, then, is it so popular? What follows is a conjecture about the history of this very curious puzzle.

Perhaps someone was browsing through an old dictionary or a book on unusual and interesting words, and came across the word "meagry," meaning meager. Perhaps he or she noticed that this old word had an unusual ending, an ending it shared with only two other words: "angry" and "hungry." Perhaps he or she were inspired to make up a puzzle, and send it to a newspaper columnist or a popular radio show. Perhaps the puzzle was published or broadcast. Perhaps the rest, as they say, is history.

This puzzle first appears in print in Anita Richterman's "Problem Line" column in *Newsday* on May 9, 1975. Several correspondents reported in this article that they had heard the puzzle on the Bob Grant Talk Show on WMCA-AM in New York City. The original form of the puzzle was: There are only three words in the English language, all adjectives, which end in "-gry." Two are "angry" and "hungry"; the third word describes the state of the world today. What is it?

This appears to be the origin of this puzzle. Additional evidence for this hypothesis is found in the correspondence files of Merriam-Webster. These files contain letters to the editors of Merriam-Webster (formerly G. & C. Merriam Co.), publishers of *Webster's Collegiate Dictionary* and *Webster's International Dictionary*. These files go back over 100 years. Letters asking for the third word ending in "-gry" do not appear until 1975, but there is a steady stream thereafter.

However, the word "meagry" is not in any current dictionary. Nor are any of the words on the list below. So, people could not find an answer. Nature abhors a vacuum, so people resorted to trick solutions. Thus the modern versions of this puzzle were born. Everyone is confident that the versions they originally heard were the true and correct versions. The plain facts are that there is no good answer, and that there is no one version that is correct. Some of the trick versions are enumerated below.

1. This version only works when spoken: There are three words in English that end in "gree." The first two are "angry" and "hungry," and if you've listened closely, you'll agree that I've already told you the third one.

The answer is "agree." The object is to make the listener think about the letters g-r-y instead of the sound "gree."

2. There are three words in the English language that end in the letters g-r-y. Two are "hungry" and "angry." Everyone knows what the third word means, and everyone uses it every day. What is the third word?

The answer is "energy." The riddle says that the word ends in the letters g-r-y; it says nothing about the order of the letters. Energy is something everyone uses everyday, and everyone probably knows what it means.

3. The "Ask Marilyn" (Marilyn Vos Savant) column in *Parade* magazine on March 9, 1997 featured this spoken version: There are at least three words in the English language that end in g or

y. One of them is "hungry," and another one is "angry." There is a third word, a short one, which you probably say every day. If you are listening carefully to everything I say, you just heard me say it three times. What is it?

The answer is "say." This version depends upon the listener confusing the spoken word "or" and the spoken letter r.

4. There are three words in the English language that end in "gry." Two words that end in "gry" are "hungry" and "angry." Everyone knows what the third word means, and everyone uses them every day. If you listened very carefully, I have already stated to you what the third word is. The three words that solve this riddle are ...?

The answer is the three-word sentence "I am hungry." This version asks for three words that end in "gry," not three words each of which end in "gry."

The remaining versions are a form of meta-puzzle, in the sense that they make no use of the actual letters "gry" themselves, which therefore are a red herring. The red herring only works because there is another puzzle that does use these letters (even though that puzzle has no good answer).

5. On March 28, 1996, one such version was broadcast on WHTZ in New York City during "The Elvis Duran Afternoon Show." The person asking the question was a caller who worked in a beauty salon at a mall somewhere in New Jersey: Think of words ending in "-gry." Angry and hungry are two of them. There are only three words in "the English language." What is the third word? The word is something that everyone uses everyday. If you have listened carefully, I have already told you what it is.

The answer to this version is "language"—the third word in the phrase "the English language." There are quotation marks needed to make this answer correct when the puzzle is printed, but they give away the trick.

6. Angry and hungry are two words in the English language that end in "-gry." "What" is the third word. The word is something that everyone uses everyday. If you have listened carefully, I have already told you what it is.

The answer is "what." But again, the quotation marks spoil the puzzle when it is printed.

7. This version is usually stated with certain words capitalized, for no apparent reason but historical accident: There are three words in the English language that end in "-gry." ONE is angry and the other is hungry. Every ONE knows what the third ONE means and what it stands for. Every ONE uses them every day. And if you listened carefully I've given you the third word. What is it?

The answer is "three," the third word in the paragraph. The rest of the paragraph is a red herring.

Here is the list of obsolete words, phrases and names (see the end of the list for the meaning of the references in brackets).

This list was gathered from the following articles:

George H. Scheetz, In Goodly Gree: With Goodwill, *Word Ways* 22:3 (Nov. 1989)

Murray R. Pearce, Who's Flaithbhertach MacLoingry?, *Word Ways* 23:1 (Feb. 1990)

Harry B. Partridge, Gypsy Hobby Gry, *Word Ways* 23:1 (Feb. 1990)

A. Ross Eckler, -Gry Words in the OED, *Word Ways* 25:4 (Nov. 1992)

Darryl Francis, Some New -Gry Words, *Word Ways* 30:3 (Aug. 1997)

References: Many references are of the form [Source:volume:page] or [Source:page]. They are listed after the -gry words.

affect-hungry [OED (see "sado-masochism")]

aggry [OED:1:182;W2;W3]

Agry [OED (see "snappily")]

Agry Dagh (Mount Agry) [EB11]

ahungry [OED:1:194; FW;W2]

air-hungry [OED (see "Tel Avivian")]

angry [OED; FW;W2;W3]

anhungry [OED:1:332;W2]

Badagry [Johnston; EB11; OED (see "Dahoman")]

Ballingry [Bartholomew:40; CLG:151; RD:164, pl.49]

begry [OED:1:770,767]

bewgry [OED:1:1160]

boroughmongry [OED (see "boroughmonger")]

bowgry [OED:1:1160]

braggry [OED:1:1047]

Bugry [TIG]

Chockpugry [Worcester]

Cogry [BBC]

cony-gry [OED:2:956]

conyngry [OED:2:956]

cottagry [OED (see "cottagery")]

Croftangry [DFC, as "Chrystal Croftangry"; OED (see "way")]

diamond-hungry [OED (see "Lorelei")]

dog-hungry [W2]

dogge-hungry [OED (see "canine")]

Dshagry [Stieler]

Dzagry [Andree]

eard-hungry [CED (see "yird"); CSD]

Echanuggry [Century:103–104, on inset map, Key 104 M 2]

Egry [France;TIG]

euer-angry [OED (see "ever")]

ever-angry [W2]

fenegry [OED (see "fenugreek")]

fire-angry [W2]

Gagry [EB11]

girl-hungry [OED (see "girl")]

gonagry [OED (see "gonagra")]

gry (from Latin gry) [OED:4/2:475;W2]

gry (from Romany grai) [W2]

haegry [EDD (see "hagery")]

half-angry [W2]

hangry [OED:1:329]

heart-angry [W2]

heart-hungry [W2]

higry pigry [OED:5/1:285]

hogry [EDD (see "huggerie"); CSD]

hogrymogry [EDD (see "huggerie"); CSD (as "hogry-mogry")]

hongry [OED:5/1:459; EDD:3:282]

hound-hungry [OED (see "hound")]

houngry [OED (see "minx")]

huggrymuggry [EDD (see "huggerie"); CSD (as "huggry-muggry")]

hund-hungry [OED (see "hound")]

hungry [OED; FW;W2;W3]

Hungry Bungry [Daily Illini, in ad for The Giraffe, Spring 1976]

hwngry [OED (see "quart")]

iggry [OED]

Jagry [EB11]

job-hungry [OED (see "gadget")]

kaingry [EDD (see "caingy")]

land-hungry [OED;W2]

Langry [TIG;Times]

leather-hungry [OED]

ledderhungry [OED (see "leather")]

life-hungry [OED (see "music")]

Lisnagry [Bartholomew:489]

losengry [OED (see "losengery")]

MacLoingry [Phillips (as "Flaithbhertach MacLoingry")]

mad-angry [OED:6/2:14]

mad-hungry [OED:6/2:14]

magry [OED:6/2:36, 6/2:247–48]

malgry [OED:6/2:247]

man-hungry [OED]

managry [OED (see "managery")]

mannagry [OED (see "managery")]

Margry [Indians (see "Pierre Margry" in bibliog., v.2, p.1204)]

maugry [OED:6/2:247–48]

mawgry [OED:6/2:247]

meagry [OED:6/2:267]

meat-hungry [W2; OED (see "meat")]

menagry [OED (see "managery")]

messagry [OED]

music-hungry [OED (see "music")]

nangry [OED]

overangry [RH1; RH2]

Pelegry [CE (in main index as "Raymond de Pelegry")]

Pingry [Bio-Base; HPS:293–94, 120–21]

Podagry [OED;W2 (below the line)]

Pongry [Andree (Supplement, p.572)]

pottingry [OED:7/2:1195; Jamieson:3:532]
power-hungry [OED (see "power")]
profit-hungry [OED (see "profit")]
puggry [OED:8/1:1573; FW; W2]
pugry [OED:8/1:1574]
red-angry [OED (see "sanguineous")]
rungry [EDD:5:188]
scavengry [OED (in 1715 quote under "scavengery")]
Schtschigry [LG/1:2045; OSN:97]
Seagry [TIG; EB11]
Segry [Johnston; Andree]
self-angry [W2]
selfe-angry [OED (see "self-")]
sensation-hungry [OED (see "sensation")]
sex-angry [OED (see "sex")]
sex-hungry [OED (see "cave")]
Shchigry [CLG:1747; Johnson:594; OSN:97,206; Times:185,pl.45]
shiggry [EDD]
Shtchigry [LG/1:2045; LG/2:1701]
Shtshigry [Lipp]
sight-hungry [OED (see "sight")]
skugry [OED:9/2:156, 9/1:297; Jamieson:4:266]

Sygry [Andree]
Tangry [France]
Tchangry [Johnson:594; LG/1:435,1117]
Tchigry [Johnson:594]
tear-angry [W2]
th'angry [OED (see "shot-free")]
tike-hungry [CSD]
Tingry [France; EB11 (under "Princesse de Tingry"); OED (see "parquet")]
toggry [Simmonds (as "Toggry," but all entries are capitalized)]
ulgry [Smith:24–25]
unangry [OED; W2]
vergry [OED:12/1:123]
Vigry [CLG:2090]
vngry [OED (see "wretch")]
war-hungry [OED (see "war")]
Wigry [CLG:2090; NAP:xxxix; Times:220, pl.62; WA:948]
wind-hungry [W2]
yeard-hungry [CED (see "yird")]
yerd-hungry [CED (see "yird"); OED]
yird-hungry [CED (see "yird")]
Ymagry [OED:1:1009 (col. 3, 1st "boss" verb), (variant of "imagery")]

References
Andree, Richard. *Andrees Handatlas* (index volume). 1925.
Bartholomew, John. *Gazetteer of the British Isles: Statistical and Topographical.* 1887.
BBC = *BBC Pronouncing Dictionary of English Names.*
Bio-Base. (Microfiche) Detroit: Gale Research Company. 1980.
CE = *Catholic Encyclopedia.* 1907.
CED = *Chambers English Dictionary.* 1988.
Century = "India, Northern Part." *The Century Atlas of the World.* 1897, 1898.
CLG = *The Colombia Lippincott Gazetteer of the World.* L.E. Seltzer, ed. 1952.
CSD = *Chambers Scots Dictionary.* 1971 reprint of 1911 edition.
Daily Illini (University of Illinois at Urbana-Champaign).
DFC = *Dictionary of Fictional Characters.* 1963.
EB11 = *Encyclopedia Britannica,* 11th ed.
EDD = *The English Dialect Dictionary.* Joseph Wright, ed. 1898.
France = Map Index of France. G.H.Q. American Expeditionary Forces. 1918.
FW = *Funk & Wagnalls New Standard Dictionary of the English Language.* 1943.
HPS = *The Handbook of Private Schools: An Annual Descriptive Survey of Independent Education,* 66th ed. 1985.
Indians = *Handbook of American Indians North of Mexico.* F.W. Hodge. 1912.
Jamieson, John. *An Etymological Dictionary of the Scottish Language.* 1879–87.
Johnston, Keith. *Index Geographicus...* 1864.
LG/1 = *Lippincott's Gazetteer of the World: A Complete Pronouncing Gazetteer or Geographical Dictionary of the World.* 1888.
LG/2 = *Lippincott's New Gazetteer: ...* 1906.

Lipp = *Lippincott's Pronouncing Gazetteer of the World*. 1861, undated edition from late 1800's; 1902.

NAP = *Narodowy Atlas Polski*. 1973–1978 [Polish language]

OED = *The Oxford English Dictionary*. 1933. [Form: OED:volume/part number if applicable:page]

OSN: U.S.S.R. Volume 6, S-T. Official Standard Names Approved by the United States Board on Geographic Names. Gazetteer #42, 2nd ed. June 1970.

Partridge, Harry B. "Ad Memoriam Demetrii." *Word Ways*, 19 (Aug. 1986): 131.

Phillips, Lawrence. *Dictionary of Biographical Reference*. 1889.

RD = *The Reader's Digest Complete Atlas of the British Isles*, 1st ed. 1965.

RH1 = *Random House Dictionary of the English Language, Unabridged*. 1966.

RH2 = *Random House Dictionary of the English Language, Second Edition Unabridged*. 1987.

Simmonds, P.L. *Commercial Dictionary of Trade Products*. 1883.

Smith, John. *The True Travels, Adventvres and Observations: London* 1630.

Stieler, Adolph. *Stieler's Handatlas* (index volume). 1925.

TIG = *The Times Index-Gazetteer of the World*. 1965.

Times = *The Times Atlas of the World*, 7th ed. 1985.

W2 = *Webster's New International Dictionary of the English Language, Second Edition, Unabridged*. 1934.

W3 = *Webster's Third New International Dictionary of the English Language, Unabridged*. 1961.

WA = *The World Atlas: Index-Gazetteer. Council of Ministries of the USSR*, 1968.

Worcester, J.E. *Universal Gazetteer, Second Edition*. 1823.

C

c—longest common head 'n' tail centered on letter c (1)—longest common palindrome centered on letter c (1)—longest common word with typewriter letters from bottom row (1-t)

caaba—uncommon word with lowest letter sum for length 5 (8-t)—*from the Islamic shrine in Mecca*

cabbage—common word with lowest letter sum for length 7 (21)—longest common word spelled with piano notes (7-t)

cabbaged—longest uncommon word spelled with piano notes (8-t)—*stolen*

cabbagehead—uncommon word with lowest letter sum for length 11 (39)—*stupid person*

cabbageheads—uncommon word with lowest letter sum for length 12 (58)

cabled—highest ratio of consecutive alphabetic letters to length for a common word (0.83-t)

cacafugo—see "acacetin"—*braggart*

cachaca—uncommon word with lowest letter sum for length 7 (20)—*Brazilian rum*

cad—shortest common word with last letter next in alphabet after first for letter c (3-t)

caeca—longest uncommon head 'n' tail centered on letter e (5-t)—*cavities open at one end*

caesious—shortest uncommon word containing each vowel once in order (8)—*dark blue*

calcium hydrogen sulfite—phrase with the lowest ratio length to number of different letters for length 22 (1.29)—*disinfectant*

calcium hydrogen sulfites—phrase with the lowest ratio length to number of different letters for length 23 (1.35)

calliopes—longest common alternade [clips & aloe] (9-t)

callous—example of homophones differing by letter o [callus]

callus—see "callous"

calpullec—example of a plural that ends with letter c—*Aztec clan*

calycal—longest uncommon head 'n' tail centered on letter y (7)—*cup shaped*

canal—longest sum pair with common words [canal → doom] (5-t)

cane—longest common progressive sum pair [cane → dos → sh → a] (4-t)

canfuls—longest sum pair with an uncommon word [canfuls → dotage] (7-t)—*amounts that fill a can*

cannibalized—common word containing most consecutive letters in the alphabet after letter z (6-t)

canola—example of an acronym that has become uncapitalized, beginning with letter c [CANada Oil + Low Acid]

canthari—see "cantharidates"—*Greek cup*

cantharidaes—see "cantharidates"—*soldier beetles*

cantharidates—longest uncommon progressive delete letter from any position to form another word [cantharidates → cantharidaes → cantharides → cantharids → cantharis → canthari → cathari → cathar → athar → thar → har → ar → r] (13)

canthari

cantharides—see "cantharidates"—*Spanish flies*

cantharids—see "cantharidates"—*Spanish flies*

cantharis—see "cantharidates"

capitalizations—longest common roller-coaster (15-t)

carbomethoxyglycines—uncommon word with the lowest ratio length to number of different letters for length 20 (1.25-t)

carbonized—common word containing most consecutive letters in the alphabet after letter z (6-t)

carboxyhemoglobins—uncommon word with the lowest ratio length to number of different letters for length 18 (1.20-t)

carers—see "cares"—*those who care*

cares—longest uncommon hospitable [scares & chares & cadres & caries & carers & caress] (5-t)—see "caress"

caress—shortest common word in which dropping s makes a plural [caress → cares] (6-t)

caries—see "carries"

carouser—see "carousers"—*loud partygoer*

carousers—longest uncommon alternating terminal elision [carousers → carouser → arouser → arouse → rouse → rous → ous → ou → u] (9-t)—longest uncommon progressive terminal elision [carousers → arouser → rouse → ous → u] (9-t)

carpetweeds—longest uncommon alternade [crewes & apted] (11-t)—*North American weed*

carries—example of homophones differing by letter r [caries]

caseous—example of a word that sounds like letters, beginning with letter k sound [KSES]—*with damaged tissues resembling cheese*

cata-cornered—see "catercorner"

catacorner—see "catercorner"

catastrophist—common word with most consecutive runs of consecutive alphabetic letters (3-t)

catchphrase—longest consonant string for an uncommon word (6-t)—*popular phrase*

catenate—example of a false antonym beginning with letter c [concatenate]

catercorner—non-foreign uncommon word with most variant spellings [cater-corner & cater-cornered & catacorner & cata-cornered & catty-corner & catty-cornered & kitty-corner & kitty-cornered] (9)—*in a corner on a diagonal line*

cater-corner—see "catercorner"

cater-cornered—see "catercorner"

cathar—see "cantharidates"—*medieval religious sect*

cathari—see "cantharidates"—*members of medieval European sect*

catty-cornered—see "catercorner"

catty-corner—see "catercorner"

caza—see "spoon"—*Turkish administrative unit*

CD—shortest phrase with last letter next in alphabet after first for letter c (2)—*compact disk*

cent—see "scent"

centrifugalisation—longest well-mixed uncommon transubstitution [centrifugalisation → intercartilaginous] (18-t)—*processing in a centrifuge*

cereals—longest uncommon multiplicative offset shift pair [kanauri] [factor of 21] (7-t)

ceresin—uncommon homophones that have the fewest letters in common for their combined length [ceresin → Saracen] (2 out of 14)—*white wax*

certification—longest metathesis with common words [certification → rectification] (13-t)

ces—see "cess"—*letter c's*

cesium—example of a word that sounds like letters, beginning with letter c sound [CZM]—*element with atomic number 55*

cess—shortest uncommon word in which dropping s makes a plural [cess → ces] (4-t)—*tax*

CFC—shortest phrase that starts and ends with letter c (3)—*chlorofluorocarbon*

chachalaca—uncommon word with lowest letter sum for length 10 (41-t)—*Central American bird*

chacking—longest full vowel substitution with an uncommon word [checking & chicking & chocking & chucking] (8-t)—*Scottish for pinching*

chares—see "cares"—*chores*

charoseth—longest uncommon progressive terminal elision [charoseth → haroset → arose → ros → o] (9-t)—*Jewish ceremonial meal*

charpoy—longest sum pair with an uncommon word [charpoy → kishen] (7-t)—*Indian rope bed*

chasses—see "classes"—*ballet steps*

chauffeur—see "shofar"

chechen—longest rot-13 pair with an uncommon word [purpura] (7-t)—*people of Dagestan, U.S.S.R.*

checkbook—longest common word spelled with horizontal symmetry letters (9)

checkbook journalism—phrase containing most consecutive letters in the alphabet after letter h (8)—phrase containing most consecutive letters in the alphabet after letter i (7)—*paying for news coverage*

checking—see "chacking"

chemotherapeutic—longest common word that starts and ends with letter c (16-t)

chenodeoxycholic acid—see "chenodesoxycholic acids"—*bile acid*

chenodesoxycholic acids—longest letter subtraction for a phrase [chenodesoxycholic acids → chenodeoxycholic acid] (22)

chic—shortest common word that starts and ends with letter c (4)

chichi—longest common tautonym beginning with letter c (6)

chicking—see "chacking"—*sprouting*

chimps—longest common word with letters in alphabetical order (6-t)

chinos—longest common word with letters in alphabetical order (6-t)

chintz—longest common word with letters in alphabetical order (6-t)

chiquichiqui—longest tautonym for an uncommon word (12-t)—longest uncommon tautonym beginning with letter c (12)—*South American palm*

chlorofluorocarbon—common word containing the most repeats of letter o (5)

chlorofluorocarbons—longest common word without ET (19)

chlorophyll—longest common word without ETAINS (11)

chlorpromazine—see "breathtakingly"

chocking—see "chacking"

chortle—example of a portmanteau, beginning with letter c [chuckle, snort]

christocentric—longest uncommon word with consecutive letters adjacent on phone keypad beginning with letter c (14)—*based upon Christ*

chroococcaceae—uncommon word containing the most repeats of letter c (5-t)—*family of blue-green algae*

chroococcaceous—uncommon word containing the most repeats of letter c (5-t)—*type of algae*

chucking—see "chacking"

chylophyllously—uncommon word with the most infrequently used letters for length 15 (637)—longest uncommon word without ETAIN (15-t)—*growing thick leaves*

cineangiocardiographic—longest uncommon word that starts and ends with letter c (22)—*moving x-rays of the heart*

cinematographers—longest well-mixed transposal with an uncommon word [megachiropterans] (16-t)—*cameramen*

cinerins—longest uncommon progressive delete-reverse [cinerins → sirenic → ineris → siren → neri → ire → er → r] (8-t)—*naturally occurring insecticides*

cinq-cents—example of a word that contains silent letter q—*card game*

circa—longest sum pair with common words [circa → laud] (5-t)

civic—longest common palindrome beginning with letter c (5)—longest common palindrome centered on letter v (5-t)

civies—see "civvies"—*civilian clothing*

civvies—example of homophones differing by letter v [civies]—*variant of civies*

clacking—longest full vowel substitution with an uncommon word [clecking & clicking & clocking & clucking] (8-t)

clashes—longest common progressive beheadment [clashes → lashes → ashes → shes → hes → es → s] (7-t)

classes—longest uncommon onalosi [glasses & chasses & clesses & clauses & clashes & classis & classed] (7-t)

classis—see "classes"—*church governing body*

cleave—example of a self-antonym, beginning with letter c [separate, join]

clecking—see "clacking"—*hatching*

clesses—see "classes"—*Scottish for classes*

clicking—see "clacking"

cline—longest common onalosi [aline & chine & clone & clime & cling] (5-t)

clink—longest common onalosi [blink & chink & clank & click & cline] (5-t)

clobbers—see "clovers"

clocking—see "clacking"

close—example of an antonym of four different words, beginning with letter c [open, remote, aloof, liberal]

clotheshorse—longest two-syllable word beginning with letter c (12)—*a frame on which to hang clothes*

clovers—longest common well-mixed digital charade pair [clobbers] (8-t)

clucking—see "clacking"

coadministration—see "coadministrations"—*joint government*

coadministrations—longest uncommon progressive transdeletion [coadministrations → coadministration → romanticisation → ratiocinations → narcotisation → notarisation → nitrosation → intortions → sortition → tortonis → risotto → stroot → trots → tots → tot → to → t] (17-t)

coccaceae—longest uncommon word containing one type of consonant for consonant c (9)—*family of bacteria*

coccidiocide—longest uncommon word spelled with horizontal symmetry letters (12)—*death from certain parasitical protozoans*

coccidioidomycosis—longest uncommon word without ETA (18-t)—*infection of the lungs and skin*

cockles—example of a word that exists only in an idiom, beginning with letter c [cockles of the heart]

cod—shortest common word with last letter next in alphabet after first for letter c (3-t)

codefendant—uncommon word containing most consecutive letters in order after letter c (4-t)—*defendant joined with other defendants in a single action*

code flag—phrase containing most consecutive letters in order after letter c (5)—*nautical signal flag*

coffer—longest difference pair with common words [coffer → nizam] (6-t)

coining—closest to five million letter product for a common word (5000940)

comb—example of a word that ends with silent letter b

commitment—common word containing the most repeats of letter m (3-t)

committee—most doubled letters for a common word (3-t)

communism—common word containing the most repeats of letter m (3-t)

compartmentalizing—common word with the lowest ratio length to number of different letters for length 18 (1.38-t)

comprehensibility—common word with the lowest ratio length to number of different letters for length 17 (1.21-t)—most different letters for a common word (14-t)

comprehensible—longest common well-mixed isomorph [counterexample] (14-t)

comprehensivisation—see "atmospheric inversion"—*opening of a secondary school to all levels of ability*

comprising—longest common well-mixed isotel pair [conspiring] (10)

compurgator—longest uncommon well-mixed isotel pair [constrictor] (11-t)—*person who vouches for another*

computerized axial tomography scanner—most different letters for a phrase (19-t)—*X-ray machine that creates a 3D image*

concatenate—see "catenate"

concierge—example of a word spelled with i before e after c, beginning with letter c

concord—example of a word pronounced differently when capitalized, beginning with letter c [agree, New Hampshire capital]

conjoin—see "join"—*join*

conscientiousness—longest common word containing four types of consonants (17)

consciousnesses—longest common word containing three types of consonants (15-t)

conspiring—see "comprising"

constitutionality—common word containing the most repeats of letter t (4-t)

constitutive—common word containing most consecutive letters in order after letter s (4-t)

constrictor—see "compurgator"

constructive—common word containing most consecutive letters in order after letter s (4-t)—common word containing most consecutive letters in order after letter t (3-t)

contour—see "amounts"

convallarias—longest uncommon word spelled with two-letter U.S. postal codes (12)—*lily of the valley*

convallarias

convexo-convex—longest hyphenated head 'n' tail (13-t)—longest hyphenated head 'n' tail centered on letter o (13)—*convex on both sides*

cooperatively—most letters in alphabetical place with shifting alphabet for a common word (6-t)

coops—longest common charitable [oops & cops & cops & coos & coop] (5-t)

corespondent—longest uncommon homophone with no removable prefix or suffix [corespondent → correspondent] (25)—*codefendant to the adulterous spouse in a divorce proceeding*

cornrowed—see "alarmedly"—*braided hair in parallel rows*

corocoro—longest fixed offset shift pair with an uncommon word [wiliwili] [shift of 20] (8)—*Malay boat*

correspondent—see "corespondent"

cotter—uncommon homophones that have the fewest letters in common for their combined length [cotter → Kadir] (1 out of 11)

cough—uncommon homophones that have the fewest letters in common for their combined length [cough → Kaf] (0 out of 8)—example of a common word with the most variably pronounced suffix [see "Pronunciation Variants" article, page 135]

councilman—longest common word with consecutive letters adjacent on phone keypad beginning with letter c (10)

countercountermeasure—longest nontrivial internal tautonym for an uncommon word (14)—longest repeated prefix for an uncommon word (14)—*preparation for retaliation*

counterexample—see "comprehensible"

counterfeit—example of a word spelled with e before i, beginning with letter c

countermanding—longest common word containing each vowel once (14-t)

counterreconnaissances—longest uncommon word containing five types of consonants (22-t)—*ways to prevent being observed*

counterrevolutionaries—common word with the lowest ratio length to number of different letters for length 22 (1.83-t)

coup—example of a word that ends with silent letter p

courie—see "curie"—*marine mollusk*

cow—longest common word that has no letters in common with its plural [cow → kine] (3/4)

coxalgia—longest uncommon iskot pair [alimentation] (12)—*disease of the hip joint*

crabbing—see "craving"

cramps—longest length four linkade with common words [cram & ramp & amps] (6-t)

crankshafts—longest common word containing one type of vowel for vowel a (11-t)

crashes—longest common progressive beheadment [crashes → rashes → ashes → shes → hes → es → s] (7-t)

craters—longest common alternating terminal elision [craters → crater → rater → rate → ate → at → t] (7-t)—longest common progressive terminal elision [craters → rater → ate → t] (7-t)

craunched—longest one-syllable word beginning with letter c (9)—*crunched*

craving—longest common well-mixed digital charade pair [crabbing] (8-t)

crazily—longest common word with no contiguous subsequence that is a word (7)

creatine phosphokinases—longest well-mixed subtransposition for a phrase [as different as chalk and cheese] (27-t)—*muscle enzymes*

creel—longest rot-13 pair with common words [perry] (5-t)

crewes—see "carpetweeds"—*pots*

crushed—see "astride"

crux—shortest common word that cannot have a letter added and transposed to form another word (4-t)

cry—shortest common stingy word (3-t)

crystallographic—longest common word that starts and ends with letter c (16-t)

ctene—example of a word that is a confusing code for letter c [teen]—*row of strong cilia with fused bases*

cud—shortest common word with last letter next in alphabet after first for letter c (3-t)

cuffing—closest to two million letter product for a common word (2000376-t)

cui-ui—longest hyphenated word with no subsequence that is a word (5)—*fish found only in Lake Pyramid, Nevada*

cui-ui

culmination—common word containing most consecutive letters in order after letter l (4-t)

cuirie—see "curie"—*Medieval breast plate*

cullies—see "collies"—*cohorts*

cunette—example of an uncommon word formed by borrowing or lending letters to frequent

Longest Word

What is the longest word in the English language?
> But then one day I learned a word
> that saved me achin' nose,
> the biggest word you ever 'eard,
> and this is 'ow it goes:
> "Supercalifragilisticexpialidocious"
> [from Walt Disney's film *Mary Poppins*]

As mentioned in the Preface, some odd properties of words are so obvious that they inevitably will be abused. No property has been abused more than word length. Every child wants to know what the longest word is. The temptation to coin a new record holder has proven irresistible. Few of these coined words make their way into dictionaries, but some do, and every few generations the canonical longest "word" changes.

In ancient Greece, Aristophanes was fond of concocting long words to amuse his audiences. His longest comes from the play *Ecclesiazusae* and basically means "hash": lopadotemachoselachogaleokranioleiosanodrimhypotrimmatosilphioparaomelitokatakechymenokichlepikossyphopattoperisteralektryonoptekephalliokigklopeleiolagoiosiraiobaphetraganopterygon.

In Shakespeare's school days he learned the longest Latin word, which the clown Costard pontificates in *Love's Labor's Lost*: honorificabilitudinitatibus.

In Sir Walter Scott's youth he learned the longest word and repeated it to his diary (though he mangled it a bit by replacing the first n with a p): floccinaucinihilipilification.

In the nineteenth and early twentieth centuries, students learned that the longest word was: antidisestablishmentarianism.

And so on.

Suppose we ignore these coined examples. Then what is the longest word? As technical knowledge accumulates, ever more complicated experimental apparatus, chemical compounds, medical conditions, etc. are invented or discovered. These need to be named, and these names tend to be quite long. Words like: anhydrohydroxyprogesterone, dichlorodiphenyltrichloroethane, electroencephalographically, ethylenediaminetetraacetate, hydroxydesoxycorticosterone, octamethylpyrophosphoramide, and trinitrophenylmethylnitramine come into use. The longest medical-sounding word in the major dictionaries is the 45-letter name of a supposed lung disease: pneumonoultramicroscopicsilicovolcanoconiosis.

However, it turns out that this word is a hoax perpetrated by the members of the National Puzzlers' League, the world's oldest wordplay association. The word is unknown to medical science. The League President (Everett M. Smith) coined the word at the 103rd meeting of the League, held on February 22, 1935 in New York City. It was picked up by a newspaper reporter for the *Herald Tribune* and printed the next day in the headline of an article on the League meeting. Frank Scully, author of a series of puzzle books and later one of the early UFO enthusiasts, read the newspaper article and repeated the word in *Bedside Manna; The Third Fun in Bed Book*, (Simon and Schuster, 1936, p. 87). On the strength of this citation, League members (with a wink from the editors?) got the word into both the *OED Supplement* and *Webster's Third*. There it remains even to this day.

Suppose we ignore these technical terms. Then what is the longest word? Dictionaries contain many long words such as: countercountermeasures, counterrevolutionaries, deinstitutionalization, intercomprehensibility, interdenominationalism, overintellectualization, postimpressionistically, semimicrodetermination, transubstantiationalist.

However, in order to save space, dictionaries do not explicitly list all such words, which are called "closed compounds." In the explanatory sections of most dictionaries, the editors explicitly state that since the meanings of these words can be deduced from their component parts, the space they would consume can be put to better use. So, for example, many verbs can have "re-" added to them to form other verbs, and many nouns, adjectives, and adverbs can likewise be modified by the application of prefixes and suffixes. If these prefixes or suffixes can be added once, why can't they be added again? "Countercountermeasures" is a word; is "countercounter-countermeasures" one too?

And so on.

Suppose we strip off the prefixes and suffixes. Then what is the longest word? The problem now is that it's not easy to say what is a prefix or a suffix, because most words were formed sometime in history by compounding shorter words. For example, in the word "alphabet," is "alpha" a prefix?

So the only reasonable conclusion is that there is no longest word. Mathematicians have known for millennia that there is no largest number. They have adjusted to the disappointment. I suppose we can too. But if a small child (or newspaper reporter) pleads with you to please, please, tell what the longest word is, perhaps a 45-letter lung disease will be good enough for a few generations.

companions, beginning with letter c [lacunetta → la cunetta]—*small channel dug in the bottom of a large channel*

curbing—closest to two million letter product for a common word (2000376-t)

curie—longest uncommon hospitable [ecurie & courie & cuirie & curnie & curiae & curies] (5-t)

curing—closest to one million letter product for a common word (1000188)

curiosity—example of a word that sounds like letters, beginning with letter q sound [QRESET]

curnie—see "curie"—*group of people*

curtainless—longest uncommon alternade [cranes & utils] (11-t)—*without curtains*

curvaceousnesses—longest uncommon word spelled with short lowercase letters (16)—*qualities of having a well-rounded body*

customizable—common word containing most consecutive letters in order after letter z (3-t)

cutter classification—longest well-mixed transdeletion for a phrase [cutter classification → facilities contracts] (20-t)—*library classification scheme*

cut the ground from under someone's feet—longest phrase containing three types of vowels (33-t)—*undermine*

cyclo—see "hexachlorocyclohexane"—*three-wheeled taxi*

cymba—longest uncommon progressive sum pair [cymba → bloc → nar → os → h] (5-t)—*boat-shaped palm seedpod*

czar—example of a word that begins with silent letter c

D

d—longest common head 'n' tail centered on letter d (1)

dab—example of a common word formed by borrowing or lending letters to frequent companions, beginning with letter d [adept → a dab]

dabbed—common word with lowest letter sum for length 6 (18-t)

dactinomycin—longest phrase nontrivial one letter head-to-tail shift [dactinomycin → actinomycin D] (12)—*poisonous drug*

dad—longest common head 'n' tail centered on letter a (3-t)—shortest common word that starts and ends with letter d (3-t)

daimon—longest digital reversal pair with common words [domain] (6-t)

dam—see "damn"

damn—example of homophones differing by letter n [dam]

damndest—common word with most consecutive runs of consecutive alphabetic letters (3-t)

darns—see "dearns"—*swears*

day—example of a word that ends with silent letter y

DD—shortest phrase that starts and ends with letter d (2)—*doctor of divinity*

de—shortest uncommon word with last letter next in alphabet after first for letter d (2)—see "aides" and "amides"—*letter d*

dead-endednesses—longest hyphenated pyramid word (15)—*qualities of being fruitless*

dead-freight—hyphenated word containing most consecutive letters in order after letter d (5)—*loss due to unoccupied space on a cargo ship*

deadheaded—uncommon word with lowest letter sum for length 10 (41-t)—*acted dumb*

deafening—common word containing most consecutive letters in order after letter d (4-t)

dearn—see "dearns"—*mild oath*

dearns—longest uncommon charitable [earns & darns & derns & deans & dears & dearn] (6-t)—*secrecies*

debagged—longest uncommon word spelled with piano notes (8-t)—*removed the pants from someone*

debar—see "bar"—*suspend*

debt—example of a word that contains silent letter b

debug—longest digital reversal pair with common words [gabbed] (6-t)

decaffeinated—common word with lowest letter sum for length 13 (83)

decontamination—longest common roller-coaster (15-t)

deed—longest common palindrome centered on letter e (4-t)

deeded—longest common word with typewriter letters from one finger (6)—longest common word containing one type of consonant for consonant d (6-t)—longest common trio isogram (6)

deedeed—longest uncommon palindrome centered on letter d (7-t)—longest uncommon word with typewriter letters from one finger (7)—*damned*

defaced—longest common word spelled with hexadecimal letters (7-t)—longest common word spelled with piano notes (7-t)

defeating—common word containing most consecutive letters in order after letter d (4-t)

defending—common word containing most consecutive letters in order after letter d (4-t)

deficient—example of a word spelled with i before e after c, beginning with letter d

defining—common word containing most consecutive letters in order after letter d (4-t)

degas—example of a word pronounced differently when capitalized, beginning with letter d [remove gas from, French artist]

degauss—see "assuage" and "assuaged"

degged—longest uncommon palindrome centered on letter g (6)—*sprinkled*

dehaired—longest uncommon numberdrome (8-t)—*shorn*

deified—longest common palindrome beginning with letter d (7)—longest common palindrome centered on letter f (7)—longest palindrome for a common word (7-t)—longest common numberdrome (7)

deinstitutionalized—longest uncommon word that starts and ends with letter d (19)—*released from an institution*

deity—example of a word spelled with e before i, beginning with letter d

delated—see "delater"—*accused*

delater—longest uncommon onalosi [relater & dilater & debater & deleter & delayer & delator & delated] (7-t)—*informer*

delator—see "delater"—*informer*

delayer—see "delater"—*one that delays*

deleter—see "delater"—*one that deletes*

delightful—common word containing most consecutive letters in the alphabet after letter d (6-t)—common word containing most consecutive letters in the alphabet after letter e (5-t)

delivers—longest delete-reverse with common words [delivers → reviled] (8-t)

delivery—longest delete-reverse with common words [delivery → reviled] (8-t)

demander—longest delete-reverse with common words [demander → renamed] (8-t)

demi—see "demitasse"—*half*

demilitarizing—longest common well-mixed isomorph [municipalities] (14-t)

demitasse—longest length four linkade with an uncommon word [demi & emit & mita & itas & tass & asse] (9-t)—*small cup of strong black coffee*

dent—example of a false antonym beginning with letter d [indent]

denude—see "nude"

denunciate—longest uncommon nontrivial one letter head-to-tail shift [denunciate → enunciated] (10)—*denounce*

denunciation—see "enunciation"

denunciations—see "discontinuance"

deports—longest common progressive delete-reverse [deports → stoped → depot → tope → pot → to → o] (7-t)

dermatoglyphics—longest uncommon isogram (15-t)—*prints of the hands and feet*

derns—see "dearns"—*Scottish for hides*

derrings-do—example of a plural that ends with letter o—*daring actions*

des—see "aides" and "amides" and "dess" and "thanatopsides"

desegregated—longest common word with typewriter letters from left hand (12-t)

desertress—longest uncommon word with typewriter letters from adjacent keys (10-t)—*female who deserts*

desiccate—most difficult uncommon word to spell [see "Misspelled Words" article, page 125]—*remove water*

despots—longest common progressive delete-reverse [despots → stoped → depot → tope → pot → to → o] (7-t)

dess—shortest uncommon word in which dropping s makes a plural [dess → des] (4-t)—*pile*

desserts—longest common reversal pair [stressed] (8)

destructive—common word containing most consecutive letters in order after letter s (4-t)—common word containing most consecutive letters in order after letter t (3-t)

determinations—longest common changeover [exterminations] (14-t)

detractors—longest common double progressive beheadment [detractors → tractors → actors → tors → rs] (10-t)

devil-devil—longest hyphenated tautonym beginning with letter d (10)—*magic spell*

devious—example of a word that sounds like letters, beginning with letter d sound [DVS]

devolutionists—see "evolutionists"—*persons believing in local control*

devolve—longest common nontrivial one letter head-to-tail shift [devolve → evolved] (7-t)

devoved—longest uncommon palindrome centered on letter o (7)—*devoted*

d-gluco-pentahydroxy-pentyls—hyphenated word with the lowest ratio length to number of different letters for length 25 (1.56)—*chemicals*

diacetylmorphines—uncommon word with the lowest ratio length to number of different letters for length 17 (1.13-t)—*narcotic*

dichlorodiphenyltrichloroethane—uncommon word containing the most repeats of letter h (4-t)—most repeated letters for an uncommon word (10-t)—*DDT*

did—longest common palindrome centered on letter i (3-t)—shortest common word that starts and ends with letter d (3-t)

diddle-daddled—hyphenated word containing the most repeats of letter d (7)—*dawdled*

didst—longest common multiplicative offset shift pair [rural] [factor of 11] (5-t)

die—shortest common word with last letter next in alphabet after first for letter d (3-t)

diiodide—longest uncommon word containing one type of consonant for consonant d (8)—*compound of iodine*

diiodohydroxyquins—longest uncommon word without ETA (18-t)—*medicines for amebic dysentery*

diketopiperazines—longest alternating vowels and consonants for an uncommon word (17-t)—*chemicals that break down in water into amino acids*

dilater—see "delater"—*one that dilates*

dimethyltubocurarines—uncommon word with the lowest ratio length to number of different letters for length 21 (1.31-t)—*muscle relaxants*

dinaphthothiophene—uncommon word containing the most repeats of letter h (4-t)—*derivative of coal tar used in moth balls*

diphenylthiocarbazones—uncommon word with the lowest ratio length to number of different letters for length 22 (1.37-t)—*chemicals*

disabuse—see "abuse"

disciplining—longest common word containing one type of vowel for vowel i (12-t)

discombobulated—longest common word that starts and ends with letter d (15-t)

discontinuance—longest common well-mixed transdeletion [discontinuance → denunciations] (14-t)

discreetness—see "discreteness"—*prudence*

discreteness—longest uncommon homophones that are transposals [discreteness → discreetness] (12)—*separateness*

discriminative—longest common well-mixed isomorph [simplification] (14-t)

discussions—longest common four-cadence (3-t)

disenfranchised—longest common word that starts and ends with letter d (15-t)

disenfranchising—common word containing most consecutive letters in the alphabet after letter c (7-t)—common word that contains the most consecutive letters in alphabet (7-t)

disjunct tetrachords—longest phrase containing each vowel once (19-t)—*non-overlapping four-tone chords*

dismantlement—longest common word with typewriter letters from alternating hands (13)

disspreading—longest uncommon isomorse pair, measured in number of dots and dashes [bessemerizing] (31-t)—longest uncommon well-mixed isomorse pair [bessemerizing] (13-t)—*expanding*

distribution—longest common four-cadence (3-t)

distributive—common word containing most consecutive letters in order after letter s (4-t)

distributive law—phrase containing most consecutive letters in order after letter s (5)—phrase containing most consecutive letters in order after letter t (4)—*mathematical law for combining operations*

divas—longest common multiplicative offset shift pair [lance] [factor of 3] (5-t)

dividivi—longest uncommon tautonym beginning with letter d (8)—*tropical American tree*

divisibility—longest common two-cadence (5-t)

djin—example of a word that is a confusing code for letter d [gin]—*variant of djinni*

djinni—example of a word that begins with silent letter d—*genie*

docility—longest common word with consecutive letters adjacent on phone keypad beginning with letter d (8-t)

dodo—longest common tautonym beginning with letter d (4)

doe—shortest common word with last letter next in alphabet after first for letter d (3-t)

dogwoods—longest common word where each letter is three symbols in Morse code (8-t)

dollop—longest common lowercase upside-down word (6-t)

domain—see "daimon"

don't halloo till you're out of the wood—phrase containing the most repeats of letter o (8)—*keep quiet until safety is assured*

doodad—longest common word containing one type of consonant for consonant d (6-t)

doom—see "canal"

dooms—longest common lowercase upside-down word pair [swoop] (5)

dopa—example of an acronym that has become uncapitalized, beginning with letter d [DihydrOxyPhenylAlanine]—*organic chemical*

doppler effect—longest shiftgram pair for a phrase [tertius gaudet] [shift of 11] (13-t)—*change in frequency due to motion of sound source*

dos—longest progressive charitable with common words [dos & do & ds & os] (3-t)

do-se-dos—longest hyphenated head 'n' tail centered on letter e (7)—*movement in square-dance*

dotage—see "canfuls"

dotty—longest sum pair with common words [dotty → sins] (5-t)

double wingback formations—phrase with the lowest ratio length to number of different letters for length 24 (1.33-t)—*football formation*

doubloon—example of a word that sounds like letters, beginning with letter w sound [WN]—*old Spanish gold coin*

doubloon

dough—longest common multiplicative offset shift pair [twain] [factor of 5] (5-t)

doux—example of a word that ends with silent letter x—*very sweet*

download—longest common word with consecutive letters adjacent on phone keypad beginning with letter d (8-t)

downstream—longest consonant string for a common word (5-t)

downthrusts—longest uncommon word with consecutive letters adjacent on phone keypad beginning with letter d (11)—*downward movements*

downtown—longest common word with consecutive letters adjacent on phone keypad beginning with letter d (8-t)

downy false foxglove—phrase containing most consecutive letters in the alphabet after letter v (4)—*plant that looks like a foxglove*

dowts—longest uncommon progressive difference pair [dowts → orca → wob → hm → u] (5-t)—*Scottish for a cigarette butt*

dramedy—example of a portmanteau, beginning with letter d [drama, comedy]—*comedy with dramatic scenes*

draughtboards—longest two-syllable word beginning with letter d (13)—*checkerboards*

draughts—longest one-syllable word beginning with letter d (8)

dresser—longest common switchback [presser] (7-t)

druthers—example of a word that exists only in an idiom, beginning with letter d [if I had my druthers]—*prefer-ence*

dresser

dry—shortest common stingy word (3-t)

duchenne's muscular dystrophy—longest phrase with balanced letter sum (26)—*common form of a genetic disease of the muscles*

dud—longest common palindrome centered on letter u (3-t)—shortest common word that starts and ends with letter d (3-t)

due—shortest common word with last letter next in alphabet after first for letter d (3-t)

dull—example of an antonym of three different words, beginning with letter d [sharp, clear, interesting]

dumbbell—most difficult common word to spell [see "Misspelled Words" article, page 125]

dunderheadededness—uncommon word containing the most repeats of letter d (5)—*stupidity*

dust—example of a self-antonym, beginning with letter d [remove fine particles, cover with fine particles]

dybbuk—common word with the most infrequently used letters for length 6 (128)

dye—shortest common word with last letter next in alphabet after first for letter d (3-t)

E

e—longest common word containing all vowels (1-t)

earthed—longest one-syllable word beginning with letter e (7)

earthtongues—longest two-syllable word beginning with letter e (12)—*type of fungus*

eastern diamondback rattlesnake—longest phrase changeover [western diamondback rattlesnake] (29)

eat—see "ate"

eats—see "seats"

eaux—example of a plural that ends with letter x—*watery solution*

ecce—longest uncommon palindrome beginning with letter e (4-t)—*behold*

echevarria—example of a word that sounds like letters, beginning with letter h sound [HAVREA]

echinoders—uncommon word with most consecutive runs of consecutive alphabetic letters (4)—*small marine worms*

ecurie—see "curie"—*team of car racers*

ed—see "stop order"—*education*

edged—longest common head 'n' tail centered on letter g (5-t)

edutainment—example of a portmanteau, beginning with letter e [education, entertainment]—*educational entertainment*

ee—uncommon word with the most frequently used letters for length 2 (236)—shortest uncommon word that starts and ends with letter e (2)—see "beens"—*Scottish for eye*

een—see "beens"—*Scottish for evening*

eens—see "beens"

eensie-weensie—longest hyphenated head 'n' tail (13-t)—longest hyphenated head 'n' tail centered on letter w (13)—*very small*

e'er—see "aer"—*ever*

eerie—common word with the most frequently used letters for length 5 (486-t)—highest ratio vowels to consonants for a common word (4-t)—longest common word containing one consonant (5-t)

ees—see "beens"—*letter e's*

ef—shortest uncommon word with last letter next in alphabet after first for letter e (2)—*letter f*

efe—longest uncommon head 'n' tail centered on letter f (3-t)—*native of central Africa*

effaced—longest common word spelled with hexadecimal letters (7-t)—longest common word spelled with piano notes (7-t)

effeminacy—example of a word that sounds like letters, beginning with letter f sound [FMNSE]

effervescence—longest common three-cadence (5-t)

efficient—example of a word spelled with i before e after c, beginning with letter e

egg—shortest common stingy word (3-t)

eider—example of a word that begins with silent letter e

eighty-eight—longest hyphenated head 'n' tail centered on letter y (11-t)

einsteins—longest uncommon head 'n' tail (9-t)—longest uncommon head 'n' tail centered on letter t (9)—*units of radiation*

either—example of a word spelled with e before i, beginning with letter e

eldest—longest difference pair with common words [eldest → shyly] (6-t)

electroencephalogram—longest common word containing three types of vowels (20)

electroencephalography—common word with the lowest ratio length to number of different letters for length 22 (1.83-t)—most repeated letters for a common word (8)—see "extraterrestrials"

elementarily—example of a word that sounds like letters, beginning with letter l sound [LMNTRLE]—longest common gramogram [LMNTRLE] (12)—*simply*

elf—shortest common word with last letter next in alphabet after first for letter e (3)

elhi—example of an acronym that has become uncapitalized, beginning with letter e [ELementary school + HIgh school]—*grades one through twelve*

elimination—common word containing most consecutive letters in order after letter l (4-t)

ellipse—longest common backswitch [spilled] (7-t)

ellipses—example of a colliding plural [ellipse, ellipsis]

els—longest progressive charitable with common words [els & el & es & ls] (3-t)

emanate—longest common nontrivial one letter head-to-tail shift [emanate → manatee] (7-t)

emcees—longest common word containing all letters restricted to primes (6-t)

eminency—example of a word that sounds like letters, beginning with letter m sound [MNNC]—*importance*

emony—example of an uncommon word formed by borrowing or lending letters to frequent companions, beginning with letter e [anemone → an emony]—*anemone*

emus—longest common word torture [emu & mus & em & mu & us] (4-t)

en—common word with the most frequently used letters for length 2 (186)

en banc—example of a word that ends with silent letter c—*with judicial authority*

enchaicnements—longest uncommon word with consecutive letters adjacent on phone keypad beginning with letter e (14)—*ballet steps*

enchantments—longest common word with consecutive letters adjacent on phone keypad beginning with letter e (12-t)

encourage—longest common word in which changing one letter radically changes the pronunciation [encourage → entourage] (9-t)

enfeeblement—common word containing the most repeats of letter e (5-t)

enjoin—example of a self-antonym, beginning with letter e [direct or impose, prohibit or forbid]

ennui—longest common word containing one type of consonant for consonant n (5-t)

enraged—see "angered"

entailments—see "artefacts"

entente—common word with the most frequently used letters for length 7 (672)—longest common word with Morse code that is entirely dot-dashes (7)

entertainment—common word with the most frequently used letters for length 13 (1071)

entertainments—common word with the most frequently used letters for length 14 (1137)

entêtée—uncommon word with the most frequently used letters for length 7 (722)—*French for infatuated*

entitlements—longest common word with consecutive letters adjacent on phone keypad beginning with letter e (12-t)

entourage—see "encourage"

entreaties—common word with the most frequently used letters for length 10 (882)

entwicklungsroman—uncommon word with the lowest ratio length to number of different letters for length 17 (1.13-t)—longest uncommon word containing each vowel once (17-t)—*autobiographical novel*

entwicklungsromane—uncommon word with the lowest ratio length to number of different letters for length 18 (1.20-t)—*variant of entwicklungsroman*

enumerable—example of common homophonic contranyms [enumerable: countable & innumerable: uncountable]

enunciated—see "denunciate"

enunciation—longest common hydration [denunciation & renunciation] (0.11)

environment—common word with most consecutive alphabetic letters in reverse order consecutively (3-t)

envy—shortest common isolano (4-t)

eosinophilous—example of a word that sounds like letters, beginning with letter e sound [ESNFLS]—longest uncommon gramogram [ESNFLS] (13)—*relating to white blood cells*

epee—shortest common isolano (4-t)

epidemiology—shortest seven-syllable word (12)

epieikeia—longest uncommon word containing two consonants (9-t)—*exception to the law due to hardship*

epizootiological—shortest nine-syllable word (16)

epizootiologically—shortest 10-syllable word (18)

epizootiology—shortest eight-syllable word (13)—*disease of animals*

epopoeia—longest uncommon word containing one type of consonant for consonant p (8-t)—*epic poetry*

equalization—longest common word containing five consonants (12-t)

equiprobable—common word containing most consecutive letters in the alphabet after letter o (4-t)

equivalent evaporations—phrase containing most consecutive letters in the alphabet after letter n (9)—*rates at which water would evaporate at normal boiling temperature and pressure*

er—see "amusers" and "blowers" and "cinerins"—*expression of hesitation*

eradicate—example of uncommon homophonic contranyms [eradicate: pull up by the roots & irradicate: root deeply]

erasers—longest common progressive letter subtraction [erasers → eases → ass → a] (7-t)

ere—longest common palindrome beginning with letter e (3-t)—longest common palindrome centered on letter r (3)—shortest common word that starts and ends with letter e (3-t)—see "aer"

err—see "aer"

ers—see "amusers" and "blowers"—*type of plant used for fodder*

erupt—example of uncommon homophonic contranyms [erupt: burst out & irrupt: burst in]

es—see "as"

escutcheon—example of a word that exists only in an idiom, beginning with letter e [blot on the escutcheon]

esse—longest uncommon palindrome beginning with letter e (4-t)—*essence*

establish—example of an antonym of four different words, beginning with letter e [disprove, abolish, repeal, abrograte]

estates—longest common progressive letter subtraction [estates → stats → tat → a] (7-t)

estimable—example of a false antonym beginning with letter e [inestimable]

etamine—see "ketamines"—*fabric*

etamines—see "ketamines"

ethylenediaminetetraacetate—uncommon word containing the most repeats of letter e (7)— uncommon word containing the most repeats of letter t (5-t)—longest uncommon word that starts and ends with letter e (27)—*chemical used to treat lead poisoning*

etymologizable—uncommon word containing most consecutive letters in order after letter y (4-t)—*able to be traced through history*

eukaryotic—shortest common word containing each vowel (including y) once (10)

eunoia—shortest uncommon word containing each vowel once (6)—*alertness*

euouae—highest vowels minus consonants for an uncommon word (6-t)—longest uncommon word containing all vowels (6-t)—*Gregorian cadence*

euouaes—highest ratio vowels to consonants for an uncommon word (6-t)—longest uncommon word containing one consonant (7-t)—longest vowel string for an uncommon word (6-t)

european—example of a word that sounds like letters, beginning with letter u sound [UROPN]

euxoa—longest uncommon word containing one type of consonant for consonant x (5-t)—*cutworm*

euxoa

eve—longest common head 'n' tail centered on letter v (3)—longest common palindrome beginning with letter e (3-t)— shortest common word that starts and ends with letter e (3-t)

everywhere—common word containing most consecutive letters in order after letter v (2-t)

evil—shortest common isolano (4-t)

evolutionist—see "revolutionists"

evolutionists—longest uncommon hydration [devolutionists & revolutionists] (0.13-t)

evolved—see "devolve"

evovae—longest uncommon word containing one type of consonant for consonant v (6)—*variant of euouae*

ewe—example of a word pronounced differently when capitalized, beginning with letter e [female sheep, African language]—example of a word that is a confusing code for letter e [you]—longest common head 'n' tail centered on letter w (3)—longest common palindrome beginning with letter e (3-t)—longest common palindrome centered on letter w (3)—shortest common word that starts and ends with letter e (3-t)

exchange stabilization fund—phrase containing most consecutive letters in the alphabet after letter z (10)—*monetary reserve used to maintain official exchange rate*

expediency—example of a word that sounds like letters, beginning with letter x sound [XPDNC]

exploitation—longest nontrivial internal palindrome for a common word (7-t)

expressiveness—longest common changeover [repressiveness] (14-t)

expressway—common word containing most consecutive letters in the alphabet after letter w (3-t)

Hangman

What is the best word to play in Hangman?

In Hangman, there are two apparently contradictory strategies for picking a word: choose a word with only rare letters, or choose a word with only common letters. Both strategies have something to argue for them: if you choose only rare letters, your opponent will have to spend time asking for common letters. On the other hand, if you choose common letters, your opponent will have to test for all the words that can contain these letters. Which strategy is better?

When presented with a difficult problem, one approach is to solve a simple version of the problem. In Hangman, you can reduce the number of letters in the word and simplify the game. Suppose we start with the simplest possible game of Hangman: one-letter words.

Contrary to popular belief, there are 26 one-letters words in English. The word consisting of a single letter is the name for that letter. Thus, for example, "z" is the word for the letter z. Some of these words also have other meanings, but each one-letter word has at least this meaning.

The strategy for one-letter Hangman is not complicated. The frequency of letters makes no difference, since each word contains exactly one unique letter. The distribution of letters within a word makes no difference, since each letter occurs in the only available position in each word. The best that your opponent can do is get your word in one guess; the worst is 26 guesses; the average is 13.5 guesses. It makes no difference which one-letter words you pick.

Moving up to two-letter words, the situation is a bit more complex. There are about 330 two-letter words; that is too many to analyze simply, so reduce that number to a more manageable level, say, seven. Consider the best word to pick when playing Hangman with the lexicon: am, an, be, no, on, of, we.

This is the count of words containing a specific letter in a specific position in this list:

letter	missing	first position	second position
a	5	2	0
b	6	1	0
e	5	0	2
f	6	0	1
m	6	0	1
n	4	1	2
o	4	2	1
w	6	1	0

You may know that your opponent always guesses vowels, or has a limited vocabulary, or some other piece of specific knowledge, but for the sake of this analysis assume that your opponent knows this lexicon and will play optimally. This means that your opponent will attempt to get as much information as possible out of each guess. This is done by using the guess to split the lexicon into sets that are as nearly equal in size as possible. Further guesses will be used to subdivide each set, and subdivide again, and so on until there is only one word left in each set.

For example, suppose the first guess is the letter n. This subdivides the lexicon into these sets:

no n	n in the first position	n in the second position
am	no	an
be		on
of		
we		

The first of these sets (no n) requires two more guesses to subdivide down to one word. The second set (n in the first position) requires no more guesses. The third set (n in the second position) requires only one more guess. The maximum total number of guesses required is three.

Consider the case where the first guess is o instead of n; the corresponding sets are:

no o	o in the first position	o in the second position
am	of	no
an	on	
be		
we		

Again, the maximum total number of guesses required is three.

What happens if the first guess is the letter b? The sets are:

no b	b in the first position	b in the second position
am	be	
an		
no		
on		
we		

B is not a good choice for the first guess, because it requires three more guesses to break the no-b set down into single words, and thus it requires four guesses overall.

Now we have a way of deciding which letters are good first guesses, and which letters are not. Good guess letters are letters that divide the lexicon up into more sets of more equal sizes. Such divisions give our opponent more information. Can we reduce this idea to a formula? We can.

If a letter divides a set into two exactly equal subsets, we'll say this letter gives us one bit of information. If a letter divides a set into four equal subsets, that's the same as dividing it into two twice, so that should equal two bits of information. If a letter divides a set into eight equal subsets, that should be three bits, and so on. Is there a formula that, given the sizes of these subsets, computes the number of bits of information? Fortunately, there is a well-known formula from information theory that does just this. We won't go into the details of the formula here, but using it we get the following information associated with each letter:

letter	subsets sizes	information
a	5, 2, 0	.86
b	6, 1, 0	.59
e	5, 0, 2	.86
f	6, 0, 1	.59
m	6, 0, 1	.59
n	4, 1, 2	1.38
o	4, 2, 1	1.38
w	6, 1, 0	.59

From this table, you can deduce which letter your opponent will pick for the first guess. Once this letter is picked, your opponent will apply the same formula again to deduce the next best letter to pick, given the results of the first letter. For example, if the first guess is n and if your word contains no n, your opponent will have to decide between "am," "be," "of," and "we." For these words the information content of each letter is:

letter	subsets sizes	information
a	3, 1, 0	.81
b	3, 1, 0	.81
e	2, 0, 2	1.00
f	3, 0, 1	.81
m	3, 0, 1	.81
o	3, 1, 0	.81
w	3, 1, 0	.81

So e has the highest information content, and your opponent will pick it. Your opponent will continue in this way, picking the most informative letters, until your word is uncovered.

Your best strategy is to pick words that resist this procedure until the bitter end. Which word out of the seven is the best to pick? The answer is: any word in the no-n, no-o set, namely, "am," "be," or "we." We see now why the two strategies mentioned at the start of the article are neither quite right. If you pick only rare letters, your opponent will quickly discover this. If you pick only common letters, your opponent will get them all in the first few guesses. The trick is to mix common letters with rare letters. Also, although we cannot see this from the simple examples we have looked at, you want to pick words that have common letters in common patterns, so that the distribution of common letters does not give away too much.

Moving now from our toy lexicon to the real English lexicon, if we use this algorithm to deduce the best words to pick in Hangman for each word length, we get these results:

2: ys, zs
3: wat, wes, xat, yes
4: yill, zill
5: yills, zills
6: coxing, cozing, wagged, zagged
7: tilling, willing
8: bummings, buzzings
9: quakering, quavering

One caveat: If your opponent knows that you are using this procedure to pick words, it is possible that in some cases it is no longer the best procedure and requires some modification. This becomes a problem in game theory. Specifically, if your opponent has read this article, don't use these words!

ex-servicewoman—hyphenated word containing most consecutive letters in the alphabet after letter v (3-t)—*former servicewoman*

extemporaneously—common word with the lowest ratio length to number of different letters for length 16 (1.23-t)

exterminations—see "determinations"

extractors—longest common double progressive beheadment [extractors → tractors → actors → tors → rs] (10-t)

extracurricular—common word containing the most repeats of letter r (4-t)

extraordinaire—longest common word that starts and ends with letter e (14)

extraterrestrial—common word containing the most repeats of letter r (4-t)

extraterrestrials—longest well-mixed common words with same letter sum [electroencephalography] (22)

extraterritorial—common word containing the most repeats of letter r (4-t)

extraterritoriality—common word containing the most repeats of letter r (4-t)

eyas—example of an uncommon word formed by borrowing or lending letters to frequent companions, beginning with letter e [a neyas → an eyas]—*baby hawks*

eye—longest common head 'n' tail centered on letter y (3)—longest common palindrome beginning with letter e (3-t)—shortest common word that starts and ends with letter e (3-t)

eyre—see "aer"—*court with a traveling judge*

F

f—longest common head 'n' tail centered on letter f (1)—longest common palindrome beginning with letter f (1)

fabaceae—uncommon word with lowest letter sum for length 8 (24)—longest uncommon word spelled with hexadecimal letters (8)—*beans and peas*

fable—see "birds"

fabricated—common word containing most consecutive letters in the alphabet after letter a (6-t)—common word containing most consecutive letters in the alphabet after letter b (5-t)

face-bedded—hyphenated word with lowest letter sum for length 10 (39)—longest hyphenated word spelled with hexadecimal letters (10)—longest hyphenated word spelled with piano notes (10)—*with natural face showing*

facetious—longest and shortest common word containing each vowel once in order (9)

facetiously—longest and shortest common word containing each vowel (including y) once in order (11)

facilities contracts—see "cutter classification"—*agreements to maintain a building or equipment*

fads—longest common word torture [ads & fad & ad & ds & fa] (4-t)

fag—shortest common word with last letter next in alphabet after first for letter f (3-t)

falaj—example of switching first two letters to make plural with an uncommon word [falaj → aflaj]—*Arabian waterwork*

farsighted—common word containing most consecutive letters in the alphabet after letter d (6-t)

fast—example of a self-antonym, beginning with letter f [rapid, unmoving]

fatty—longest sum pair with common words [fatty → guns] (5-t)

fauteuil—example of a word that ends with silent letter l—*upholstered armchair*

fauxbourg—example of a word that contains silent letter x—*suburb*

fauteuil

feedback—common word containing most consecutive letters in the alphabet after letter a (6-t)—common word containing most consecutive letters in the alphabet after letter b (5-t)

feedingstuff—longest uncommon word that starts and ends with letter f (12)—*animal food*

feisty—example of a word spelled with e before i, beginning with letter f

feoffee—longest uncommon word containing one type of consonant for consonant f (7)—*trustee of public land*

ferriprotoporphyrin—uncommon word containing the most repeats of letter r (5-t)—*chemical in hemoglobin*

ferroprotoporphyrin—uncommon word containing the most repeats of letter r (5-t)—*variant of ferriprotoporphyrin*

festschrift—longest consonant string for an uncommon word (6-t)—*collection of honorary essays*

few—shortest common stingy word (3-t)

fez—shortest common stingy word (3-t)

FF—longest palindrome beginning with letter f (2)—shortest phrase that starts and ends with letter f (2)—*first family*

fiancé—example of common homophonic contranyms [fiancé: male betrothed & fiancée: female betrothed]

fiancée—see "fiancé"

fido—example of an acronym that has become uncapitalized, beginning with letter f [Freaks + Irregulars + Defects + Oddities]—*coin with minting error*

fief—longest common word containing one type of consonant for consonant f (4-t)—shortest common word that starts and ends with letter f (4)

fife—longest common word containing one type of consonant for consonant f (4-t)

fifty-fifty—longest hyphenated tautonym beginning with letter f (10)—*even*

fig—shortest common word with last letter next in alphabet after first for letter f (3-t)

fighter—common word containing most consecutive letters in the alphabet after letter e (5-t)

figurehead—common word containing most consecutive letters in the alphabet after letter d (6-t)

fiji—highest ratio dotted to undotted letters for an uncommon word (0.75-t)—*from an island in the South Pacific*

filid—example of a plural that ends with letter d—*Irish poets*

filling knittings—longest phrase containing one type of vowel for vowel i (16-t)—*knitting with crosswise loops*

financier—example of a word spelled with i before e after c, beginning with letter f

fireplaces—longest common double progressive beheadment [fireplaces → replaces → places → aces → es] (10-t)

fivepence—example of a word that contains silent letter v—*five-cent piece*

flagship—common word containing most consecutive letters in order after letter f (4)

flagsticks—longest uncommon word with consecutive letters adjacent on phone keypad beginning with letter f (10)—*flag sticks*

flamenco—common word containing most consecutive letters in order after letter l (4-t)—longest common word with consecutive letters adjacent on phone keypad beginning with letter f (8-t)

flameproof—longest common word that starts and ends with letter f (10)

flameproofed—longest two-syllable word beginning with letter f (12)

flammable—example of a false antonym beginning with letter f [inflammable]

flashes—longest common progressive beheadment [flashes → lashes → ashes → shes → hes → es → s] (7-t)

flashlights—longest common word containing two vowels (11-t)

flax—see "qwerty"

flibbertigibbet—uncommon word containing the most repeats of letter b (4-t)—*fool*

flinched—longest one-syllable word beginning with letter f (8)—*recoiled*

floccinaucinihilipilification—example of a sesquipedalian word [see "Longest Word" article, page 106]—longest uncommon word without E (29)—uncommon word containing the most repeats of letter i (9)—uncommon word with the most repeats of any one letter [i] (9-t)—see "strongylocentrotus"—*worthless*

floodlight projector—phrase containing most consecutive letters in the alphabet after letter c (8)—phrase containing most consecutive letters in the alphabet after letter d (7)—*searchlight*

florist's chrysanthemums—longest phrase containing each vowel (including y) once (22)—*a Chinese flower*

flourish—longest common word with consecutive letters adjacent on phone keypad beginning with letter f (8-t)

fluffy-ruffle—hyphenated word containing the most repeats of letter f (5)—*with a fluffy ruffled margin*

flunk—example of a portmanteau, beginning with letter f [flinch, funk]

flyby—longest common word where each letter is four symbols in Morse code (5)

foci—shortest stingy and hostile common word (4-t)

fog—shortest common word with last letter next in alphabet after first for letter f (3-t)

forebay—longest uncommon multiplicative offset shift pair [pavings] [factor of 7] (7-t)—*where water runs out of a pond*

forecastle—example of a word that contains silent letter r—*superstructure in the bow of a merchant ship where the crew is housed*

foreshadowing—common word containing most consecutive letters in the alphabet after letter d (6-t)

forest—example of a word pronounced differently when capitalized, beginning with letter f [area with trees, town in Belgium]—longest length four linkade with common words [fore & ores & rest] (6-t)

foresting—see "reafforesting"—*establishing a forest*

forthrightness—longest common word containing three vowels (14)

fouquieriaceae—highest vowels minus consonants for an uncommon word (6-t)—longest uncommon word containing four consonants (14)—*spiny shrubs or trees of southwestern United States*

fourthly—longest common word with consecutive letters adjacent on phone keypad beginning with letter f (8-t)

foyer—example of a word that ends with silent letter r

fracas—longest common changing offset shift pair [oblong] [shift of 9] (6)

fractionation—longest nontrivial internal head 'n' tail for a common word (9-t)

fracture—longest Morse code reversal pair with common words [intertwined] (11-t)

frays—example of a word that is a confusing code for letter f [phrase]

fredericksburg—uncommon word containing most consecutive letters in the alphabet after letter b (6-t)—*an era of geologic time*

free—example of an antonym of two different words, beginning with letter f [costly, enslaved]

freight—common word containing most consecutive letters in the alphabet after letter e (5-t)

freshman compositions—longest roller-coaster for a phrase (20)

frighten—common word containing most consecutive letters in the alphabet after letter e (5-t)

frightened—common word containing most consecutive letters in the alphabet after letter d (6-t)

fritz—example of a word that exists only in an idiom, beginning with letter f [on the fritz]

froufrou—longest uncommon tautonym beginning with letter f (8)—*frivolous*

frowzy—see "jumbling"—*unkempt*

fuddy-duddy—hyphenated word with the most infrequently used letters for length 10 (292)—*stuffed shirt*

funiculars—longest uncommon Morse code reversal pair, measured in number of dots and dashes [secularized] (30)—*cable railways*

fusion—longest fixed offset shift pair with common words [layout] [shift of 6] (6-t)

fuzzy—common word with the most infrequently used letters for length 5 (73)

fuzzy-wuzzy—hyphenated word with the most infrequently used letters for length 10 (145)—*from Sudan*

G

gabbed—see "debug"

gaelicists—longest uncommon word with consecutive letters adjacent on phone keypad beginning with letter g (10)—*experts in Celtic Highlanders of Scotland*

gag—longest common head 'n' tail centered on letter a (3-t)—longest common palindrome beginning with letter g (3-t)—shortest common word that starts and ends with letter g (3-t)

gaga—longest common tautonym beginning with letter g (4)

gagging—common word containing the most repeats of letter g (4-t)

gairtens—see "angriest"—*garters*

galanases—longest length four linkade with an uncommon word [gala & alan & lana & anas & nase & ases] (9-t)—*Medieval fines for murder*

galengale—longest uncommon head 'n' tail (9-t)—longest uncommon head 'n' tail centered on letter n (9-t)—*East Indian ginger*

gamecocks—longest common word with consecutive letters adjacent on phone keypad beginning with letter g (9)

game of chance—longest phrase with consecutive letters adjacent on phone keypad beginning with letter g (12)—*gambling game*

ganggang—longest uncommon tautonym beginning with letter g (8-t)—*Australian cockatoo*

ganggang

ganister—see "angriest"—*quartzite*

gantries—see "angriest"—*steel structures used to bridge over something*

garnish—example of a self-antonym, beginning with letter g [add to food, subtract from wages]

gash—shortest common word with last letter next in alphabet after first for letter g (4-t)

gastrointestinal—see "transliterations"

gathering—common word containing most consecutive letters in order after letter g (3-t)

gathering-ground—longest hyphenated word containing each vowel once in order (15)—*area that feeds a river*

gauge—longest common word containing one type of consonant for consonant g (5-t)

gazelle-faced wallaby—hyphenated phrase containing most consecutive letters in the alphabet after letter y (9)—*New Guinea kangaroo*

gee-gee—longest hyphenated word containing one type of consonant for consonant g (6-t)—*child's word for horse*

geiger—example of a word spelled with e before i, beginning with letter g—*charged particle*

generalizations—longest common roller-coaster (15-t)

genius—example of a false antonym beginning with letter g [ingenious]

gentleman's gentleman—longest head 'n' tail phrase centered on letter s (19)—longest head 'n' tail phrase (19)—*valet*

geographic—common word containing most consecutive letters in order after letter g (3-t)

gerrymander—example of a portmanteau, beginning with letter g [Gerry, salamander]

gerrymandering—longest common word that starts and ends with letter g (14)

ghost—example of a word that contains silent letter h

gig—longest common palindrome beginning with letter g (3-t)—longest common palindrome centered on letter i (3-t)—shortest common word that starts and ends with letter g (3-t)

gigging—common word containing the most repeats of letter g (4-t)

giggling—common word containing the most repeats of letter g (4-t)

gillotti—example of a word that sounds like letters, beginning with letter g sound [GLOT]

gird—example of a word that exists only in an idiom, beginning with letter g [gird one's loins]

girding—closest to four million letter product for a common word (4000752-t)

glacier—example of a word spelled with i before e after c, beginning with letter g

glamour—example of a common multisyllabic American word ending "our" but pronounced like "or"

glycosphingolipids—longest uncommon word without ETA (18-t)—*types of fat*

gnaw—example of a word that begins with silent letter g

gnu—example of a word that is a confusing code for letter g [new]

go—example of an antonym of two different words, beginning with letter g [stop, come]

goatsbeard—longest uncommon iskot pair measured in number of dots and dashes [infamatory] (25-t)—*European weed*

go from strength to strength—highest consonants minus vowels for a phrase (14)—*experience one success after another*

goggling—common word containing the most repeats of letter g (4-t)

goldfinches—common word containing most consecutive letters in the alphabet after letter c (7-t)—common word that contains the most consecutive letters in alphabet (7-t)

gong—longest common progressive difference pair [gong → rag → qt → w] (4-t)

goody-goody—longest hyphenated tautonym beginning with letter g (10)—*person who behaves in an overly good manner*

goog—longest uncommon palindrome beginning with letter g (4)—*egg*

goo-goo—longest hyphenated word containing one type of consonant for consonant g (6-t)—*amorous*

gosh—shortest common word with last letter next in alphabet after first for letter g (4-t)

gouge—longest common word containing one type of consonant for consonant g (5-t)

goutte à goutte—longest head 'n' tail phrase centered on letter a (13-t)—*drop by drop*

governmentalising—longest uncommon word that starts and ends with letter g (17-t)—*variant of governmentalizing*

governmentalizing—longest uncommon word that starts and ends with letter g (17-t)—*controlling by a government*

gox—example of an acronym that has become uncapitalized, beginning with letter g [Gaseous OXygen]

goyim—example of a plural that ends with letter m—*non-Jews*

grandstands—longest common word containing one type of vowel for vowel a (11-t)—longest nontrivial internal head 'n' tail for a common word (9-t)

granites—see "angriest"—*igneous rocks*

granulocytopenias—see "breakdown voltages"—*diseases resulting in loss of white blood cells*

graphic—common word containing most consecutive letters in order after letter g (3-t)

graphical—common word containing most consecutive letters in order after letter g (3-t)

grass—longest common onalosi [brass & glass & gross & grabs & grasp] (5-t)

gratifications—longest terminal elision with common words [gratifications → ratification] (14-t)

grave-wax—hyphenated word containing most consecutive letters in order after letter v (3)—hyphenated word containing most consecutive letters in the alphabet after letter v (3-t)—*white substance produced in dead bodies*

great crested grebes—longest phrase with typewriter letters from left hand (18)—*European birds*

greegree—longest uncommon tautonym beginning with letter g (8-t)—*African amulet*

green—longest rot-13 pair with common words [terra] (5-t)

griffin—longest common nontrivial one letter head-to-tail shift [griffin → riffing] (7-t)

groszy—example of a plural that ends with letter y—*monetary unit of Poland*

Grothendieck K-theory—longest hyphenated homophonic phrase with no removable prefix or suffix [Grothendieck K-theory → growth-and-decay theory]—*mathematical theory*

grouched—longest one-syllable word beginning with letter g (8)—*complained*

groundsheets—longest two-syllable word beginning with letter g (12)—*waterproofed ground covers*

growth-and-decay theory—see "Grothendieck K-theory"

gry—example of an uncommon word ending -gry [see "Words Ending in -Gry" article, page 96]—*trifle*

guglia—example of an uncommon word formed by borrowing or lending letters to frequent companions, beginning with letter g [l'aguglia → la guglia]—*obelisk*

gunpowdery—see "blacksmith"—*explosive*

guns—see "fatty"

gush—shortest common word with last letter next in alphabet after first for letter g (4-t)

guy—example of a word pronounced differently when capitalized, beginning with letter g [male, Flemish ruler]

gyp—longest common word spelled with descending letters (3)

gyppy—longest uncommon word spelled with descending letters (5)—*diarrhea*

h—see "cymba" and "hexachlorocyclohexane"

haberdine—example of an uncommon word formed by borrowing or lending letters to frequent companions, beginning with letter h [labordean → l'abordean]—*salted dried cod*

habited—example of a false antonym beginning with letter h [inhabited]—*resided*

hacienda—example of a word spelled with i before e after c, beginning with letter h

hagigah—longest uncommon palindrome beginning with letter h (7-t)—longest uncommon palindrome centered on letter i (7-t)—*Jewish ritual sacrifices*

hah—longest common head 'n' tail centered on letter a (3-t)—longest common palindrome beginning with letter h (3-t)—longest common word containing one type of consonant for consonant h (3-t)—shortest common word that starts and ends with letter h (3-t)

hail columbia—longest phrase with consecutive letters adjacent on phone keypad beginning with letter h (12-t)—*trouble*

hains—see "hairns"—*puts aside*

hairn—see "hairns"—*Scottish for brain*

hairns—longest uncommon charitable [airns & hirns & harns & hains & hairs & hairn] (6-t)

hairsbreadths—longest two-syllable word beginning with letter h (13)—*widths of a hair*

haji—see "hajji"—*a pilgrim to Mecca*

hajji—example of homophones differing by letter j [haji]—*variant of haji*

halalah—longest uncommon palindrome beginning with letter h (7-t)—*monetary unit of Saudi Arabia*

haleru—example of a plural that ends with letter u—*monetary unit of Czechoslovakia*

half-Christian—longest hyphenated phrase with consecutive letters adjacent on phone keypad beginning with letter h (13)

Misspelled Words

The World Wide Web provides a new way of measuring how difficult it is to spell a word. The Web consists of millions of documents containing billions of words. Each Web page is usually prepared with some care, since it is expected that it will be read by strangers. It is the modern equivalent of the edited document, or at least as close as we can come to it. These Web pages represent the combined written output of hundreds of thousands of fairly well-educated people. Presumably, a word that is hard to spell will be misspelled frequently on the Web.

There are programs called "spiders" that walk the Web, visiting every page, extracting and indexing every word. The index produced by the spider is used for full-text searching of the Web. As a by-product of this process, these spiders compute word counts for every word on every page on the Web. This database is then freely accessible to everyone over the Web itself. It consists of word counts for several billion word instances.

One definition of the hardest word to spell is the word that is misspelled most often on the Web. Below we exhibit a table that consists of the word counts for several words that are well-known to be difficult to spell, provided that they occur at least 100 times on the Web. We require that they occur at least 100 times to avoid statistical anomalies. We also require that the documents they occur in be written in English.

The first column of the list is the ratio of the count of the word in the second column (the correct spelling) divided into the sum of the counts of the words in the subsequent columns (various incorrect spellings). It is, in short, the misspelling ratio. The list is sorted by increasing value of this ratio.

At the top of the list we find extremely obscure words that are never misspelled. This does not mean they are easy to spell; rather it means that anyone who knows the word either already knows how to spell it, or looks it up in the dictionary every time. We cannot tell which is the case, so we cannot accurately award the title of "hardest word to spell" to these words. To avoid this ambiguity we refine the definition of "hardest word to spell" to be "word most frequently misspelled."

Proceeding down the list, we come to the .500 ratio. Below this point are words that are misspelled half as often as they are correctly spelled. We find, however, that in almost every case, the spellings in column three are listed in many dictionaries as variant spellings. These cannot be considered as true misspellings.

However, one word stands out: "desiccate." This is the only word with a misspelling ratio greater than 1.000, which means that it is misspelled more often than it is correctly spelled. Surprisingly, no dictionary lists either of its common misspellings as a variant. These two facts combine to justify the awarding of the title "hardest word to spell" to the word "desiccate."

Ratio	Correct Spelling	Incorrect (or Variant) Spelling(s)
0.000	eisteddfodau (114)	–
0.000	kwashiorkor (963)	–
0.001	irritable (22889)	irritible (20), iritable (20)
0.005	development (1626032)	developement (8380)
0.006	rijsttafel (296)	risttafel (1), ristafel (1)
0.007	dissipate (22873)	disipate (160), disippate (3)
0.010	Orszaggyules (949)	Orszagyules (8), Orzaggyules (2)
0.010	similar (3000671)	similiar (31176)
0.011	Houyhnhnm (259)	Houhnhnm (3)
0.011	a lot (2549399)	alot (30399)
0.011	tyranny (55802)	tyrrany (626)
0.011	yield (301799)	yeild (3466)
0.017	Phacochoerus (112)	Phacocoerus (1)

0.017	exceed (26813)	excede (460)
0.017	privilege (234299)	privelege (3040), priviledge (1143)
0.017	vichyssoise (857)	vichysoise (11), vishyssoise (4)
0.018	recommend (88674)	reccomend (1616)
0.018	repetition (109451)	repitition (2005)
0.020	pursue (33067)	persue (675)
0.021	subpoena (29864)	subpena (657)
0.023	seize (108891)	sieze (2593)
0.025	despair (138430)	dispair (3563)
0.028	dyspnoea (769)	dyspnoia (17), dispnoea (5)
0.029	independent (324037)	independant (9484)
0.032	occasion (36851)	ocassion (1186)
0.037	consensus (24106)	concensus (914)
0.038	receive (358934)	recieve (13860)
0.041	broccoli (52005)	brocolli (1182), broccolli (970)
0.050	eschscholtzia (236)	escholtzia (12)
0.053	desperate (13189)	desparate (702)
0.054	momento (238363)	memento (13053)
0.055	inadvertent (21369)	inadvertant (1189)
0.060	all right (229496)	alright (13879)
0.063	separate (163658)	seperate (10318)
0.071	battalion (11672)	batallion (832)
0.080	Nietzschean (1600)	Nietzchean (118), Nietschean (10)
0.083	embarrassment (84998)	embarassment (7088)
0.084	existence (49575)	existance (4213)
0.084	gauge (219212)	guage (18604)
0.085	anoint (6839)	annoint (586)
0.091	bouillabaisse (3611)	bouillabaise (323), bouilabaisse (7)
0.091	drunkenness (10445)	drunkeness (954)
0.098	liaison (35270)	liason (3470)
0.104	harass (20802)	harrass (2184)
0.116	embarrass (14239)	embarass (1652)
0.124	cemetery (38521)	cemetary (4781)
0.125	indispensable (8109)	indispensible (1014)
0.127	inoculate (3440)	innoculate (437)
0.132	weird (45715)	wierd (6055)
0.137	occurrence (155168)	occurence (21358)
0.142	insistent (25102)	insistant (3567)
0.148	definitely (37261)	definately (5534)
0.149	sacrilegious (3381)	sacreligious (505)
0.151	irresistible (50955)	irresistable (7744)
0.154	ecstasy (78335)	ecstacy (12105)
0.155	accidentally (180112)	accidently (28000)
0.190	accommodate (409589)	accomodate (77902), acomodate (100)
0.261	coolly (10893)	cooly (2849)
0.279	carillonneur (261)	carilloneur (68), carrillonneur (5)
0.340	judgment (35243)	judgement (11996)
0.363	peddler (10564)	pedlar (2737), pedler (1102)
0.499	millennium (198547)	millenium (97015), milenium (2178)
0.527	praemunire (91)	premunire (48)

0.562	liquify (988)	liquefy (556)
0.696	dumbbell (4419)	dumbell (3076)
0.705	supersede (1378)	supercede (972)
0.894	minuscule (502)	miniscule (449)
1.090	desiccate (528)	dessicate (361), desicate (215)

half islands—longest Morse code reversal pair for a phrase, measured in number of dots and dashes [superhelices] (33)—*peninsulas*

half-joking—hyphenated word containing most consecutive letters in the alphabet after letter f (7)

halfpenny—example of a word that contains silent letter f—*English coin*

halftimes—see "specials"

halve—example of homophones differing by letter l [have]

hamamelidaceae—uncommon word with lowest letter sum for length 14 (81)—longest uncommon word with letters from first half of alphabet (14)—*witch hazel*

hamamelidaceae

han—see "thanatopsides"—*people of Central Asia*

handcraftsmanships—highest consonants minus vowels for an uncommon word (10-t)

hand gallops—longest phrase isomorse pair, measured in number of dots and dashes [signature loans] (34)—longest well-mixed isomorse pair for a phrase [signature loans] (14-t)—*moderate gallops*

handle blanks—longest phrase with consecutive letters adjacent on phone keypad beginning with letter h (12-t)—*lumber for making handles*

handsome—example of a word that contains silent letter d

handstands—longest nontrivial internal head 'n' tail for a common word (9-t)

happed—longest full vowel (including y) substitution with an uncommon word [happed & hepped & hipped & hopped & hupped & hypped] (6)

har—see "cantharidates"—*thick cold sea fog*

hard—example of an antonym of two different words, beginning with letter h [soft, easy]

harlequin opal—longest shiftgram pair for a phrase [presumptively] [shift of 4] (13-t)—*reddish opal*

harns—see "hairns"—*Scottish for brains*

haroset—see "charoseth"—*Jewish symbolic food*

hashish—common word containing the most repeats of letter h (3-t)

haunched—longest one-syllable word beginning with letter h (8)—*with hips or hindquarters*

have—see "halve"

haw—example of a word that exists only in an idiom, beginning with letter h [hem and haw]

hazy—shortest common word that cannot have a letter added and transposed to form another word (4-t)

heading cabbage—phrase with lowest letter sum for length 14 (69)—*type of cabbage*

heading cabbages—phrase with lowest letter sum for length 15 (88)

hee-hee—longest hyphenated word containing one type of consonant for consonant h (6-t)—*giggle*

hegari—example of a word that ends with silent letter i—*Sudanese sorghums*

heiau—longest uncommon word containing one type of consonant for consonant h (5)—*Hawaiian temple*

heiau

height—example of a word spelled with e before i, beginning with letter h

heir—example of a word that is a confusing code for letter h [air]—see "aer"

hela—example of an acronym that has become uncapitalized, beginning with letter h [HEnrietta LAcks]—*cancerous cell in a particular strain*

hephthalites—see "highbinders"—*White Huns*

hepped—see "happed"—*enthusiastic*

herb—example of a word pronounced differently when capitalized, beginning with letter h [plant, short for Herbert]

hertz—example of a plural that ends with letter z

heterogeneratae—uncommon word with the most frequently used letters for length 15 (1267)—*brown algae*

heteronereises—uncommon word with the most frequently used letters for length 14 (1200)—*free-swimming worms*

heterotransplantation—longest uncommon reverse snowball [hetero & trans & plan & tat & io & n] (21-t)—*tissue graft from a different species*

hexachlorocyclohexane—longest uncommon snowball [h & ex & ach & loro & cyclo & hexane] (21)—*chemical*

hexahydroxycyclohexane—uncommon word containing the most repeats of letter x (3)—*chemical*

hi—shortest common word with last letter next in alphabet after first for letter h (2)

hiccough—example of an uncommon word with the most variably pronounced suffix [see "Pronunciation Variants" article, page 135]—*hiccup*

hiders—common word with most consecutive runs of consecutive alphabetic letters (3-t)

highbinders—longest uncommon isomorse pair, measured in number of dots and dashes [hephthalites] (31-t)—*corrupt politicians*

highlight—common word containing the most repeats of letter h (3-t)—longest common word spelled with tall lowercase letters (9-t)

highlighting—longest common word containing one type of vowel for vowel i (12-t)

high-muck-a-mucks—hyphenated word with the most infrequently used letters for length 14 (540)—*important people*

high-muckety-muck—hyphenated word with the most infrequently used letters for length 15 (623)—*important person*

high-mucky-muck—hyphenated word with the most infrequently used letters for length 13 (414)—*variant of high-muckety-muck*

highty-tighty—longest hyphenated word spelled with tall lowercase letters (12)—*frivolous*

hijack—common word containing most consecutive letters in order after letter h (4)—common word containing most consecutive letters in order after letter i (3-t)—common word containing most consecutive letters in the alphabet after letter h (4-t)

hijacking—common word containing most consecutive letters in the alphabet after letter g (5-t)

hillbilly—longest common word spelled with tall lowercase letters (9-t)

hipped—see "happed"—*having hips*

hirns—see "hairns"—*corners*

hirschsprung's disease—longest consonant string for a phrase (7)—*congenital dilation of the colon*

hitchhike—common word containing the most repeats of letter h (3-t)

hitter—longest common fixed offset shift pair that are reversals [napped] [shift of 22] (6-t)

hm—see "dowts"—*sound made when thinking*

hodgepodge—longest nontrivial internal head 'n' tail for a common word (9-t)

hoe—longest common word containing one type of consonant for consonant h (3-t)

hokum—example of a portmanteau, beginning with letter h [hocus-pocus, bunkum]

hold with the hare and run with the hounds—phrase containing the most repeats of letter h (7-t)—*have it both ways*

homophony—longest common word with typewriter letters from right hand (9-t)

homotaxia—longest uncommon word spelled with vertical symmetry letters (9-t)—*similarity in arrangement*

honest—longest length four linkade with common words [hone & ones & nest] (6-t)

honorificabilitudinitatibus—example of a sesquipedalian word [see "Longest Word" article, page 106]—*honorableness*

honorificabilitudinity—longest alternating vowels and consonants for an uncommon word (including y) (22)—*variant of honorificabilitudinitatibus*

hoochie-coochie—longest hyphenated word spelled with horizontal symmetry letters (14)—*sensuous dance style*

hoo-hah—longest hyphenated word containing one type of consonant for consonant h (6-t)—*laugh or fuss*

hoo-oo—longest hyphenated word spelled with full symmetry letters (5)—*interjection expressing strong emotion*

hopped—see "happed"

horseradish—longest common word that starts and ends with letter h (11)

hotbeds—longest common isotel pair with no letters in common [invader] (7-t)

hotshot—longest common head 'n' tail centered on letter s (7)—longest common head 'n' tail (7)

hotshots—longest common tautonym beginning with letter h (8)—longest tautonym for a common word (8)

hour—example of homophones differing by letter h [our]—example of a word that begins with silent letter h

housey-housey—longest hyphenated tautonym beginning with letter h (12-t)—*gambling game*

housie-housie—longest hyphenated tautonym beginning with letter h (12-t)—*variant of housey-housey*

hovel—longest digital reversal pair with common words [bobber] (6-t)

hovels—longest common equidistant word (6-t)

hubbub—longest common word containing all letters restricted to Fibonacci sequence (6-t)

hue—longest common word containing one type of consonant for consonant h (3-t)

huggermuggering—uncommon word containing the most repeats of letter g (5)—*in confused secrecy*

huh—longest common palindrome beginning with letter h (3-t)—longest common palindrome centered on letter u (3-t)—longest common word containing one type of consonant for consonant h (3-t)—shortest common word that starts and ends with letter h (3-t)

humanlike—longest common word with consecutive letters adjacent on phone keypad beginning with letter h (9)

humuhumunukunukuapuaa—uncommon word containing the most repeats of letter u (9)—uncommon word with the most repeats of any one letter [i] (9-t)—shortest 12-syllable word (21)—longest uncommon two-cadence (8)—*Hawaiian fish*

humuhumunukunukuapuaas—longest uncommon word containing two types of vowels (22-t)

hungry—example of a common word ending -gry [see "Words Ending in -Gry" article, page 96]

hupped—see "happed"—*sat down*

hustlements—longest uncommon word with consecutive letters adjacent on phone keypad beginning with letter h (11)—*household goods*

hydrochlorofluorocarbon—uncommon word containing the most repeats of letter o (6-t)—longest uncommon word without ET (23)—*refrigerant*

hydrolyzable—uncommon word containing most consecutive letters in order after letter y (4-t)—*capable of having hydrogen added chemically*

hydromagnetic waves—phrase with the lowest ratio length to number of different letters for length 18 (1.12)—*waves in a plasma*

hydrometallurgists—longest uncommon word containing each vowel (including y) once (18)—*experts in treating ores with water*

hydrosulphurous—longest uncommon word without ETAIN (15-t)—*from a type of acid*

hydroxydeoxycorticosterones—see "hydroxydesoxycorticosterones"

hydroxydesoxycorticosterones—longest uncommon word that can nontrivially delete letter from any position to form another word [hydroxydesoxycorticosterones → hydroxydeoxycorticosterones] (28)

hygroexpansivity—longest uncommon well-mixed isomorph [hypermasculinity] (16-t)—*tendency to expand due to moisture*

hygrothermograph—longest uncommon word that starts and ends with letter h (16)—*instrument recording both humidity and temperature*

hypermasculinity—see "hygroexpansivity"—*extreme masculinity*

hyperpolysyllabically—uncommon word containing the most repeats of letter y (4-t)—*using extremely long words*

hypolimnion—longest uncommon word with typewriter letters from right hand (11-t)—*deep lake water*

hypophosphorous—longest uncommon word without ETAIN (15-t)—*from a type of acid*

hypothalamicohypophyseals—longest uncommon word spelled with chemical symbols (25)

hypped—see "happed"—*promoted*

hypsistenocephalism—longest uncommon well-mixed transdeletion [hypsistenocephalism → panmyelophthisises] (19)—*pointed headism*

hysterical—example of a self-antonym, beginning with letter h [terrified, funny]

hystero-salpingo-oophorectomies—longest well-mixed hyphenated words with same letter sum [supercalifragilisticexpialidocious] (34)—*removals of the female reproductive organs*

I

i—longest common palindrome beginning with letter i (1)—longest common word containing all vowels (1-t)

iambic—longest common word with consecutive letters adjacent on phone keypad beginning with letter i (6-t)

Iberian—example of a word that sounds like letters, beginning with letter i sound [IBREN]—*from the Spanish peninsula*

ibuprofen—example of an acronym that has become uncapitalized, beginning with letter i [Iso-BUtyl PROpionic PHENyl]—*pain reliever*

icebox—longest common word with consecutive letters adjacent on phone keypad beginning with letter i (6-t)

iceman—longest common word with consecutive letters adjacent on phone keypad beginning with letter i (6-t)

ichthyocephali—longest uncommon word that starts and ends with letter i (14-t)—*type of fish*

icicle—longest common word with consecutive letters adjacent on phone keypad beginning with letter i (6-t)

ide—shortest common word in which adding one letter adds two syllables [ide → idea] (3-t)—see "aides" and "amides" and "thanatopsides"—*type of fish*

idea—see "ide"

identical—longest Morse code reversal pair with common words [internecine] (11-t)

identifying—common word containing most consecutive letters in order after letter d (4-t)

idly—shortest stingy and hostile common word (4-t)

ie—see "aides"—*Hawaiian screw pine*

ieie—shortest four-syllable word (4)—*Pacific Islands screw pine*

ies—see "aides"

iga—see "sande"—*chemicals found in saliva, tears, and sweat*

igigi—longest uncommon palindrome beginning with letter i (5-t)—*Babylonian god*

ihi—shortest uncommon word that starts and ends with letter i (3)—*New Zealand bird*

iiwi—highest ratio dotted to undotted letters for an uncommon word (0.75-t)—*Hawaiian honeycreeper*

iiwi

ilang-ilang—longest hyphenated tautonym beginning with letter i (10)—*Philippine tree*

ileocolitis—longest uncommon word with consecutive letters adjacent on phone keypad beginning with letter i (11)—*inflammation of the intestines*

ill—example of an antonym of two different words, beginning with letter i [well, good]—example of a word pronounced differently when capitalized, beginning with letter i [sick, river in Austria]

illegally—common word containing the most repeats of letter l (4-t)

illumination—common word containing most consecutive letters in order after letter l (4-t)

imagination—longest common four-cadence (3-t)

imam—shortest common isolano (4-t)

imami—longest uncommon palindrome beginning with letter i (5-t)—longest vertical catoptron for an uncommon word (5-t)—*member of Shi'ite religious sect*

immigrants—longest common double progressive beheadment [immigrants → migrants → grants → ants → ts] (10-t)

immigrates—longest common double progressive beheadment [immigrates → migrates → grates → ates → es] (10-t)

immittance—example of a portmanteau, beginning with letter i [impedance, admittance]—*resistance of AC circuit*

immunocompromised—uncommon word containing the most repeats of letter m (4-t)—*with weakened immune system*

immunosuppression—common word containing most consecutive letters in order after letter m (4-t)

impassive—see "passive"

improvisatrici—longest uncommon word that starts and ends with letter i (14-t)—*female improvisor*

inadequacies—longest common word containing five consonants (12-t)

inamorata—see "amatorian"—*female loved one*

inane—longest common word containing one type of consonant for consonant n (5-t)

inattention—longest common word containing two types of consonants (11-t)

inauguration—longest common word containing five consonants (12-t)

incompatibilities—common word containing the most repeats of letter i (5-t)

incomprehensibility—common word with the lowest ratio length to number of different letters for length 19 (1.35)—most different letters for a common word (14-t)

incomprehensibly—common word with the lowest ratio length to number of different letters for length 16 (1.23-t)

inconveniencing—common word containing the most repeats of letter n (5-t)—longest common three-cadence (5-t)

incubi—longest common word that starts and ends with letter i (6)—shortest common word that starts and ends with letter i (6)

indent—see "dent"

indict—example of a word that contains silent letter c

individualistic—common word containing the most repeats of letter i (5-t)

inefficient—example of a word spelled with i before e after c, beginning with letter i

inequalities—longest common word containing five consonants (12-t)

ineris—see "cinerins"—*natives of Arawakan*

inert gas—see "angriest"—*gas that does not react chemically*

inestimable—see "estimable"

inevitabilities—longest uncommon four-cadence (4-t)—*things that must happen*

infamatory—see "goatsbeard"—*harming the reputation*

infectious necrotic hepatitises—longest phrase spelled with chemical symbols (29-t)

inflammable—see "flammable"

informally—longest common double progressive curtailment [informally → informal → inform → info → in] (10-t)

infrastructure—common word containing most consecutive letters in order after letter r (4-t)

ing—see "reafforesting" and "rewarehousing" and "unimmigrating"—*pasture*

ingenious—see "genius"

ingling—longest uncommon head 'n' tail centered on letter l (7-t)—*persuasive*

ingoing—longest uncommon head 'n' tail centered on letter o (7-t)—*entering*

ingot—example of a common word formed by borrowing or lending letters to frequent companions, beginning with letter i [lingot → l'ingot]

ingrain—closest to two million letter product for a common word (2000376-t)

ingrates—see "angriest"

inhabited—see "habited"

initialization—common word containing the most repeats of letter i (5-t)

initializing—common word containing the most repeats of letter i (5-t)

innumerable—see "enumerable"

inoperative—most letters in alphabetical place with shifting alphabet for a common word (6-t)

inquest—see "quest"

inscribe—see "scribe"

instantiations—longest uncommon tetrahedron word (14-t)—*individuals that represent a class*

instinctivistic—longest uncommon word containing one type of vowel for vowel i (15)—*inborn*

institution—longest common four-cadence (3-t)

institutionalization—common word containing the most repeats of letter t (4-t)—longest common word containing five types of consonants (20-t)—longest common word without E (20)

instructive—common word containing most consecutive letters in order after letter s (4-t)

insulins—longest uncommon numberdrome (8-t)—*metabolic hormones*

in tears—see "anestri"—*crying*

intellectually—common word containing the most repeats of letter l (4-t)

intemperate—see "preempted"

intend—see "tend"

intenerations—see "internationalised"—*softenings*

intensities—longest common polygram (11)

intercartilaginous—see "centrifugalisation"—*inside the soft part of the bones*

interdependence—common word containing the most repeats of letter e (5-t)

interdependencies—common word containing the most repeats of letter e (5-t)

interlineations—see "internationalised"—*things between the lines*

intermediate range ballistic missile—longest phrase containing three types of vowels (33-t)

intermittent—common word containing the most repeats of letter t (4-t)

internationalise—see "internationalised"

internationalised—longest uncommon progressive transdeletion [internationalised → internationalise → interlineations → renointestinal → intenerations → internations → trentonians →

stentorian → tontiners → trentons → rottens → otters → trots → tots → tot → to → t] (17-t)

internationalities—longest well-mixed uncommon transubstitution [internationalities → tetranitroanilines] (18-t)

internationalization—longest common word containing five types of consonants (20-t)

internations—see "internationalised"—*medical trainings*

internecine—see "identical"

interpenetrated—common word with the most frequently used letters for length 15 (1211)

interpret—longest nontrivial internal palindrome for a common word (7-t)

intertwined—see "fracture"

interventionism—longest common reverse snowball [inter & vent & ion & is & m] (15-t)

interventionist—longest common reverse snowball [inter & vent & ion & is & t] (15-t)

interview—common word containing most consecutive letters in order after letter v (2-t)

intestinal calculuses—longest polygram for a phrase (20)—*balls of solid matter in the intestines*

intestines—longest common pair isogram (10)

intestinointestinal—longest nontrivial internal head 'n' tail for an uncommon word (17)—*involving only the intestine*

inthralled—longest two-syllable word beginning with letter i (10)—*totally fascinated*

into—example of a self-antonym, beginning with letter i [divided into, multiplied by]

intortions—see "coadministrations"—*spiralings inward*

intransigence—longest palindrome in Morse code for a common word (13)

intuitive—common word containing most consecutive letters in order after letter t (3-t)

invader—see "hotbeds"

invaluable—see "valuable"

invisibility—common word containing the most repeats of letter i (5-t)

inweave—see "weave"—*weave together*

io—see "heterotransplantation"—*Hawaiian hawk*

iodide—longest common word containing one type of consonant for consonant d (6-t)

ipilipil—longest uncommon tautonym beginning with letter i (8)—*Philippine shrub*

irelessnesses—longest uncommon hydration [tirelessnesses & wirelessnesses] (0.13-t)—*states without anger*

irises—longest length four linkade with common words [iris & rise & ises] (6-t)

irradicate—see "eradicate"—*to put down long roots*

irrupt—see "erupt"—*intrude*

is—see "as"

ish—example of a word that exists only in an idiom, beginning with letter i [ish kabibble]

island—longest common word with consecutive letters adjacent on phone keypad beginning with letter i (6-t)

isobutyronitrile—see "subternatural"—*chemical*

isocheim—example of a word spelled with e before i, beginning with letter i—*line of equal average winter temperature*

itas—see "demitasse"—*native people of the Philippines*

itched—longest one-syllable word beginning with letter i (6)—*rubbed*

ius—example of a word that begins with silent letter i—example of a word that is a confusing code for letter i [use]—*legal principle*

J

j—longest common head 'n' tail centered on letter j (1)—longest common palindrome beginning with letter j (1)—longest common palindrome centered on letter j (1)—longest common word containing one type of consonant for consonant j (1)

jack—shortest common word with last letter next in alphabet after first for letter j (4-t)

jackal—common word containing most consecutive letters in order after letter j (3-t)

jacklight—uncommon word containing most consecutive letters in the alphabet after letter g (6-t)—uncommon word containing most consecutive letters in the alphabet after letter h (5-t)—*flashlight*

jack salmon—phrase containing most consecutive letters in order after letter j (5)—*freshwater perch*

jacky-jacky—longest hyphenated tautonym beginning with letter j (10)—*aborigine*

jacuzzi—example of a word that sounds like letters, beginning with letter j sound [JQZ]—*bath with jets*

jailbreak—common word containing most consecutive letters in the alphabet after letter i (4-t)

jak—shortest uncommon word with last letter next in alphabet after first for letter j (3)—*East Indian fruit*

jake—example of a self-antonym, beginning with letter j [uncouth, fine]

jakhalsbessie—uncommon word containing most consecutive letters in the alphabet after letter h (5-t)—*African tree*

jangadeiro—example of a word spelled with e before i, beginning with letter j—*Brazilian fisherman*

japanese hemlock—phrase containing most consecutive letters in the alphabet after letter j (7)

jararaca—longest digital reversal pair with an uncommon word [maharaja] (8)—*South American pit vipers*

jasminelike—uncommon word containing most consecutive letters in the alphabet after letter i (6)—uncommon word containing most consecutive letters in the alphabet after letter j (5)—*resembling jasmine*

jato—example of an acronym that has become uncapitalized, beginning with letter j [Jet-Assisted TakeOff]

jaywalking—common word containing most consecutive letters in the alphabet after letter i (4-t)

jealously—longest common word with consecutive letters adjacent on phone keypad beginning with letter j (9-t)

jejune—common word containing the most repeats of letter j (2-t)

jerk—shortest common word with last letter next in alphabet after first for letter j (4-t)

jerkily—common word containing most consecutive letters in order after letter j (3-t)—common word containing most consecutive letters in the alphabet after letter i (4-t)

jetfighter—uncommon word containing most consecutive letters in the alphabet after letter e (6)—uncommon word containing most consecutive letters in the alphabet after letter f (5)

jews—shortest common word that cannot have a letter added and transposed to form another word (4-t)

jib—highest ratio dotted to undotted letters for a common word (0.67-t)

jibi—highest ratio dotted to undotted letters for an uncommon word (0.75-t)—*extinct Hawaiian bird*

jig—example of a word that exists only in an idiom, beginning with letter j [the jig is up]—highest ratio dotted to undotted letters for a common word (0.67-t)

jigjig—longest uncommon tautonym beginning with letter j (6)—*jerky*

jingling—longest uncommon isotel pair with no letters in common [khoikhoi] (8-t)

job—example of a word pronounced differently when capitalized, beginning with letter j [occupation, Bible character]

Pronunciation Variants

What sequence of letters has the most different pronunciations?

The sequence "ough" has an incredible 28 different pronunciations, 10 of which occur in common words.

These phonetic symbols are used in describing the different pronunciations:

ə: e in "the," u in "humdrum"; ä: o in "bother" and "cot"; aů: ow in "now," ou in "loud"; ō: o in "bone" and "snow"; ȯ: a in "saw" and "all"; ü: u in "rule," oo in "fool"; ů: u in "pull," oo in "wood"; <u>k</u>: German ch in "ich-laut"

The ten common words, together with the pronunciation of "ough," are:

ə	BOROUGH, THOROUGH
əf	TOUGH
əp	HICCOUGH
ä	NOUGHT
aů	BOUGH
äf	TROUGH
ō	THOUGH
ȯ	OUGHT
ȯf	COUGH
ü	THROUGH

The remaining eighteen uncommon words are:

ə<u>k</u>	TURLOUGH (dialectical, obsolete)
ə<u>k</u>	BROUGH (dialectical)
əw	BOROUGH, THOROUGH
äft	TROUGH (dialectical)
ä<u>k</u>	LOUGH (dialectical)
ä<u>k</u>	DOUGHT, LOUGH (dialectical)
äth	TROUGH (dialectical)
ōg	SKEOUGH (dialectical, obsolete)
ō<u>k</u>	WOUGH (dialectical, obsolete)
ō<u>k</u>	BOUGHT, HOUGH (dialectical)
ȯft	TROUGH (dialectical)
ȯth	TROUGH (dialectical)
üf	SOUGH (dialectical, obsolete)
üg	SLOUGHI
ük	OUGH (obsolete)
ü<u>k</u>	OUGH
ůf	SOUGH (dialectical, obsolete)
ů<u>k</u>	OUGH

jock—shortest common word with last letter next in alphabet after first for letter j (4-t)

johnny-jump-up—longest hyphenated word with typewriter letters from right hand (12-t)—*wild pansy*

join—example of a false antonym beginning with letter j [conjoin]

jokingly—common word containing most consecutive letters in order after letter j (3-t)—common word containing most consecutive letters in the alphabet after letter i (4-t)

jolt—example of a portmanteau, beginning with letter j [joll, jot]

jounced—longest one-syllable word beginning with letter j (7)—*bounced*

joviality—longest common word with consecutive letters adjacent on phone keypad beginning with letter j (9-t)

jovicentric—longest uncommon word with consecutive letters adjacent on phone keypad beginning with letter j (11-t)—*centered around Jupiter*

juca—example of a word that is a confusing code for letter j [yuca]—*melon*

jug—common word with the most infrequently used letters for length 3 (54)

jug-jug—hyphenated word with the most infrequently used letters for length 6 (108)—*song of the nightingale*

juicier—example of a word spelled with i before e after c, beginning with letter j

jujitsu—common word containing the most repeats of letter j (2-t)

jujutsu—common word containing the most repeats of letter j (2-t)

jumblements—longest uncommon word with consecutive letters adjacent on phone keypad beginning with letter j (11-t)—*jumbled actions*

jumbling—one of three common words that together contain the most different letters [frowzy & sketchpad] (23)

juneteenths—longest two-syllable word beginning with letter j (11)—*holiday in Texas*

junk—shortest common word with last letter next in alphabet after first for letter j (4-t)

just—example of an antonym of two different words, beginning with letter j [unfair, extremely]

justice courts—longest phrase with consecutive letters adjacent on phone keypad beginning with letter j (13)

justitiae—example of a word that begins with silent letter j—*rights*

jynx—see "waqf"—*abnormal neck twisting*

K

k—longest common head 'n' tail centered on letter k (1)—longest common palindrome centered on letter k (1)

Kadir—see "cotter"—*from a primitive Indian people*

Kaf—see "cough"—*eleventh Hebrew letter*

kahikateas—longest uncommon changing offset shift pair [nemoricole] [shift of 3] (10)—*New Zealand white pine*

kajak—longest uncommon palindrome centered on letter j (5)—*variant of kayak*

kakistocracies—example of a word spelled with i before e after c, beginning with letter k—*governments by the worst men*

kakkak—uncommon word containing the most repeats of letter k (4-t)—*Guam bird*

kaleidoscope—example of a word spelled with e before i, beginning with letter k

kamchadale—longest uncommon word with consecutive letters adjacent on phone keypad beginning with letter k (10-t)—*natives of Kamchatka*

kamchadals—longest uncommon word with consecutive letters adjacent on phone keypad beginning with letter k (10-t)

kana-majiris—longest hyphenated word with consecutive letters adjacent on phone keypad beginning with letter k (11)—*Japanese writing system*

kanauri—see "cereals"—*Indian language*

kayak—longest common palindrome beginning with letter k (5)—longest common palindrome centered on letter y (5)

kazak—longest uncommon palindrome centered on letter z (5-t)—*natives of Kazakhstan*

keel—shortest common word with last letter next in alphabet after first for letter k (4-t)

keep—example of an antonym of three different words, beginning with letter k [release, break, neglect]

ketamines—longest uncommon alternating terminal elision [ketamines → etamines → etamine → tamine → tamin → amin → ami → mi → m] (9-t)—*anesthetic*

khalkha—longest uncommon head 'n' tail centered on letter l (7-t)—*natives of Outer Mongolia*

khawarij—example of a plural that ends with letter j—*Muslim religious sects*

khoikhoi—see "jingling"—*people of southern Africa*

khuskhus—longest uncommon tautonym beginning with letter k (8-t)—*Indian grass*

kick—shortest common word that starts and ends with letter k (4-t)

kickback—common word containing the most repeats of letter k (3)—longest common word that starts and ends with letter k (8-t)

kick off—example of a self-antonym, beginning with letter k [begin, die]

kill—shortest common word with last letter next in alphabet after first for letter k (4-t)

killickinnick—longest uncommon word that starts and ends with letter k (13)—*Indian ceremonial food*

killjoy—common word containing most consecutive letters in the alphabet after letter i (4-t)

kilojoules—common word containing most consecutive letters in the alphabet after letter i (4-t)

kilovolts—longest common word with consecutive letters adjacent on phone keypad beginning with letter k (9)

kin—example of a word pronounced differently when capitalized, beginning with letter k [relatives, Manchu ancestors]

kine—see "cow"

kink—shortest common word that starts and ends with letter k (4-t)

kinnikinnick—longest delete-reverse with an uncommon word [kinnikinnick → kinnikinnik] (12-t)—*variant of killickinnick*

kinnikinnik—longest palindrome for an uncommon word (11)—longest uncommon palindrome beginning with letter k (11)—longest uncommon palindrome centered on letter k (11)—longest uncommon word with typewriter letters from right hand (11-t)—see "kinnikinnick" and "kinnikinniks"—*variant of killickinnick*

kinnikinniks—longest delete-reverse with an uncommon word [kinnikinniks → kinnikinnik] (12-t)—longest nontrivial internal palindrome for an uncommon word (11-t)

kinsfolk—longest common word that starts and ends with letter k (8-t)

kip—example of an acronym that has become uncapitalized, beginning with letter k [KIlo- + Pound]—*monetary unit of Laos*

kirk—shortest common word that starts and ends with letter k (4-t)

kishen—see "charpoy"—*Manx unit of capacity*

kith—example of a word that exists only in an idiom, beginning with letter k [kith and kin]

kitty-corner—see "catercorner"

kitty-cornered—see "catercorner"

kjeldahlizing—uncommon word containing most consecutive letters in the alphabet after letter g (6-t)—*chemical method for determining the amount of nitrogen in a sample*

kleptomaniac—common word containing most consecutive letters in order after letter k (4)—common word containing most consecutive letters in the alphabet after letter k (6-t)

klompen—highest ratio of consecutive alphabetic letters to length for an uncommon word (0.85)—*wooden shoe*

klompen

klop-klop—longest hyphenated equidistant word (8)—*repeated clops*

knapsack—longest common word that starts and ends with letter k (8-t)

knickknacks—longest two-syllable word beginning with letter k (11)—*novelties*

knight of st. john of jerusalem—phrase containing most consecutive letters in the alphabet after letter e (11-t)—phrase containing most consecutive letters in the alphabet after letter f (10-t)—phrase containing most consecutive letters in the alphabet after letter g (9-t)—phrase that contains the most consecutive letters in alphabet (11-t)—*military religious group*

knights—longest one-syllable word beginning with letter k (7)

knights commanders—longest well-mixed phrase isomorph [meadow spittlebugs] (17-t)—*second class in certain honorary groups*

knights of st. john of jerusalem—same records as "knight of st. john of jerusalem"

knot—example of homophones differing by letter k [not]—example of a word that is a confusing code for letter k [not]

know—example of a word that begins with silent letter k

knurl—example of a portmanteau, beginning with letter k [knur, gnarl]—*snarl*

kohl—shortest common word with last letter next in alphabet after first for letter k (4-t)

kol—shortest uncommon word with last letter next in alphabet after first for letter k (3)—*people of India*

kook—longest common palindrome centered on letter o (4-t)—longest common word containing one type of consonant for consonant k (4)—shortest common word that starts and ends with letter k (4-t)

kronen—example of a plural that ends with letter n—*monetary unit of Norway*

kroner—example of a plural that ends with letter r

kukukuku—uncommon word containing the most repeats of letter k (4-t)—uncommon word with the most infrequently used letters for length 8 (160)—highest ratio length to letters for an uncommon word (4)—longest uncommon tautonym beginning with letter k (8-t)—longest uncommon word containing one type of consonant for consonant k (8)—longest uncommon tetrad isogram (8)—*natives of New Guinea*

kukukukus—uncommon word with the most infrequently used letters for length 9 (226)—longest uncommon word where each letter is three symbols in Morse code (9-t)

kumbuk—uncommon word with the most infrequently used letters for length 6 (125)—*tropical Asian tree*

kvetchy—see "browzing"—*complaining*

ky—uncommon word with the most infrequently used letters for length 2 (29)—*Scottish for cow*

L

lackadaisically—common word with lowest letter sum for length 15 (123)

laets—see "atles"—*freedmen in ancient Kent*

lam—example of a word that exists only in an idiom, beginning with letter l [on the lam]—shortest uncommon word with last letter next in alphabet after first for letter l (3-t)—see "lamb"—*escape*

lamb—example of homophones differing by letter b [lam]

lamentation—see "nostalgia"

laments—longest common alternating terminal elision [laments → lament → ament → amen → men → me → e] (7-t)

laminae—see "animals"

laminar—see "animals"

lana—see "galanases"—*wood of a West Indian tree*

lance—see "divas"

lapulapu—longest uncommon tautonym beginning with letter l (8-t)—*Philippine grouper*

lar—see "alares"—*Malayan gibbon*

lardizabalaceae—uncommon word with lowest letter sum for length 15 (101)—*shrubs*

lare—see "alares"—*lore*

lares—see "alares"—*Roman spirits*

laser—example of an acronym that has become uncapitalized, beginning with letter l [Light Amplification by Stimulated Emission of Radiation]

lates—see "atles"—*Nile perch*

latitudinarianisms—see "attitudinarianisms"—*tolerant beliefs*

laud—see "circa"

laudation—see "adulation"—*praising*

laugh and lay down—longest phrase with typewriter letters from alternating hands (15-t)—*card game*

laughing—common word containing most consecutive letters in order after letter g (3-t)

laughing jackass—phrase containing most consecutive letters in order after letter g (5)—*Australian kingfisher*

launched—longest one-syllable word beginning with letter l (8)

lavalava—longest uncommon tautonym beginning with letter l (8-t)—*Polynesian kilt*

layout—see "fusion"

lavalava

LDL—shortest phrase that starts and ends with letter l (3)—*low-density lipoprotein*

leadership—most letters in alphabetical place without shifting alphabet for a common word (4-t)

least—see "atles"

leats—see "atles"—*trenches for mill water*

lecithality—longest uncommon word with consecutive letters adjacent on phone keypad beginning with letter l (11-t)—*having a yolk*

leisure—example of a word spelled with e before i, beginning with letter l

lens—longest common hospitable [glens & liens & leans & lends & lense] (4)

lethal—longest common fixed offset shift pair that are reversals [shoals] [shift of 19] (6-t)

leucocytozoans—longest uncommon word with typewriter letters from alternating hands (14-t)—*bird parasites*

level—longest common palindrome beginning with letter l (5)—longest common palindrome centered on letter v (5-t)

levitators—longest uncommon backswitch [rotatively] (10)—*one that levitates*

lexicographical—longest common word that starts and ends with letter l (15)

liar—example of a word that contains silent letter a

lidar—example of a portmanteau, beginning with letter l [light, radar]

lierre—example of an uncommon word formed by borrowing or lending letters to frequent companions, beginning with letter l [l'ierre → lierre]—*olive color*

lighttight—longest uncommon word spelled with tall lowercase letters (10-t)—*not admitting light*

lightweights—longest two-syllable word beginning with letter l (12)

like—most different parts of speech for a common word (8)

lillypilly—longest uncommon word spelled with tall lowercase letters (10-t)—*Australian tree*

lima—example of a word pronounced differently when capitalized, beginning with letter l [bean, Peru city]

links-links—longest hyphenated tautonym beginning with letter l (10)—*knitting machine*

lint—longest common progressive difference pair [lint → cut → ha → g] (4-t)

liquefacient—example of a word spelled with i before e after c, beginning with letter l—*something that turns something into a liquid*

liroth—example of a plural that ends with letter h—*monetary unit of Israel*

lisente—see "sente"—*monetary unit of Lesotho*

list—shortest common word that has two different synonymous meanings with another word [roll: set of names; tilt] (4)

listerelloses—longest uncommon reversed embedded word [sollerets] (9-t)

listerellosis—longest uncommon reversed embedded word [sollerets] (9-t)—*animal disease*

listerize—longest synonymous transposal with an uncommon word [listerize → sterilize] (9-t)—*sterilize*

literally—example of a self-antonym, beginning with letter l [actually, figuratively]

litiscontestational—longest uncommon word that starts and ends with letter l (19)—*legal process*

little—example of an antonym of three different words, beginning with letter l [big, great, important]

liverwurst—common word containing most consecutive letters in the alphabet after letter r (6)—common word containing most consecutive letters in the alphabet after letter s (5)—common word containing most consecutive letters in the alphabet after letter t (4-t)—common word containing most consecutive letters in the alphabet after letter u (3-t)

llareta—example of a word that is a confusing code for letter l [yareta]—*Andean herb*

LM—shortest phrase with last letter next in alphabet after first for letter l (2)—*lunar module*

loam—shortest common word with last letter next in alphabet after first for letter l (4-t)

locational—see "allocation"

loll—shortest common word that starts and ends with letter l (4-t)

lomilomi—longest uncommon tautonym beginning with letter l (8-t)—*Hawaiian massage*

lone—example of a common word formed by borrowing or lending letters to frequent companions, beginning with letter l [alone → a lone]

loom—shortest common word with last letter next in alphabet after first for letter l (4-t)

loosen—example of a false antonym beginning with letter l [unloosen]

loro—see "hexachlorocyclohexane"—*parrot fish*

lose—common word with most antonyms [win & find & gain] (3)

loti—example of an uncommon word in which adding letters to beginning makes it plural [loti → maloti]—*monetary unit of Lesotho*

lots to blanks—longest phrase with consecutive letters adjacent on phone keypad beginning with letter l (12)—*sure thing*

loxolophodonts—longest uncommon word containing one type of vowel for vowel o (14)—*extinct hoofed animals* lull—shortest common word that starts and ends with letter l (4-t)

lulliloo—longest uncommon word containing one type of consonant for consonant l (8-t)—*African celebratory cry*

lum—shortest uncommon word with last letter next in alphabet after first for letter l (3-t)—*chimney*

lowe—see "blowers"—*Scottish for glow*

lumberjack—common word containing most consecutive letters in the alphabet after letter j (4)

luminous—common word containing most consecutive letters in order after letter l (4-t)

luring—closest to four million letter product for a common word (4000752-t)

luxuriant—longest common word with consecutive letters adjacent on phone keypad beginning with letter l (9)

luxuriantly—longest uncommon word with consecutive letters adjacent on phone keypad beginning with letter l (11-t)

lym—shortest uncommon word with last letter next in alphabet after first for letter l (3-t)—*bloodhound*

m—longest common palindrome centered on letter m (1)—longest common word with typewriter letters from bottom row (1-t)

ma—shortest full vowel (including y) substitution with multi-letter uncommon words [me & mi & mo & mu & my] (2-t)

macacahuba—longest uncommon word containing all letters restricted to Fibonacci sequence (10)—*tropical American tree*

macassar agar-agars—longest hyphenated phrase containing one type of vowel for vowel a (17)—*East Indian algae gelatins*

mad—example of an antonym of two different words, beginning with letter m [calm, sane]

madam—longest common palindrome beginning with letter m (5-t)

magma—longest common head 'n' tail centered on letter g (5-t)

magnetoencephalogram—longest uncommon word that starts and ends with letter m (20)—*recording of magnetic brain waves*

magnetosphere—common word containing most consecutive letters in order after letter m (4-t)

maharaja—see "jararaca"—*Indian ruler*

mahimahi—longest uncommon tautonym beginning with letter m (8-t)—*Hawaiian fish*

mainland—longest common word spelled with two-letter U.S. postal codes (8-t)

maintenance—see "urgently"

makomako—longest uncommon tautonym beginning with letter m (8-t)—*New Zealand wine berry*

maladjustment—longest common word with consecutive letters adjacent on phone keypad beginning with letter m (13)

malariae malaria—longest head 'n' tail phrase centered on letter e (15)—*type of malaria*

malayalam—longest uncommon palindrome beginning with letter m (9)—longest uncom-

Pangrams

Is it possible to construct a list of words containing 26 different letters?

There are several ways that this can be accomplished: with a limited number of words, with fixed-length words, with no repeated letters, with the letters introduced in alphabetical order, etc. The ultimate challenge is to find a simple, meaningful sentence that contains all the 26 letters exactly once. Before we get to that, let's visit some of the other milestones on the journey.

Limited Number of Words with Most Distinct Letters with No Repeated Letters
    1: uncopyrightable (15 in 15)
    2: poldavy thumbscrewing (20 in 20)
    3: frowzy backvelds thumping (23 in 23)
    4: jynx vozhd backswept grimful (25 in 25)
    5: waqf jynx speltz vugh mockbird (26 in 26)

Limited Number of Words with Most Distinct Letters
    1: psychogalvanometric (16 in 19)
    2: sympathizingly backfurrowed (22 in 26)
    2: judgment-proof blacky-whites (22 in 25 + hyphen)
    3: zanthoxyl buckjumped fevertwigs (25 in 29)
    3: quick-fix overbejeweled sympathizing (26 in 33 + hyphen)
    4: qwerty flax buckjumping vozhds (26 in 27)

Fixed Length Words with Most Distinct Letters with No Repeated Letters
    3: vex adz cwm fir sky lob nth pug (24 in 24, 8 words)
    4: next jock whiz flag dumb spry (24 in 24, 6 words)
    5: waqfs bronx klutz gyved chimp (25 in 25, 5 words)
    6: poxing jumbly kvetch dwarfs (24 in 24, 4 words)
    7: braving mudflow sketchy (21 in 21, 3 words)

Fixed Length Words with Most Distinct Letters
    3: qts box jak viz wyn pfc rhm ged lug (26 in 27, 9 words)
    4: qoph lynx jamb fuzz vest wick drug (26 in 28, 7 words)
    5: quick vexed jazzy frown blimp sight (26 in 30, 6 words)
    6: jiquis flexed kwanza botchy grumpy (25 in 30, 5 words)
    7: quartzy lockbox jewfish vamping (25 in 28, 4 words)
    8: judgment lazyback prowfish (23 in 24, 3 words)
    8: squeezer xylotomy whipjack vagabond (25 in 32, 4 words)
    9: zanthoxyl buckjumps fevertwig (25 in 27, 3 words)

Letters Introduced in Alphabetical Order
    ABC def ghi jak limn op qre st uva wax yez (26 in 32, 11 words)

Letters Introduced in Reverse Alphabetical Order
    zyme oxbow vauts iraq pon milk jig hog fed caba (26 in 38, 10 words)

Sentences
Here are several sentences that contain each letter of the alphabet:
    Sympathizing would fix Quaker objectives. (36 letters)
    Quick brown fox, jump over the lazy dogs. (32 letters)

Pack my box with five dozen liquor jugs. (32 letters)
Jackdaws love my big sphinx of quartz. (31 letters)
Quick waxy bugs jump the frozen veldt. (31 letters)
The five boxing wizards jump quickly. (31 letters)
Judges vomit; few quiz pharynx block. (30 letters)
How quickly daft jumping zebras vex. (30 letters)
Foxy nymphs grab quick-lived waltz. (29 letters)

The following sentences contain each letter exactly once, but either the words used are very uncommon or the syntax is very strained, or both:

Cwm, fjord-bank glyphs quiz vext.
Jack vends frowzy Qum, PBX light.
Jynx flight browzed quack MVPs.
Kluxing vozhd jambs PFC qwerty.
Nth quark biz gyps cwm fjeld vox.
Quartz glyph job vex'd cwm finks.
Squdgy fez, blank jimp crwth vox.
Veldt jynx grimps waqf zho buck.
Waqf vozhd trecks, jumbling pyx.

The following pangrammatic sentence uses words found in college-level dictionaries, although they are not common words. It has a fairly straightforward syntax, although it is a compound sentence:

Gyps balk nth fjord cwm quiz, vex.
Gyps are college students in Britain. Thus the sentence means that the college students refused to take the nth fjord cwm quiz (a "fjord cwm" is a basin at the end of a steep-walled valley leading to the sea), and that this annoyed someone.

Finally, this simple sentence contains all the 26 letters of the alphabet, each exactly once:

Jumbling vext frowzy hacks PDQ.
This means that being bounced about quickly annoyed the disheveled taxi drivers.

mon palindrome centered on letter y (9)—*Dravidian language spoken in southwest India*

maloti—see "loti"—*monetary unit of Lesotho*

mamma—longest common head 'n' tail centered on letter m (5)—longest common word containing one type of consonant for consonant m (5-t)

mammie—longest uncommon word containing one type of consonant for consonant m (6-t)—*Tropical American tree*

mammogram—uncommon word containing the most repeats of letter m (4-t)—*X-ray of the breast*

man—shortest common word with last letter next in alphabet after first for letter m (3-t)

manana—longest uncommon word where each letter is two symbols in Morse code (6-t)

manatee—see "emanate"

mandarin—longest common word spelled with two-letter U.S. postal codes (8-t)

mandibulopharyngeals—uncommon word with the lowest ratio length to number of different letters for length 20 (1.25-t)—*relating to the jaw and mouth*

manxman—longest uncommon head 'n' tail centered on letter x (7)—*from the Isle of Man*

martels—longest uncommon multiplicative offset shift pair [mundari] [factor of 21] (7-t)—*pointed hammer weapons*

maser—example of an acronym that has become uncapitalized, beginning with letter m

[Microwave Amplification by Stimulated Emission of Radiation]

mathematically—see "athematically"

mattering—see "smatterings"

matters—longest common progressive curtailment [matters → matter → matte → matt → mat → ma → m] (7-t)

matzot—example of a plural that ends with letter t—*unleavened bread*

maximum—common word containing the most repeats of letter m (3-t)

maximum and minimum thermometer—phrase containing the most repeats of letter m (8)—*device that records the highest and lowest temperatures reached*

mazedly—see "bonniest"—*completely confused*

me—see "ma"

meadow spittlebugs—see "knights commanders"—*North American insects*

megachiropterans—see "cinematographers"—*European fruit bats*

megalomaniacal — common word with lowest letter sum for length 14 (107)

megachiropteran

memorial—longest common word spelled with two-letter U.S. postal codes (8-t)

men—shortest common word with last letter next in alphabet after first for letter m (3-t)

menopause—common word containing most consecutive letters in order after letter m (4-t)

merge—example of a false antonym beginning with letter m [immerge]

mesomes—longest uncommon head 'n' tail centered on letter o (7-t)—*parts of an embryo*

messes—longest common word containing all letters restricted to primes (6-t)

metallics—longest uncommon switchback [oscillate] (9)—*substances made of metal*

mi—see "ma"

miamian—longest uncommon word where each letter is two symbols in Morse code (7-t)—*from the city of Miami, Florida*

microencapsulated—common word with the lowest ratio length to number of different letters for length 17 (1.21-t)—most different letters for a common word (14-t)

microspectrophotometers—longest metathesis with an uncommon word [microspectrophotometers → microspectrophotometres] (23)—*small devices for measuring spectra*

microspectrophotometres—see "microspectrophotometers"—*variant of microspectrophotometers*

mide—see "amides"—*Native American secret society*

mides—see "amides"

milky way galaxy—phrase with the most infrequently used letters for length 14 (536)—*Earth's galaxy*

minicomputer—common word containing most consecutive letters in order after letter m (4-t)

minim—longest common palindrome beginning with letter m (5-t)—longest common palindrome centered on letter n (5-t)

minima—longest uncommon word where each letter is two symbols in Morse code (6-t)

minimum—common word containing the most repeats of letter m (3-t)

misinterpret—longest nontrivial internal palindrome for a common word (7-t)

mita—see "demitasse"—*Spanish conscription of Peruvian natives*

mm—longest uncommon word with typewriter letters from bottom row (2-t)—shortest uncommon word that starts and ends with letter m (2)—*sound expressing satisfaction*

MNC—longest phrase with typewriter letters from bottom row (3)—*multinational corporation*

mnemic—example of a word that is a confusing code for letter m [nemic]—*effected by past experience*

mnemonic—example of a word that begins with silent letter m

mo—see "ma"—*moment*

moats—longest common charitable [oats & mats & mots & moas & moat] (5-t)

mockbird—see "waqf"—*mockingbird*

moldy corn poisonings—longest phrase without ETA (19)—*diseases of farm animals*

mole—example of a word pronounced differently when capitalized, beginning with letter m [birthmark, Sudanese people]

mom—longest common head 'n' tail centered on letter o (3-t)—longest common uppercase upside-down word pair [wow] (3-t)—shortest common word that starts and ends with letter m (3-t)

momentum—common word containing the most repeats of letter m (3-t)

momma—longest common word containing one type of consonant for consonant m (5-t)

mommie—longest uncommon word containing one type of consonant for consonant m (6-t)—*mother*

monogonoporous—uncommon word containing the most repeats of letter o (6-t)—*having a single genital opening for both male and female organs*

monsieur—example of a word that contains silent letter n

mooched—longest one-syllable word beginning with letter m (7)—*borrowed*

moosetongues—longest two-syllable word beginning with letter m (12)—*willow herbs*

moot—example of a self-antonym, beginning with letter m [debatable, not worthy of debate]

morituri te salutamus—longest alternating vowels and consonants for a phrase (19-t)—*we who are about to die salute you*

motel—example of a portmanteau, beginning with letter m [motor, hotel]

motmot—longest uncommon word with Morse code that is entirely dashes (6)—*tropical American bird*

motto—longest common word with Morse code that is entirely dashes (5)

mouth-to-mouth—longest hyphenated word spelled with vertical symmetry letters (12)—*artificial respiration*

mozambican—uncommon word containing most consecutive letters in order after letter z (4-t)—*from Mozambique*

mozambique—common word containing most consecutive letters in order after letter z (3-t)

mozarabic—uncommon word containing most consecutive letters in order after letter z (4-t)—*from medieval Spanish Christians*

mu—see "ma"

muchness—example of a word that exists only in an idiom, beginning with letter m [much of a muchness]—*greatness of quantity*

muckamuck—longest uncommon head 'n' tail centered on letter a (9-t)—*important person*

muddleheaded—common word containing the most repeats of letter d (4)

mudflaps—see "browzing"

mugwump—common word with the most infrequently used letters for length 7 (181)

mugwumps—common word with the most infrequently used letters for length 8 (247)

multicentricity—longest uncommon word with consecutive letters adjacent on phone keypad beginning with letter m (15)—*coming from many places*

multiculturalism—longest common word that starts and ends with letter m (16)

multilateralization—longest uncommon rollercoaster (19)—*opening up to all parties*

multimillionaire—see "multimillionairess"

multimillionaires—see "multimillionairess"

multimillionairess—longest uncommon word in which deleting consecutively repeated letters forms word [multimillionairess → multimillionaire] (18)—longest uncommon word in which dropping s makes a plural [multimillionairess → multimillionaires] (18)—longest letter subtraction with an uncommon word [multimillionairess → multimillionaire] (18)—*female multimillionaire*

mum—longest common palindrome centered on letter u (3-t)—shortest common word that starts and ends with letter m (3-t)

mundari—see "martels"—*Indian dialect*

municipalities—see "demilitarizing"

murdrum—longest uncommon palindrome centered on letter d (7-t)—*secret murder*

murein—example of a word spelled with e before i, beginning with letter m—*chemical in bacterial cell walls*

murmur—longest common tautonym beginning with letter m (6)

murmured—longest repeated prefix for a common word (6-t)

muroidea—shortest uncommon word containing each vowel once in reverse order (8)—*rodents*

musers—see "amusers"—*persons that are absorbed in thought*

mutafacient—example of a word spelled with i before e after c, beginning with letter m—*causing mutation*

muzzy—uncommon word with highest letter sum for length 5 (111)—*fuzzy*

my—see "ma"

myomotomy—longest sequence of repeated dashes in Morse code for an uncommon word (17)—longest uncommon word spelled with vertical symmetry letters (9-t)—*cutting a muscle*

myrrh—example of a word that ends with silent letter h

mythically—longest common double progressive curtailment [mythically → mythical → mythic → myth → my] (10-t)

N

n—longest common word with typewriter letters from bottom row (1-t)

nagnag—longest uncommon tautonym beginning with letter n (6)—*nag*

nailers—longest common backswitch [reliant] (7-t)

nain—example of an uncommon word formed by borrowing or lending letters to frequent companions, beginning with letter n [mine ain → my nain]—*Scottish for own*

napped—see "hitter"

nar—see "cymba"—*near*

narcotisation—see "coadministrations"—*drugging*

nase—see "galanases"—*high point of land*

nastier—see "anestri"

nat—see "thanatopsides"—*Burmese spirit*

nationalization—longest common word that starts and ends with letter n (15-t)

naughts—longest one-syllable word beginning with letter n (7)—*nothings*

nauruan—longest uncommon palindrome beginning with letter n (7)—longest uncommon palindrome centered on letter r (7)—*from Nauru*

nauseousnesses—longest uncommon word containing two types of consonants (14-t)—*feelings of sickness*

necromancers—longest common word spelled with short lowercase letters (12-t)

necropoli—see "necropolis"

necropolis—example of an uncommon word that makes its own plural by dropping s [necropolis → necropoli]—*cemetery*

neither—example of a word spelled with e before i, beginning with letter n

nek—see "oriel"—*low ridge between two hills*

nemoricole—see "kahikateas"—*living in groves*

neothalamus—longest uncommon word with consecutive letters adjacent on phone keypad beginning with letter n (11)—*part of the thalamus*

neri—see "cinerins"—*Medieval Italian political faction*

neritas—see "anestri"—*marine snails*

nervy—example of a self-antonym, beginning with letter n [showing calm courage, excitable]

nescience—example of a word spelled with i before e after c, beginning with letter n

nestles—example of a word pronounced differently when capitalized, beginning with letter n [snuggles, chocolate maker]

neurochemistries—longest uncommon well-mixed isomorph [postchlorination] (16-t)—*chemistries of the nerves*

never-never—longest hyphenated tautonym beginning with letter n (10)—*imaginary*

newt—example of a common word formed by borrowing or lending letters to frequent companions, beginning with letter n [an ewt → a newt]

Ngo—example of a word that begins with silent letter n—*from a city in the Congo*

Niceno-Constantinopolitan—longest hyphenated phrase that starts and ends with letter n (24)—*member of a religious sect*

nickelodeon—example of a portmanteau, beginning with letter n [nickel, melodeon]—*jukebox*

nickname—example of a common word formed by borrowing or lending letters to frequent companions, beginning with letter n [an ekename → a nekename]

nicotinamide adenine dinucleotide phosphate—see "transmission electron microscopes"—*chemical used as heart medicine*

nightclothes—longest two-syllable word beginning with letter n (12)

nighty-night—longest hyphenated head 'n' tail centered on letter y (11-t)—*good-night*

nip—example of a word that exists only in an idiom, beginning with letter n [nip and tuck]

nitinol—example of an acronym that has become uncapitalized, beginning with letter n [NIckel + TIn + Naval Ordinance Laboratory]—*alloy of titanium and nickel*

nitrosation—see "coadministrations"—*chemical process of adding nitrogen and oxygen*

nizam—see "coffer"

no—shortest common word with last letter next in alphabet after first for letter n (2)

noble—example of an antonym of three different words, beginning with letter n [cheap, base, ignoble]

noncondensing engine—phrase containing the most repeats of letter n (7)—*steam engine without a condenser*

nondenominational—common word containing the most repeats of letter n (5-t)

nonindustrialization—longest uncommon word that starts and ends with letter n (20)—*development without industry*

noninstitutionalized—longest uncommon word with balanced letter sum (20-t)—*not committed to an institution*

nonintervention—common word containing the most repeats of letter n (5-t)—longest common word that starts and ends with letter n (15-t)

nonis—longest uncommon uppercase upside-down word pair [sinon] (5)—*East Indian shrub*

nonny-nonny—hyphenated word containing the most repeats of letter n (6)—*refrain in songs*

nonopaque—uncommon word containing most consecutive letters in order after letter n (4-t)—*clear*

nonsupports—longest uncommon word containing letters from last half of alphabet (11-t)—*failures to support*

nontortuous—longest uncommon word containing letters from last half of alphabet (11-t)—*straight*

nonunion—longest uncommon word containing one type of consonant for consonant n (8-t)—*not in a union*

Pangrammatic Window

What is the shortest pangrammatic window?

A pangrammatic window is a sequence of letters in a work of literature that contains all of the letters of the alphabet. How long would we expect a pangrammatic window to be? If we assume that each letter occurs independently of each other letter, then the average length will be determined by the frequency of the letters. These can be measured from samples of English literature, and when the math is worked through, we find even odds of all the letters occurring in a window about 1000 letters long.

The British turn-of-the-century puzzlist A. Cyril Pearson reported what is to this day the shortest known pangrammatic window. Here's what *The Twentieth Century Standard Puzzle Book* by Pearson (George Routledge & Sons, London, 1907, Part II, p. 149) says in its entirety about pangrammatic windows:

ALL THE ALPHABET!

Many of us know that there is a long verse in the Book of Ezra in which all the letters of the alphabet are used, taking "j" as "i" (Ezra vii., v. 21).

A very curious coincidence also occurs in a comparatively short sentence in "The Beth Book," by Sarah Grand:—"It was an exquisitely deep blue just then, with filmy white clouds drawn up over it like gauze"; and here "j" is itself in evidence.

All of the letters of the alphabet occur in the 67 letters between the x in "exquisitely" and the z in "gauze." What are the expected odds of a window of 67 letters? The answer is: 1 in 200,000! Could this truly be a coincidence? Is this an innocent citation, or did Grand construct this sentence with the explicit purpose of including all the letters of the alphabet? And how did anyone notice this in the first place? Could Grand be in cahoots with Pearson? Is this a hoax? Inquiring minds want to know.

Sarah Grand was the pseudonym of Frances Elizabeth Clarke McFall. *The Beth Book* was published in New York in 1897, and London during the following year. Here is the paragraph containing the window (*The Beth Book*, Virago Modern Classics edition, Dial Press, New York, 1980, p. 200):

"And were you happy?" Beth asked solemnly.

Aunt Victoria gazed at her vaguely. She had never asked herself the question. Then Beth sat with her work on her lap for a little, looking up at the summer sky. It was an exquisite deep blue just then, with filmy white clouds drawn up over it like gauze to veil its brightness. The red roofs and gables and chimneys of the old house below, the shrubs, the dark Scotch fir, the copper-beech, the limes and the chestnut stood out clearly silhouetted against it; and Beth felt the forms and tints and tones of them all, although she was thinking of something else.

But wait! Something is amiss here. The passage actually contains the word "exquisite," not "exquisitely." Thus the true window is 65 letters, not 67. How could Pearson have misquoted the passage? After making so remarkable a discovery, he must have counted the letters two or three times, at least. A clue to how this could have happened is in the introduction to the *Standard Puzzle Book*. He explains that the book contains material that has been submitted to him by his readers. Probably a reader noticed the pangrammatic window and reported it, erroneously, to Pearson. Since the page number is not recorded (as it is for the Bible verse), perhaps the reader did not provide it. Pearson can be forgiven for not scanning the entire *Beth Book* looking for this passage.

So while Pearson has in all likelihood been exonerated from any charge of colluding with McFall, the suspicion now falls upon some unknown correspondent of Pearson. But, as we shall see, logic dictates that these suspicions are likely to be groundless.

Is this passage innocent? The language is a bit flowery, but not overly contrived. If McFall were trying to construct a short pangrammatic window, she could do two letters better by dropping the word "up" from the sentence. But the clincher is the two-letter mistake substituting the word "exquisitely" for "exquisite." Why would a partner in crime to McFall misquote the passage, to the detriment of the record? That would make no sense at all.

No, I think logic forces us to conclude that there was no collusion, and if so, that the passage was entirely innocent and coincidental.

If this 65-letter window is accidental, then perhaps there are other short windows that just have not been noticed. Indeed, a 76-letter window was noticed by Eric Albert (*Word Ways*, November 1981, p. 216) in *Paradise Lost* by Milton (line 812):

Likening his Maker to the gra[zed ox—
Jehovah, who, in one night, when he passed
From Egypt marching, equalled with one stroke
B]oth her first-born and all her bleating gods.

Surely the great Milton did not contrive a passage in Latin that translated to English would form a short pangrammatic window. I set about to look for other windows. The easiest way to look for windows was to scan the readily available texts. These revealed the following minimal pangrammatic and near-pangrammatic windows:

25 in 64 in John 11,12 in the King James version of the Bible:

John 11:57 Now both the chief priests and the Pharisees had given a commandment, that, if any man knew where he were, he should shew it, that they mi[ght take him.

John 12:1 Then Jesus six days before the passover came to Bethany, where Laz]arus was, which had been dead, whom he raised from the dead.

25 in 65 in Chapter 94 of *Moby Dick* by Herman Melville:

Would that I could [keep squeezing that sperm for ever! For now, since by many prolonged, repeated ex]periences, I have perceived that in all cases man must eventually lower, or at least shift, his conceit of attainable felicity; not placing it anywhere in the intellect or the fancy; but in the wife, the heart, the bed, the table, the saddle, the fire-side, the country; now that I have perceived all this, I am ready to squeeze case eternally.

24 in 42 at Act I, Scene I of *Titus Andronicus* by Shakespeare:
Suffer thy brother Marcus to inter
His noble nephew here in virtue's nest,
That died in honour and Lavinia's cause.
Thou art a Roman; be not barbarous:
The [Greeks upon advice did bury Ajax
That slew himself]; and wise Laertes' son
Did graciously plead for his funerals:
Let not young Mutius, then, that was thy joy
Be barr'd his entrance here.

25 in 73 at Act V, Scene II of *Love's Labours Lost* by Shakespeare:
O, sir, you have overthrown
Alisander the conqueror! You will be scraped out of
the painted cloth for this: your lion, that holds
his poll-axe sitting on a close-stool, will be [given
to Ajax: he will be the ninth Worthy. A conqueror,
and afeard to speak! run away for sham]e, Alisander.

26 in 73 in Chapter XVIII of Don Quixote of the Mancha by Cervantes:
"Therein is nothing else to be done," said the curate, "but that Sir
Don Quixote say at once; for in these matters of chivalry, all these
noblemen and myse[lf do give unto him the prick and the prize." "I
swear unto you by Jove, good sirs," quoth Don Quix]ote, "that so many
and so strange are the things which have befallen me in this castle,
these two times that I have lodged therein, as I dare avouch nothing
affirmatively of anything that shall be demanded of me concerning the
things contained in it; for I do infallibly imagine that all the
adventures which pass in it are guided by enchantment."

Again, Cervantes could not have contrived this passage in Spanish.

26 in 66 in the Introduction to *Poems of Henry Timrod*:
Or we smo[ked, conversing lazily between the puffs,
"Next to some pine whose antique roots j]ust peeped
From out the crumbling bases of the sand."

This 66-letter window nearly ties that of *The Beth Book*. I conclude that there are many
undiscovered pangrammatic windows out there hidden in the pages of English literature. If the
odds of a 65-letter window are 1 in 200,000, and a typical page of text contains about fifty
65-letter windows, then we should find a 65-letter window every 4,000 pages. Remember that
the next time you settle down with a thick book.

noon—longest common palindrome beginning with letter n (4)—longest common palindrome centered on letter o (4-t)

nos—longest common uppercase upside-down word pair [son] (3-t)

nostalgia—longest common iskot pair measured in number of dots and dashes [lamentation] (22)—longest common iskot pair [lamentation] (11)

not—see "knot"

notarisation—see "coadministrations"—*notarizing*

not to put too fine a point on it—longest phrase containing four types of consonants (25)—*to be blunt*

nought—example of a common word with the most variably pronounced suffix [see "Pronunciation Variants" article, page 135]

nouveau—longest common word containing two consonants (7-t)—shortest common word with no matching vowel pattern (7-t)

nowhere—see "abjurer"

nth—longest common word containing all consonants (3-t)

nude—example of a false antonym beginning with letter n [denude]

numbskulls—longest common word containing one type of vowel for vowel u (10-t)

nun—longest common palindrome centered on letter u (3-t)—shortest common word that starts and ends with letter n (3)

nunchaku—example of a word that ends with silent letter u—*martial arts weapon*

nuptials—longest common word with consecutive letters adjacent on phone keypad beginning with letter n (8)

nunchaku

O

o—longest common palindrome beginning with letter o (1)—longest common word containing all vowels (1-t)

oar—example of homophones differing by letter a [or]

obbligato—longest common word that starts and ends with letter o (9)

obediency—example of a word that sounds like letters, beginning with letter o sound [OBDNC]—*obeying*

obeisance—example of a word spelled with e before i, beginning with letter o

obelisks—longest common word with consecutive letters adjacent on phone keypad beginning with letter o (8)

obliviality—longest uncommon word with consecutive letters adjacent on phone keypad beginning with letter o (11)—*ignorance*

oblong—see "fracas"

obo—example of an acronym that has become uncapitalized, beginning with letter o [Oil Bulk Ore]—longest uncommon head 'n' tail centered on letter b (3-t)—*cargo vessel*

oboe—longest common word containing one type of consonant for consonant b (4-t)

obovoid—see "ovoid"—*egg-shaped*

obscure—example of an antonym of three different words, beginning with letter o [bright, famous, lucid]

obsessive—longest sequence of repeated dots in Morse code for a common word (18-t)

oedipal—example of a word that begins with silent letter o

offing—example of a word that exists only in an idiom, beginning with letter o [in the offing]

offspring—longest consonant string for a common word (5-t)

ofo—longest uncommon head 'n' tail centered on letter f (3-t)—*native of central North America*

ohio—longest uncommon word spelled with full symmetry letters (4)—*from the state of Ohio*

ohm—longest common uppercase upside-down word pair [who] (3-t)

ohms—longest common progressive difference pair [ohms → gut → la → k] (4-t)

oinked—longest one-syllable word beginning with letter o (6)—*squealed*

okeydokey—longest uncommon head 'n' tail centered on letter d (9)—*OK*

old-gold—longest hyphenated head 'n' tail centered on letter g (7)—*dark yellow color*

old world scops owl—longest phrase without ETAIN (16)—*European owl*

oleo—shortest common word that starts and ends with letter o (4-t)

olio—shortest common word that starts and ends with letter o (4-t)

old world scops owl

omniscient—example of a word spelled with i before e after c, beginning with letter o

once upon a time—see "second banana"

onga-onga—longest hyphenated tautonym beginning with letter o (8)—*New Zealand shrub*

oniomania—shortest six-syllable word (9)—*mania for shopping*

onion—longest common head 'n' tail centered on letter i (5)—longest common word containing one type of consonant for consonant n (5-t)

onomatopoeia—highest vowels minus consonants for a common word (4)—longest common word containing four consonants (12)

onto—longest common progressive difference pair [onto → ate → go → r] (4-t)—shortest common word that starts and ends with letter o (4-t)

oo—longest uncommon tautonym beginning with letter o (2)—shortest uncommon word that starts and ends with letter o (2)—*extinct Hawaiian bird*

OO gauge—longest phrase containing one type of consonant for consonant g (7)—*track size in model railroads*

ooh—longest common word containing one type of consonant for consonant h (3-t)—longest common word spelled with full symmetry letters (3)

ooze—longest common word containing one type of consonant for consonant z (4)

op—shortest uncommon word with last letter next in alphabet after first for letter o (2)—*art style*

opaque—common word containing most consecutive letters in order after letter o (3-t)—common word containing most consecutive letters in order after letter p (2-t)

opaqueness—common word containing most consecutive letters in order after letter o (3-t)

opaquers—uncommon word containing most consecutive letters in order after letter o (5)—uncommon word containing most consecutive letters in order after letter p (4-t)—*ones who make something opaque*

oppo—longest uncommon palindrome beginning with letter o (4-t)—*opposite number*

oppositionists—longest uncommon tetrahedron word (14-t)—*opponents*

ops—see "thanatopsides"—*operations*

or—see "oar"

oral—see "aural"

orange—example of a common word formed by borrowing or lending letters to frequent companions, beginning with letter o [a naranj → an aranj]

orca—see "dowts"—*killer whale*

oriel—longest uncommon progressive difference pair [oriel → wids → nek → it → o] (5-t)—*type of window*

os—see "as"

oscillate—see "metallics"

otto—longest uncommon palindrome beginning with letter o (4-t)—*flower perfume*

ou—see "carousers"—*oh*

ouabaio—highest ratio vowels to consonants for an uncommon word (6-t)—longest uncommon word containing one consonant (7-t)—longest uncommon word containing one type of consonant for consonant b (7)—*African tree*

ouagadougou—longest uncommon word containing three consonants (11-t)—*from Ouagadougou, Upper Volta*

ouch—example of a common word formed by borrowing or lending letters to frequent companions, beginning with letter o [a nouche → an ouche]

oued—example of a word that is a confusing code for letter o [wed]—*Asian river bed*

ought—example of a common word with the most variably pronounced suffix [see "Pronunciation Variants" article, page 135]

ouija—longest uncommon word containing one type of consonant for consonant j (5)—*board used to spell out magical messages*

our—example of a word pronounced differently when capitalized, beginning with letter o [belonging to us, river in Belgium]—see "hour"

ous—see "carousers"

outcrop—shortest common word with last letter next in alphabet after first for letter o (7-t)

outscouts—longest uncommon head 'n' tail centered on letter c (9-t)—*scouts*

outshouts—longest uncommon head 'n' tail centered on letter h (9)—*shouts louder*

outside—common word with most consecutive alphabetic letters in reverse order consecutively (3-t)

outstretched—longest two-syllable word beginning with letter o (12)—*fully extended*

overbravado—longest uncommon word that starts and ends with letter o (11)—*too brave*

overcompensating—common word with the lowest ratio length to number of different letters for length 16 (1.23-t)

overconservative—uncommon word containing the most repeats of letter v (3-t)—*too conservative*

overcover—longest uncommon head 'n' tail centered on letter c (9-t)—*cover completely*

overflight—common word containing most consecutive letters in order after letter e (4-t)

overlap—shortest common word with last letter next in alphabet after first for letter o (7-t)

overlook—example of a self-antonym, beginning with letter o [inspect, ignore]

overstuffed—common word with most consecutive alphabetic letters in order consecutively (4-t)

overtop—shortest common word with last letter next in alphabet after first for letter o (7-t)

overwrought—common word containing most consecutive letters in the alphabet after letter t (4-t)—common word containing most consecutive letters in the alphabet after letter u (3-t)

ovoid—example of a false antonym beginning with letter o [obovoid]

ovoviviparous—uncommon word containing the most repeats of letter v (3-t)—*producing living young from eggs that hatch within the body*

owe—longest common word containing one type of consonant for consonant w (3-t)

ower—see "blowers"—*one who owes*

owers—see "blowers"

Oxbridge—example of a portmanteau, beginning with letter o [Oxford, Cambridge]—*from Oxford or Cambridge*

oxeae—longest uncommon word containing one type of consonant for consonant x (5-t)—*part of the skeleton of a sponge*

oxygenizable—uncommon word containing most consecutive letters in order after letter x (5)—*able to be combined with oxygen*

oxygeusia—shortest uncommon word containing each vowel (including y) once (9-t)—*abnormal sensitivity to taste*

oxyopia—shortest five-syllable word (7)—*abnormal visual acuity*

oxyphenbutazone—uncommon word with highest single word score in Scrabble (1508)—*anti-inflammatory drug*

oxyuridae—shortest uncommon word containing each vowel (including y) once (9-t)—*pinworms*

oyez—example of a word that ends with silent letter z

P

p—longest common head 'n' tail centered on letter p (1)—longest common palindrome centered on letter p (1)

paeoniaceae—longest uncommon word containing three consonants (11-t)—*European and North American shrubs*

paepae—see "passe-passes"—*native Polynesian building foundation*

palapala—longest uncommon tautonym beginning with letter p (8-t)—*Hawaiian cuneiform writing*

panmnesia—example of a word that contains silent letter m—*remembering everything*

panmyelophthisises—see "hypsistenocephalism"—*diseases of the bone marrow*

panther—longest length three linkade with common words [pan & ant & nth & the & her] (7-t)

pap—longest common head 'n' tail centered on letter a (3-t)—shortest common word that starts and ends with letter p (3-t)

papaya—longest common word containing all letters restricted to squares (6-t)

papered—longest length three linkade with common words [pap & ape & per & ere & red] (7-t)

papiopio—longest uncommon word containing one type of consonant for consonant p (8-t)—*young native of South America*

pappous—longest uncommon lowercase upside-down word pair [snodded] (7-t)—*having bristles*

parables—see "parlays"

paraprofessionals—longest common word spelled with chemical symbols (17)

pares—see "apres"

parlays—longest common well-mixed digital charade pair [parables] (8-t)

parmigiana—example of a word that ends with silent letter a—*with Parmesan cheese*

parsec—example of an acronym that has become uncapitalized, beginning with letter p [PARallax SECond]—oldest common portmanteau word [PARallax SECond, 1913]

parsecs—longest common progressive curtailment [parsecs → parsec → parse → pars → par → pa → p] (7-t)

parsers—longest common progressive curtailment [parsers → parser → parse → pars → par → pa → p] (7-t)

particulate—see "particulates"

particulates—longest common dismembered word [articulates & particulate] (12-t)

pas—see "asp"

passed—longest common lowercase upside-down word (6-t)

passe-passes—longest hyphenated progressive letter subtraction [passe-passes → paepae → papa → aa] (11)—*exceptional moves in juggling*

passers—longest common progressive curtailment [passers → passer → passe → pass → pas → pa → p] (7-t)

passive—example of a false antonym beginning with letter p [impassive]

pastels—longest common progressive curtailment [pastels → pastel → paste → past → pas → pa → p] (7-t)

pasterns—length five linkade with common words [paste & aster & stern & terns] (8)

pat—longest common word that is synonymous with its reversal [pat → tap] (3)

paternalistic—see "antiparticles"

pathematically—see "athematically"—*emotionally*

patting—longest full vowel substitution with common words [petting & pitting & potting & putting] (7)

pavings—see "forebay"—*coverings on the ground*

pawpaw—longest common tautonym beginning with letter p (6)

payday—longest uncommon word containing all letters restricted to squares (6-t)—*day on which pay is distributed*

pdq—shortest uncommon word with last letter next in alphabet after first for letter p (3)—*immediately*

pears—see "apres"

peep—longest common palindrome beginning with letter p (4-t)—longest common palindrome centered on letter e (4-t)

peepe—longest uncommon head 'n' tail centered on letter e (5-t)—*dice spot*

peeweep—longest uncommon palindrome beginning with letter p (7)—longest uncommon palindrome centered on letter w (7)—*bird of Europe, Asia, and northern Africa*

peeweep

penial—example of a word that sounds like letters, beginning with letter p sound [PNEL]—*penile*

pentadactyle—longest uncommon shiftgram pair [precipitants] [shift of 15] (12)—*five-fingered*

pentaerythritol tetranitrate—phrase containing the most repeats of letter t (7)—*high explosive*

people—example of a word that contains silent letter o

pep—longest common head 'n' tail centered on letter e (3)—shortest common word that starts and ends with letter p (3-t)

pepper-upper—hyphenated word containing the most repeats of letter p (5)—*stimulant*

Perak—example of a word that ends with silent letter k—*from a state in Malaysia*

periodicities—see "products"

perpetuity—longest common word with typewriter letters from top row (10-t)

perquisite—common word containing most consecutive letters in the alphabet after letter p (6-t)

perquisition—uncommon word containing most consecutive letters in the alphabet after letter n (8-t)—uncommon word containing most consecutive letters in the alphabet after letter o (7-t)—uncommon word that contains the most consecutive letters in alphabet (8-t)—*legal search*

perry—see "creel"

per second per second—longest tautonym phrase beginning with letter p (18)—longest tautonym for a phrase (18)

peruse—example of a self-antonym, beginning with letter p [examine in detail, look over casually]

petalless—example of uncommon homophonic contranyms [petalless: lacking petals & petalous: having petals]

petalous—see "petalless"

petard—example of a word that exists only in an idiom, beginning with letter p [hoist by one's own petard]

petting—see "patting"

peyote—closest to three million letter product for a common word (3000000)

ph—see "sande"—*acidity*

phenomenal—longest common reversed embedded word [anemone] (7-t)

phenomenally—longest common reversed embedded word [anemone] (7-t)

philadelphia pepper pot—phrase containing the most repeats of letter p (6)—*type of soup*

philistinism—longest common word containing one type of vowel for vowel i (12-t)

phlebitis—longest common word with consecutive letters adjacent on phone keypad beginning with letter p (9)

phleboliths—longest uncommon word with consecutive letters adjacent on phone keypad beginning with letter p (11-t)—*blood clots*

phlegm—example of a word that contains silent letter g

photolithography—common word containing the most repeats of letter h (3-t)

phyllospondylous—longest uncommon word without ETAI (16)—*having backbones like certain extinct amphibia*

physique—common word containing most consecutive letters in order after letter p (2-t)

picturesque—common word containing most consecutive letters in the alphabet after letter p (6-t)

piggyback—common word with the most infrequently used letters for length 9 (296)

pilpulistic—longest uncommon word with consecutive letters adjacent on phone keypad beginning with letter p (11-t)—*hair-splitting*

pioupiou—longest uncommon tautonym beginning with letter p (8-t)—longest uncommon word containing one type of consonant for consonant p (8-t)—*French foot soldier*

pip—longest common palindrome centered on letter i (3-t)—shortest common word that starts and ends with letter p (3-t)

pitching niblicks—longest phrase containing one type of vowel for vowel i (16-t)—*golf clubs*

pitch nodule makers—phrase with the lowest ratio length to number of different letters for length 17 (1.06-t)—*moths*

pitting—see "patting"

pizzazz—uncommon word containing the most repeats of letter z (4-t)—*energy*

plant houses—longest well-mixed isomorse pair for a phrase [plate batteries] (14-t)—*greenhouses*

plaque—common word containing most consecutive letters in order after letter p (2-t)—example of a word that contains silent letter u

plasmoquin—uncommon word containing most consecutive letters in the alphabet after letter l (6-t)—uncommon word containing most consecutive letters in the alphabet after letter m (5-t)—*antimalarial drug*

plasmoquine—uncommon word containing most consecutive letters in the alphabet after letter l (6-t)—uncommon word containing most consecutive letters in the alphabet after letter m (5-t)—*variant of plasmoquin*

plate batteries—see "plant houses"

pleasantness-unpleasantnesses—longest hyphenated word containing five types of consonants (28)—*psychological scales of feelings*

ploughwrights—longest two-syllable word beginning with letter p (13)—*plow repairers*

plunder—longest common word whose pig Latin is also a common word [plunder → underplay] (7)

pneumocystis carinii pneumonias—longest phrase spelled with chemical symbols (29-t)—*pneumonias accompanying deficient immune systems*

pneumonoultramicroscopicsilicovolcanoconiosis—example of a sesquipedalian word [see "Longest Word" article, page 106]—*lung disease caused by volcanic dust [supposedly]*

poldavy—one of two uncommon words that together contain the most different letters [thumbscrewing] (20)—*sail material*

polish—example of a word pronounced differently when capitalized, beginning with letter p [shine, of Poland]

political executives—longest alternating vowels and consonants for a phrase (19-t)

politique—common word containing most consecutive letters in order after letter p (2-t)

polydactyly—common word containing the most repeats of letter y (3-t)

polygyny—common word containing the most repeats of letter y (3-t)

polyhydroxybutyrate—uncommon word containing the most repeats of letter y (4-t)—*chemical in biodegradable plastic*

polymerization—common word containing most consecutive letters in order after letter y (3-t)

polyphony—longest common word with typewriter letters from right hand (9-t)

poop—longest common palindrome beginning with letter p (4-t)—longest common palindrome centered on letter o (4-t)

poor—example of an antonym of two different words, beginning with letter p [wealthy, good]

pop—longest common head 'n' tail centered on letter o (3-t)—shortest common word that starts and ends with letter p (3-t)

possessed—longest nontrivial internal tautonym for a common word (6-t)

possessionlessness—most doubled letters for an uncommon word (4-t)—*utter poverty*

possessionlessnesses—uncommon word containing the most repeats of letter s (9)

possessive—longest sequence of repeated dots in Morse code for a common word (18-t)

possessiveness—common word containing the most repeats of letter s (6-t)—longest sequence of repeated dots in Morse code for a common word (18-t)—common word with the most repeats of any one letter [s] (6-t)

postchlorination—see "neurochemistries"—*after mixing with chlorine*

postscript—longest consonant string for a common word (5-t)

potting—see "patting"

powwow—common word containing the most repeats of letter w (3)

praiser—see "upraisers"—*a person that praises*

prana—see "supranasal"—*Hindu life force*

pratiques—common word containing most consecutive letters in the alphabet after letter p (6-t)

prayer—example of a word that contains silent letter y

preached—longest one-syllable word beginning with letter p (8)

preacknowledgement—longest uncommon changeover [reacknowledgements] (18-t)—see "preacknowledgements"—*acknowledgement before*

preacknowledgements—longest beheadment with an uncommon word [preacknowledgements → reacknowledgements] (19-t)—longest uncommon dismembered word [reacknowledgements & preacknowledgement] (19-t)—longest terminal elision with an uncommon word [preacknowledgements → reacknowledgement] (19-t)

preacquisitive—uncommon word containing most consecutive letters in the alphabet after letter p (7-t)—*before being acquisitive*

precipitants—see "pentadactyle"—*substances that cause precipitation*

precle—example of an uncommon word formed by borrowing or lending letters to frequent companions, beginning with letter p [l'aprecle → la precle]—*plant with rough stem used for cleaning dishes*

preconditioning—longest beheadment with common words [preconditioning → reconditioning] (15)

preempted—longest Morse code reversal pair with common words [intemperate] (11-t)

preflight—common word containing most consecutive letters in order after letter e (4-t)

preparations—longest common dismembered word [reparations & preparation] (12-t)

prepositions—longest common dismembered word [repositions & preposition] (12-t)

prerequisite—common word containing most consecutive letters in order after letter p (2-t)—common word containing most consecutive letters in the alphabet after letter p (6-t)

preserving—longest common shiftgram pair [refractive] [shift of 13] (10)

presser—see "dresser"

prestandardization—see "prestandardizations"—*before standardization*

prestandardizations—longest beheadment with an uncommon word [prestandardizations → restandardizations] (19-t)—longest uncommon dismembered word [restandardizations & prestandardization] (19-t)—longest terminal elision with an uncommon word [prestandardizations → restandardization] (19-t)—*processes that precede standardization*

prestates—longest uncommon progressive beheadment [prestates → restates → estates → states → tates → ates → tes → es → s] (9)—*guarantees*

Rhymes

What one and two syllable English words are hard to rhyme?

In *The Poet's Craft Book*, Clement Wood defines "rhyme" thus:

Rhyme is the identity in sound of an accented vowel in a word, usually the last one accented, and of all consonantal and vowel sounds following it; with a difference in the sound of the consonant immediately preceding the accented vowel.

A few pages later Wood says:

If a poet commences, October is the wildest month, he has estopped himself from any rhyme; since "month" has no rhyme in English.

"Month," "silver," and "orange" are frequently cited as words that cannot be rhymed. But this is not so. Below is a list of rhymes for words, including these three, that are frequently claimed to have no rhymes in English.

Word	Rhyme	Word	Rhyme
beards	weirds	oomph	sumph
carpet	charpit	orange	sporange
else	fels	poem	phloem, proem
fiends	teinds, piends	pregnant	regnant
filched	hilched	purple	curple, hirple
filth	spilth, tilth	puss	schuss
film	pilm	rhythm	smitham
fluxed	luxed, muxed	scalds	balds, caulds, faulds
leashed	niched	silver	chilver
lemon	Bremen, hemen, Yemen	tenth	nth
mouthed	southed	tsetse	baronetcy, intermezzi, theetsee
month	oneth [Note 1], n+1th [Note 2]	tuft	yuft
mulched	gulched	widow	kiddo
oblige	cytopyge	window	indo, lindo

Note 1: Justified by analogy with "thousandth," "hundredth," "tenth."

Note 2: Justified by analogy with "nth." A citation: "The Nature of Rationality," Robert Nozick, Princeton University Press, Princeton, NJ, 1993, p. 21

presumptively—see "harlequin opal"

presumptuously—common word with highest letter sum for length 14 (241)

pretty-prettier—longest hyphenated word with typewriter letters from top row (14)—*more gaudy*

pretty-pretty—longest hyphenated tautonym beginning with letter p (12)—*gaudy*

primer—see "primmer"

primmer—example of homophones differing by letter m [primer]—*more dainty*

primogenitureship—longest uncommon word that starts and ends with letter p (17)—*being the sole inheritor*

prissy—example of a portmanteau, beginning with letter p [prim, sissy]

procrastination—longest well-mixed subtransposition with common words [anachronistically] (17)

products—longest well-mixed common words with the same consonant order [periodicities] (13)

proficient—example of a word spelled with i before e after c, beginning with letter p

promorphology—longest uncommon word without ETAINS (13-t)—*study of embryo development*

promptscripts—longest uncommon word containing two vowels (13-t)—*scripts with stage direction*

propinquities—uncommon word containing most consecutive letters in the alphabet after letter n (8-t)—uncommon word containing most consecutive letters in the alphabet after letter o (7-t)—uncommon word that contains the most consecutive letters in alphabet (8-t)—*degrees of kinship*

propinquity—common word containing most consecutive letters in the alphabet after letter n (5-t)—common word containing most consecutive letters in the alphabet after letter o (4-t)

proprietor—longest common word with typewriter letters from top row (10-t)

proprietorship—longest common word that starts and ends with letter p (14)

proso—see "prosodiacally"—*Eurasian grass raised for its feed grain*

prosodi—see "prosodiacally"—*breathing tube in a sponge*

prosodiac—see "prosodiacally"—*relating to meter in verse*

prosodiacal—see "prosodiacally"—*relating to meter in verse*

prosodiacally—longest uncommon double progressive curtailment [prosodiacally → prosodiacal → prosodiac → prosodi → proso → pro → p] (13-t)—*rhythmically*

prostitution—common word containing most consecutive letters in order after letter r (4-t)

protein—example of a word spelled with e before i, beginning with letter p

protocorm theory—longest phrase with typewriter letters from alternating hands (15-t)—*botanical theory*

psalter—example of homophones differing by letter p [salter]—*collection of psalms*

pseudolamellibranchiata—uncommon word with the lowest ratio length to number of different letters for length 23 (1.43-t)—most different letters for an uncommon word (16-t)—*bivalve mollusks*

pseudolamellibranchiatas—uncommon word with the lowest ratio length to number of different letters for length 24 (1.50-t)

pseudolamellibranchiate—uncommon word with the lowest ratio length to number of different letters for length 23 (1.43-t)—*variant of pseudolamellibranchiata*

pseudomonocotyledonous—uncommon word containing the most repeats of letter o (6-t)—*loss of one of the first leaves during development*

pseudosaccharomycetaceae—see "reithrodontomyses"—*yeastlike fungi*

psi—example of a word that is a confusing code for letter p [sigh]

psyche—example of a word that begins with silent letter p

psychiatrists—see "astrophysicist"

psychoanalyzing—common word with highest single word score in Scrabble (1427)

psychogalvanometric—uncommon word with the lowest ratio length to number of different letters for length 19 (1.18-t)—*detecting lies*

psychologically—common word with the most infrequently used letters for length 15 (701)

ptolemaists—longest uncommon word with consecutive letters adjacent on phone keypad beginning with letter p (11-t)—*followers of Ptolemy*

pu—see "sputterers"—*Scottish for pull*

public works and ways system—phrase with the lowest ratio length to number of different letters for length 24 (1.33-t)

public works and ways systems—phrase with the lowest ratio length to number of different letters for length 25 (1.38)

puerer—see "sputterers"—*tannery worker*

pulik—example of a plural that ends with letter k—*Hungarian sheepdog*

pulik

pulmobranchiates—uncommon word with the lowest ratio length to number of different letters for length 16 (1.06-t)—*air-breathing organs*

pulquerias—uncommon word containing most consecutive letters in order after letter p (4-t)—*shops that sell Mexican alcoholic drinks*

punch—see "baron"

pungapung—longest uncommon head 'n' tail centered on letter a (9-t)—*Asian potato*

pup—longest common palindrome centered on letter u (3-t)—shortest common word that starts and ends with letter p (3-t)

pupae—longest common word containing one type of consonant for consonant p (5)

purpura—see "chechen"—*blood diseases causing bruises*

purview—common word containing most consecutive letters in order after letter u (3)—common word containing most consecutive letters in the alphabet after letter u (3-t)

put an ape in someone's hood—see "adenosine monophosphate"—*make a fool of someone*

putterer—see "sputterers"—*person who works aimlessly*

putting—see "patting"

puttyroots—uncommon word with highest letter sum for length 10 (189)—*North American orchids*

Q

q—longest common head 'n' tail centered on letter q (1)—longest common palindrome beginning with letter q (1)—longest common palindrome centered on letter q (1)

qaraqalpaq—uncommon word containing the most repeats of letter q (3)—example of a plural that ends with letter q—longest uncommon word that starts and ends with letter q (10)—*from near Lake Aral, Central Asia*

Qatar—example of a word that is a confusing code for letter q [gutter]—*from an Arab country*

qazaq—longest uncommon palindrome beginning with letter q (5)—longest uncommon palindrome centered on letter z (5-t)—shortest uncommon word that starts and ends with letter q (5)—*Caucasian rug*

QT—example of a word that exists only in an idiom, beginning with letter q [on the QT]—*quiet*

qts—longest common word containing all consonants (3-t)—*quarts*

quadraphonic—common word containing most consecutive letters in the alphabet after letter n (5-t)—common word containing most consecutive letters in the alphabet after letter o (4-t)

quadruplets—common word containing most consecutive letters in the alphabet after letter p (6-t)

quaff—longest common word containing letters in order from typewriter (5-t)

quango—example of an acronym that has become uncapitalized, beginning with letter q [QUAsi-Non Governmental Organization]

quarter-wave plates—hyphenated phrase containing most consecutive letters in the alphabet after letter p (8)—*filters that rotate polarized light one-fourth cycle*

quarts—highest ratio of consecutive alphabetic letters to length for a common word (0.83-t)

quash—longest common word containing letters in order from typewriter (5-t)

quasi-complimentary—hyphenated word containing most consecutive letters in the alphabet after letter l (10)—hyphenated word containing most consecutive letters in the alphabet after letter m (9-t)—hyphenated word that contains the most consecutive letters in alphabet (10)

quasi-important—hyphenated word containing most consecutive letters in the alphabet after letter m (9-t)

quasi-interviewed—hyphenated word containing most consecutive letters in the alphabet after letter q (7)

quasi-productive—hyphenated word containing most consecutive letters in the alphabet after letter o (8-t)

quasi-provocative—hyphenated word containing most consecutive letters in the alphabet after letter o (8-t)

queer—shortest common word with last letter next in alphabet after first for letter q (5)

quenched—longest one-syllable word beginning with letter q (8)—*satisfied thirst*

quest—example of a false antonym beginning with letter q [inquest]

questionaire—longest common word containing five consonants (12-t)

queue—highest ratio vowels to consonants for a common word (4-t)—longest common word containing one consonant (5-t)—longest common word containing one type of consonant for consonant q (5)

queueing—longest vowel string for a common word (5)

quiaquia—longest uncommon word containing one type of consonant for consonant q (8)—longest uncommon word with no contiguous subsequence that is a word (8)—*cigarfish*

quiche—example of a word pronounced differently when capitalized, beginning with letter q [egg pie, department in Guatemala]

quicken—example of an antonym of three different words, beginning with letter q [slacken, arrest, deaden]

quickthorns—longest two-syllable word beginning with letter q (11)—*European trees*

quiddity—example of a self-antonym, beginning with letter q [an inessential feature, the essence]

quiddle—example of a portmanteau, beginning with letter q [quiddity, fiddle]—*trifle*

quiescencies—example of a word spelled with i before e after c, beginning with letter q—*tranquillities*

quill—longest common word containing letters in order from typewriter (5-t)

quinaquina—longest uncommon tautonym beginning with letter q (10)—*quinine tree*

quips—longest common word containing letters in order from typewriter (5-t)

quisqueite—example of a word spelled with e before i, beginning with letter q—*naturally occurring mixture of sulfur and carbon*

quizzically—common word with the most infrequently used letters for length 11 (396)

qwerty—uncommon word that is part of a pangram using the fewest words [flax & buckjumping & vozhds] (26 in 27)—*common keyboard layout*

qwertys—longest uncommon word containing letters in order from typewriter (7-t)

R

racecar—longest uncommon palindrome centered on letter e (7-t)—*racing car*

radar—example of an acronym that has become uncapitalized, beginning with letter r [RAdio Detection And Ranging]

radiobroadcaster—longest uncommon word that starts and ends with letter r (16-t)

rainier—example of a word pronounced differently when capitalized, beginning with letter r [more rainy, U.S. mountain]

rain in—see "strainings"—*rain through a roof*

raining—closest to two million letter product for a common word (2000376-t)

rais—see "upraisers"—*Muslim leader*

raise—example of common homophonic contranyms [raise: erect & raze: tear down]

rakishly—longest common isomorse pair, measured in number of dots and dashes [aimlessly] (25)

ranas—see "supranasal"—*Hindu princes*

rangiest—see "angriest"—*lankiest*

ranties—see "anestri"—*small complaints*

rapes—see "apres"

rapport—example of a word that ends with silent letter t

raring—example of a word that exists only in an idiom, beginning with letter r [raring to go]

rasa—see "aras"—*Indian dance*

ratification—see "gratifications"

ratines—see "anestri"—*type of fabric*

ratiocinations—see "coadministrations"—*logical reasonings*

ravel—example of a false antonym beginning with letter r [unravel]—example of a self-antonym, beginning with letter r [entangle, disentangle]

ravine—longest common fixed offset shift pair that are reversals [ravine] [shift of 13] (6-t)—

longest common rot-13 pair that are reversals [ravine] (6)

raze—see "raise"

razz—longest common word with no subsequence that is a word (4-t)—shortest common word that cannot have a letter added and transposed to form another word (4-t)—shortest stingy and hostile common word (4-t)

razzamatazz—uncommon word containing the most repeats of letter z (4-t)—*double-talk*

reached—longest one-syllable word beginning with letter r (7)

reacknowledgement—see "preacknowledgements"

reacknowledgements—see "preacknowledgement" and "preacknowledgements"

re—see "rey"

readership—most letters in alphabetical place without shifting alphabet for a common word (4-t)

reafforesting—longest uncommon double progressive beheadment [reafforesting → afforesting → foresting → resting → sting → ing → g] (13-t)—*restoring a forest*

rear—shortest common word that starts and ends with letter r (4-t)

reassurances—longest common word spelled with short lowercase letters (12-t)

reasting—see "angriest"—*going rancid*

reckless—example of common homophonic contranyms [reckless: careless & wreckless: careful]

recognizability—common word containing most consecutive letters in the alphabet after letter y (5-t)

recognizable—common word containing most consecutive letters in order after letter z (3-t)

recognizably—common word containing most consecutive letters in the alphabet after letter y (5-t)

recognizing—longest nontrivial internal palindrome for a common word (7-t)

reconditioning—see "preconditioning"

reconstruction—common word containing most consecutive letters in order after letter r (4-t)

reconstructive—uncommon word containing most consecutive letters in order after letter r (5-t)—*restoring to good condition*

rectification—see "certification"

redder—longest common palindrome centered on letter d (6)

redistribute—common word containing most consecutive letters in order after letter r (4-t)

redistributive—uncommon word containing most consecutive letters in order after letter r (5-t)—*taking from some and giving to others*

redrawn—longest common backswitch [warders] (7-t)

redroots—see "stop order"—*North American flower with medicinal uses*

red rot—see "stop order"—*fungal disease of plants*

refractive—see "preserving"

refragmentations—see "antiferromagnets"

refreshing—common word containing most consecutive letters in the alphabet after letter e (5-t)

refrigerator—common word containing the most repeats of letter r (4-t)—longest common word that starts and ends with letter r (12-t)

refrigerator-freezer—hyphenated word containing the most repeats of letter r (6-t)—longest hyphenated word that starts and ends with letter r (19)

regatta—longest common switchback [wattage] (7-t)

rehabilitative—longest alternating vowels and consonants for a common word (14-t)

rehousing—see "rewarehousing"—*moving to a different house*

reign—example of homophones differing by letter g [rein]

reimbursing—longest uncommon well-mixed isotel pair [reincurring] (11-t)

rein—see "reign"

reincurring—see "reimbursing"

reindustrializer—longest uncommon word that starts and ends with letter r (16-t)

reiterate—common word with the most frequently used letters for length 9 (808)

reithrodontomyses—longest well-mixed sub-transposition with an uncommon word [pseudosaccharomycetaceae] (24)—*American harvest mice*

reliant—see "nailers"

renamed—see "demander"

rendezvous—example of a word that contains silent letter z

renointestinal—see "internationalised"—*of the kidneys and intestines*

renunciation—see "enunciation"

reparations—see "preparations"

repertoire—longest common word with typewriter letters from top row (10-t)

repositions—see "prepositions"

representativeness—common word containing the most repeats of letter e (5-t)

repressiveness—see "expressiveness"

reseeded—longest common word with typewriter letters from adjacent keys (8-t)

resiant—see "anestri"—*resident*

respond—common word with most consecutive alphabetic letters in reverse order consecutively (3-t)

response—common word with most consecutive alphabetic letters in reverse order consecutively (3-t)

responsible—common word with most consecutive alphabetic letters in reverse order consecutively (3-t)

restain—see "anestri"—*stain again*

restandardization—see "prestandardizations"

restandardizations—see "prestandardizations"

restarters—longest uncommon progressive letter subtraction [restarters → estates → stats → tat → a] (10-t)

restaurant—common word containing most consecutive letters in order after letter r (4-t)

restaurateur—longest common word that starts and ends with letter r (12-t)

retains—see "anestri"

reticulatoramoses—longest alternating vowels and consonants for an uncommon word (17-t)—*networked branches*

reticulatovenoses—longest alternating vowels and consonants for an uncommon word (17-t)—*networked veins*

retinas—see "anestri"

retsina—see "anestri"—*Greek wine*

reveille—example of a word spelled with e before i, beginning with letter r

rever—see "reversionally"—*lapel*

reverberated—longest common word with typewriter letters from left hand (12-t)

reverse-current circuit breaker—hyphenated phrase containing the most repeats of letter r (7)—*circuit breaker that trips when the voltage is reversed*

reversi—see "reversionally"—*card game*

reversional—see "reversionally"—*relating to the return of property to its original owner*

reversionally—longest uncommon double progressive curtailment [reversionally → reversional → reversion → reversi → rever → rev → r] (13-t)—*in a manner similar to the return of property to its original owner*

review—common word containing most consecutive letters in order after letter v (2-t)

reviled—see "delivers" and "delivery"

reviver—longest uncommon palindrome centered on letter i (7-t)—*stimulant*

revolutionists—longest terminal elision with common words [revolutionists → evolutionist] (14-t)—see "evolutionists"

rewarehousing—longest uncommon double progressive beheadment [rewarehousing → warehousing → rehousing → housing → using → ing → g] (13-t)—*moving to a different warehouse*

rewarewa—longest uncommon tautonym beginning with letter r (8-t)—*New Zealand tree*

rey—example of homophones differing by letter y [re]—*king*

rhadamanthus—longest uncommon word with consecutive letters adjacent on phone keypad beginning with letter r (12)—*strict judge*

rhombporphyry—longest uncommon word without ETAINS (13-t)—*igneous rock*

rhythms—longest common word containing one type of vowel for vowel y (7)

ri—see "stereophotogrammetric"—*Japanese unit of distance*

rice christian—longest phrase with consecutive letters adjacent on phone keypad beginning with letter r (13)—*hypocritical convert*

riffing—see "griffin"

riffraff—common word containing the most repeats of letter f (4)

right-about-faced—hyphenated word containing most consecutive letters in the alphabet after letter a (9)—hyphenated word containing most consecutive letters in the alphabet after letter b (8)—*turned around*

rijksdaalder—uncommon word containing most consecutive letters in order after letter i (4)—*old Dutch dollar*

rijsttafel—example of a word that contains silent letter j—*Indonesian midday meal*

ringing—longest nontrivial internal tautonym for a common word (6-t)

riroriro—longest uncommon tautonym beginning with letter r (8-t)—longest uncommon word containing one type of consonant for consonant r (8)—*New Zealand bird*

rise—example of an antonym of three different words, beginning with letter r [fall, sit, retire]

risible—longest common word with consecutive letters adjacent on phone keypad beginning with letter r (7-t)

risotto—see "coadministrations"—*Italian rice meal*

river-driver—longest hyphenated head 'n' tail centered on letter d (11)—*person who floats logs down river*

ro—see "romanisers"—*artificial language*

roar—shortest common word that starts and ends with letter r (4-t)

rocky mountain flowering raspberry—most different letters for a phrase (19-t)

roll—see "list"

roman à clef—example of a word that ends with silent letter f—*supposedly fictional novel about real people*

rom—see "romanisers"—*male gypsy*

roma—see "romanisers"—*plural of rom*

romani—see "romanisers"—*gypsy*

romanis—see "romanisers"

romanise—see "romanisers"—*to make Roman*

romaniser—see "romanisers"—*one who makes things Roman*

romanisers—longest uncommon progressive curtailment [romanisers → romaniser → romanise → romanis → romani → roman → roma → rom → ro → r] (10)

romanticisation—see "coadministrations"—*indulging in sentiment*

ros—see "charoseth"

rotatively—see "levitators"—*turning*

rotator—longest common palindrome beginning with letter r (7)—longest common palindrome centered on letter a (7)—longest palindrome for a common word (7-t)

rotavator—longest uncommon palindrome beginning with letter r (9)—longest uncommon palindrome centered on letter v (9)—*soil-tilling machine*   **rotavator**

rotor—longest common palindrome centered on letter t (5)

rottens—see "internationalised"—*rats*

roughstrings—longest two-syllable word beginning with letter r (12)—*parts of a wooden stairway*

rous—see "carousers"—*bird virus*

rouse—example of a common word formed by borrowing or lending letters to frequent companions, beginning with letter r [drink carouse → drink a rouse]

roxbury waxworks—phrase with the most infrequently used letters for length 15 (605)—*North American vines*

rs—shortest common word with last letter next in alphabet after first for letter r (2)

rubefacient—example of a word spelled with i before e after c, beginning with letter r—*ointment that reddens the skin*

ruckus—example of a portmanteau, beginning with letter r [ruction, rumpus]

ruling—closest to four million letter product for a common word (4000752-t)

rundown—longest common word with consecutive letters adjacent on phone keypad beginning with letter r (7-t)

run with the hare and hunt with the hounds—phrase containing the most repeats of letter h (7-t)—*have it both ways*

rupiahs—longest common word with consecutive letters adjacent on phone keypad beginning with letter r (7-t)

rural—see "didst"

Rzeszow—example of a word that begins with silent letter r—*from a Polish commune*

Repeated Words in a Sentence

What is a sentence with the same word repeated several times?

There is a common misconception that surrounds this problem, namely, that the following sentence has the word "had" seven times in a row: Jill, where Jack had had "had," had had "had had."

The misconception lies in not recognizing the difference between using a word and mentioning a word. When a word is used in a sentence, it is not quoted; when it is mentioned, it is quoted. The quoted word "'had'" is not the same as the unquoted word "had." Therefore, this sentence has no more than two repeats of any word.

The most satisfying case of repeated words occurs when the repeated words all mean different things in the sentence. An example of unsatisfactory repetition is intensifying an adjective or adverb by simply repeating it over and over:

The coffee was very very very very very ... very hot.

Even though the word "very" occurs arbitrarily many times, it means the same in each case. A sentence can be constructed that has a noun repeated arbitrarily many times, followed by a verb repeated the same number of times:

1. Bulldogs fight
2. Bulldogs bulldogs fight fight. (i.e., Bulldogs (that) bulldogs fight, (themselves) fight.)
3. Bulldogs bulldogs bulldogs fight fight fight. (i.e., Bulldogs (that) bulldogs (that) bulldogs fight, (themselves) fight, (themselves) fight.) ...

The inflation of this type of sentence can be accelerated by the use of the three senses of the word "buffalo":

1. oxen (noun)
2. baffle (verb)
3. from a city in Western New York (adjective, usually capitalized)

The progression becomes:

1. Buffalo buffalo buffalo. (i.e., Buffalo (from the city of) Buffalo baffle.)
2. Buffalo buffalo Buffalo buffalo buffalo buffalo. (i.e., Buffalo (from the city of) Buffalo (that) buffalo (from the city of) Buffalo baffle, (themselves) baffle.)
3. Buffalo buffalo Buffalo buffalo Buffalo buffalo buffalo buffalo buffalo. (i.e., Buffalo (from the city of) Buffalo (that) Buffalo (from the city of) Buffalo (that) Buffalo (from the city of) Buffalo baffle, (themselves) baffle, (themselves) baffle.) ...

This sentence will have an adjective-noun pair repeated arbitrarily many times, then a verb repeated the same number of times. So the word "buffalo" really only has three meanings in the sentence.

A progression using the pronoun, conjunction, and adjective meanings of the word "that" was composed by George Herbert Moberly in the 1850s.

1. I saw that C saw. (i.e., I saw the following: C saw.)
2. C saw that that I saw. (i.e., C saw the thing which I saw.)
3. I saw that that that C saw was so. (i.e., I saw the following: the thing which C saw was so.)
4. C saw that, that that that I saw was so. (i.e., C saw this fact, the following: the thing which I saw was so.)
5. I saw that, that that that that C saw was so. (i.e., I saw this fact, the following: the specific thing which C saw was so.)
6. C saw that that, that that that that I saw was so. (i.e., C saw the specific thing, the following: the specific thing which I saw was so.)
7. I saw that that, that that that that that C saw was so. (i.e., I saw the specific fact, the following: the specific thing which the specific C saw was so.)

In the final statement, the first, fourth and seventh occurrences of "that" are adjectives meaning "specific," the second and fifth are pronouns, and the third and sixth are conjunctions.

Thus there are seven uses but only three meanings.

Here is an example with five occurrences of "had" in a row, each with a different meaning. This is the longest known case of this phenomenon. As an aid to understanding, we'll build it up a step at a time.

The parents were unable to conceive, so they hired someone else to be a surrogate.

The parents had had a surrogate have their child.

The parents had had their child had.

The child had had no breakfast.

The child the parents had had had had had no breakfast.

S

s—longest common palindrome centered on letter s (1)

Saar—example of a word that is a confusing code for letter s [czar]—*from a river between France and Germany*

sagas—longest common palindrome beginning with letter s (5-t)—longest common palindrome centered on letter g (5)

said—example of a word pronounced differently when capitalized, beginning with letter s [spoke, Middle Eastern port]

salades—longest uncommon lowercase upside-down word pair [sapeles] (7-t)—*medieval helmet*

salet—see "atles"—*Medieval helmet*

salsa—longest common head 'n' tail centered on letter l (5)

salter—see "psalter"

samia—see "animates"—*silkworm moths*

sammas—longest uncommon palindrome centered on letter m (6)—*early Indian people*

sande—longest uncommon progressive sum pair [sande → tori → iga → ph → x] (5-t)—*African custom of training girls*

sangfroid—example of a word that ends with silent letter d—*imperturbability*

sank—longest common progressive sum pair [sank → toy → in → w] (4-t)

sapeles—see "salades"—*types of mahogany*

sapphire—example of a word that contains silent letter p

sara—see "aras"—*people of central Africa*

Saracen—see "ceresin"—*nomadic people of the Arabian desert*

sat—shortest common word with last letter next in alphabet after first for letter s (3-t)

satraps—see "snap traps"—*ancient Persian governors*

sawbwas—longest uncommon palindrome beginning with letter s (7-t)—longest uncommon palindrome centered on letter b (7)—*Burmese rulers*

scent—example of homophones differing by letter c [sent]—example of homophones differing by letter s [cent]

schadenfreude—uncommon word containing most consecutive letters in order after letter c (4-t)—*gloating*

schoolbooks—longest common word containing one type of vowel for vowel o (11-t)

schoolrooms—longest common word containing one type of vowel for vowel o (11-t)

schwartzbrots—longest uncommon word containing two vowels (13-t)—*black bread*

scintillescent—longest uncommon pair isogram (14)—*twinkling*

scissel—uncommon homophone that has most letters in list of homophones with no removable prefix or suffix [scissile & sicel & sisal & sisel & sissle & syssel] (42)—*metal scrap*

scissile—see "scissel"—*easily cut*

scratchbrushed—longest two-syllable word beginning with letter s (14)—*brushed with a wire brush* scribe—example of a false antonym beginning with letter s [inscribe]

scrupulously—longest common word without ETAIN (12)

scuba—example of an acronym that has become uncapitalized, beginning with letter s [Self-Contained Underwater Breathing Apparatus]

scuttlebutt—common word containing the most repeats of letter t (4-t)

'se—see "amusers"—shall

seat ring—see "angriest"—ring that forms the seal of a valve

seats—longest common charitable [eats & sats & sets & seas & seat] (5-t)

second banana—longest iskot pair for a phrase [once upon a time] (13)—longest phrase iskot pair measured in number of dots and dashes [once upon a time] (30)—second in rank

secularized—see "funiculars"

seed—example of a self-antonym, beginning with letter s [remove the seeds, distribute the seeds]

seedees—longest uncommon palindrome beginning with letter s (7-t)—longest uncommon palindrome centered on letter d (7-t)—respected African Muslims

sees—longest common palindrome centered on letter e (4-t)

seesees—longest uncommon palindrome centered on letter s (7)—Asiatic partridge

seities—longest uncommon palindrome centered on letter t (7)—individualities

seize—example of a word spelled with e before i, beginning with letter s

selfless—longest nontrivial internal palindrome for a common word (7-t)

self-naughting—hyphenated word containing most consecutive letters in order after letter e (5)—self-effacing

sememes—longest uncommon palindrome centered on letter e (7-t)—meaning of a linguistic unit

semnopitheque—uncommon word containing most consecutive letters in order after letter m (5)—uncommon word containing most consecutive letters in order after letter n (4-t)—Asiatic long-tailed monkey

semnopitheque

sense—longest common head 'n' tail centered on letter n (5)

senselessness—common word containing the most repeats of letter s (6-t)—highest ratio length to letters for a common non-tautonym (3.25)—highest ratio length to letters for a common word (3.25)—common word with the most repeats of any one letter [s] (6-t)

senselessnesses—highest ratio length to letters for an uncommon non-tautonym (3.75)—inanities

sensuousness—longest nontrivial internal palindrome for an uncommon word (11-t)—sensuous feeling

sensuousnesses—longest uncommon word containing two types of consonants (14-t)

sent—see "scent"

sente—example of an uncommon word in which adding letters to beginning makes it plural [sente → lisente]—monetary unit of Lesotho

sephardics—longest well-mixed uncommon words with the same consonant order [sphaerioidaceaes] (16-t)—Hebrew dialect

sequoia—longest common word containing two consonants (7-t)—shortest common word containing each vowel once (7)

ser—see "amusers"—Indian unit of weight

sers—see "amusers"

servomotor—longest sequence of repeated dashes in Morse code for a common word (13)

sestettes—longest uncommon trio isogram (9)—musical compositions

set—shortest common word with last letter next in alphabet after first for letter s (3-t)

setal—see "atles"—bristly

settee—common word with the most frequently used letters for length 6 (602)

settlednesses—see "shiverings"

sexes—longest common palindrome beginning with letter s (5-t)—longest common palindrome centered on letter x (5)

sexual reproduction—see "asexual reproductions"

shakalshas—longest uncommon word with typewriter letters from middle row (10)—*ancient colonizers of Sicily*

shantytown—longest common word with consecutive letters adjacent on phone keypad beginning with letter s (10)

shebang—example of a word that exists only in an idiom, beginning with letter s [the whole shebang]

shiverings—longest Morse code reversal pair with an uncommon word [settlednesses] (13)

shoals—see "lethal"

shofar—uncommon homophones that have the fewest letters in common for their combined length [shofar → chauffeur] (3 out of 15)

shoot—longest common charitable [hoot & soot & shot & shot & shoo] (5-t)

show—longest common progressive sum pair [show → awl → xi → g] (4-t)

shush—longest common head 'n' tail centered on letter u (5)

shyly—see "eldest"

sicel—see "scissel"—*ancient Sicilians*

sid—see "thanatopsides"—*husk*

signature loans—see "hand gallops"—*loans without collateral*

silence cloths—longest phrase with consecutive letters adjacent on phone keypad beginning with letter s (13)—*pads under tablecloths*

silicicolous—longest uncommon word with consecutive letters adjacent on phone keypad beginning with letter s (12-t)—*thriving on silicon-rich soil*

simplification—see "discriminative"

singers—longest common progressive curtailment [singers → singer → singe → sing → sin → si → s] (7-t)

singing—longest nontrivial internal tautonym for a common word (6-t)

sinon—see "nonis"—*betrayer*

sins—see "dotty"

sirenic—see "cinerins"—*alluring*

sirree—longest common word containing letters in reverse order from typewriter (6-t)

sis—longest common palindrome centered on letter i (3-t)—shortest common word that starts and ends with letter s (3)

sisal—see "scissel"

sisel—see "scissel"—*Eurasian squirrel*

sissies—longest common word with Morse code that is entirely dots (7)

sissle—see "scissel"—*sizzle*

sit—shortest common word with last letter next in alphabet after first for letter s (3-t)

sizable—common word containing most consecutive letters in order after letter z (3-t)

sizeable—common word containing most consecutive letters in order after letter z (3-t)

sketchpad—see "jumbling"—*drawing pad*

skillfully—common word containing the most repeats of letter l (4-t)

skullduggery—common word with the most infrequently used letters for length 12 (493)

slashes—longest common progressive beheadment [slashes → lashes → ashes → shes → hes → es → s] (7-t)

slate—see "atles"

sleeveless—longest common pyramid word (10)

sleyb—example of a plural that ends with letter b—*nomadic Arab*

slope—example of a common word formed by borrowing or lending letters to frequent companions, beginning with letter s [aslope → a slope]

sma—see "animates"—*Scottish for small*

smashes—longest common progressive beheadment [smashes → mashes → ashes → shes → hes → es → s] (7-t)

smatterings—longest letter subtraction with common words [smatterings → mattering] (11-t)

smog—example of a portmanteau, beginning with letter s [smoke, fog]

snap traps—longest phrase progressive delete-reverse [snap traps → spartans → satraps → sparts → strap → part → tap → pa → a] (9-t)—*traps that snap shut*

sniffed—longest common word with letters in reverse alphabetical order when allowing repeats (7-t)

snodded—see "pappous"—*neatened*

soccos—longest uncommon palindrome centered on letter c (6-t)—*Eastern Orthodox vestment*

soccos

soft—example of an antonym of three different words, beginning with letter s [loud, rough, harsh]

softly-softly—longest hyphenated tautonym beginning with letter s (12)—*carefully*

soiree—longest common word containing letters in reverse order from typewriter (6-t)

sollerets—see "listerelloses" and "listerellosis"—*foot armor*

solos—longest common palindrome beginning with letter s (5-t)—longest common palindrome centered on letter l (5)

son—see "nos"

sons-in-law—example of a plural that ends with letter w

sooloos—longest uncommon palindrome centered on letter l (7)—longest uncommon lowercase upside-down word (7)—*natives of New Guinea*

sophist—common word with most consecutive runs of consecutive alphabetic letters (3-t)

sortition—see "coadministrations"—*drawing lots*

sot—shortest common word with last letter next in alphabet after first for letter s (3-t)

sour gourds—longest phrase where each letter is three symbols in Morse code (10)—*Australian trees*

sous-souses—longest hyphenated word containing one type of consonant for consonant s (10)—*ballet jumps*

spa—see "asp"

spaceflight—common word containing most consecutive letters in order after letter e (4-t)

spacers—longest common progressive delete-reverse [spacers → recaps → space → caps → spa → as → s] (7-t)

spare—see "apres"

spartans—see "snap traps"—*things that are similar to those of ancient Sparta*

sparts—see "snap traps"—*grasses grown in Spain and northern Africa used for making brooms*

spear—see "apres"

specials—longest common Morse code reversal pair, measured in number of dots and dashes [halftimes] (23)

species—example of a word spelled with i before e after c, beginning with letter s

spectroheliokinematograph—uncommon word with the lowest ratio length to number of different letters for length 25 (1.66)—*camera to record the sun's features in motion*

spectrophotometers—longest common word containing two types of vowels (18)

speechlessness—longest common word containing one type of vowel for vowel e (14)

speltz—see "waqf"—*type of wheat*

spendthrifts—longest common word with a phonetic spelling identical to its regular spelling (12)—*big spenders*

sphaerioidaceaes—see "sephardics"

spilled—see "ellipse"

spoofed—longest common word with letters in reverse alphabetical order when allowing repeats (7-t)

spooked—longest common word with letters in reverse alphabetical order when allowing repeats (7-t)

spooled—longest common word with letters in reverse alphabetical order when allowing repeats (7-t)

spoon—longest common progressive difference pair [spoon → caza → bay → ab → y] (5-t)

spoonfed—longest uncommon word with letters in reverse alphabetical order when allowing repeats (8-t)

spoon-feed—longest hyphenated word with letters in reverse alphabetical order when allowing repeats (9)

sportsmanlike—common word containing most consecutive letters in the alphabet after letter k (6-t)

sportswriters—common word with highest letter sum for length 13 (219)

sputterers—longest uncommon progressive letter subtraction [sputterers → putterer → puerer → purr → pu] (10-t)—*people who sputter*

squirrelled—longest one-syllable word beginning with letter s (11)—*stored up for future use*

squirt—highest ratio of consecutive alphabetic letters to length for a common word (0.83-t)

ss—shortest uncommon word that starts and ends with letter s (2)

SSs—shortest phrase with a tripled letter (3)—*Nazi Schutzstaffels*

st—shortest uncommon word with last letter next in alphabet after first for letter s (2)—*hush*

stabbing—see "staving"

stainer—see "anestri"—*one that stains*

stale—see "atles"

stamina—see "animates"

starnie—see "anestri"—*small star*

stats—longest common palindrome beginning with letter s (5-t)

statuette—common word containing the most repeats of letter t (4-t)

statutory trust—phrase with highest letter sum for length 14 (257)—*protecting organization created by statute*

statutory trusts—phrase with highest letter sum for length 15 (276)

staving—longest common well-mixed digital charade pair [stabbing] (8-t)

steal—see "atles"

stearin—see "anestri"—*chemical contained in fat*

stearing—see "angriest"—*steering*

steeds—longest fixed offset shift pair with common words [tuffet] [shift of 1] (6-t)

stela—see "atles"—*obelisk*

stent nets—longest palindrome beginning with letter s (9)—longest palindrome centered on letter t (9)—*river-fishing net*

stereophotogrammetric—longest uncommon reverse snowball [stereo & photo & gram & met & ri & c] (21-t)—*measured using stereo photographs*

sterilize—see "listerize"

stewardesses—longest common word with typewriter letters from left hand (12-t)

stoners—longest common alternating terminal elision [stoners → stoner → toner → tone → one → on → n] (7-t)

stop order—longest phrase progressive delete-reverse [stop order → redroots → to order → red rot → order → redo → ode → ed → d] (9-t)—*order to a broker*

straightforwardness—highest consonants minus vowels for a common word (9)—longest common word that starts and ends with letter s (19)—longest common word that starts and ends with the same letter (19)

straightjacket—common word containing most consecutive letters in order after letter i (3-t)—

common word containing most consecutive letters in the alphabet after letter g (5-t)—common word containing most consecutive letters in the alphabet after letter h (4-t)

strainings—longest phrase progressive terminal elision [strainings → training → rain in → aini → in] (10)—*overexertions*

straitjacket—common word containing most consecutive letters in order after letter i (3-t)

strawberry-raspberry—hyphenated word containing the most repeats of letter r (6-t)—*Japanese plant*

strengthens—longest common word containing two vowels (11-t)

strengthlessness—highest consonants minus vowels for an uncommon word (10-t)—longest uncommon word containing three vowels (16)

strengthlessnesses—longest uncommon word containing one type of vowel for vowel e (18)

strengths—highest ratio consonants to vowels for a common word (8)—longest common word containing one vowel (9)

stressed—see "desserts"

strongholds—longest common word containing one type of vowel for vowel o (11-t)—longest common word containing two vowels (11-t)

strongylocentrotus—longest well-mixed uncommon words with same letter sum [floccinaucinihilipilification] (29)—*type of sea urchin*

stroot—see "coadministrations"—*variant of strut*

struldbrugs—longest uncommon word containing one type of vowel for vowel u (11)—*elderly people living at state expense*

stylistician—longest uncommon word with consecutive letters adjacent on phone keypad beginning with letter s (12-t)—*hairdresser*

stylization—common word containing most consecutive letters in order after letter y (3-t)

subcommittee—most doubled letters for a common word (3-t)

subcontinental—longest common word containing each vowel once (14-t)—longest and short-

est common word containing each vowel once in reverse order (14)

subpostmastership—longest uncommon word containing each vowel once (17-t)—*assistant-ship to the postmaster*

subternatural—longest well-mixed uncommon words with the same consonant order [isobutyronitrile] (16-t)—*less than natural*

successfully—most doubled letters for a common word (3-t)

successlessness—most doubled letters for an uncommon word (4-t)

succor—example of common homophonic contranyms [succor: aid & sucker: hoodwink]

succus—longest uncommon palindrome centered on letter c (6-t)—*juice*

sucker—see "succor"

superacknowledgements—uncommon word with the lowest ratio length to number of different letters for length 21 (1.31-t)

superacknowledgment—uncommon word with the lowest ratio length to number of different letters for length 19 (1.18-t)—*extreme recognition*

supercalifragilisticexpialidocious—example of a sesquipedalian word [see "Longest Word" article, page 106]—longest uncommon word that starts and ends with the same letter (34)—longest uncommon word that starts and ends with letter s (34)—most repeated letters for an uncommon word (10-t)—see "hystero-salpingo-oophorectomies"—*fantastic*

superequivalent—uncommon word containing most consecutive letters in the alphabet after letter p (7-t)—*identical in all possible ways*

supererogatory—longest alternating vowels and consonants for a common word (including y) (14-t)

superhelices—see "half islands"—*intertwined helices*

superinquisitive—uncommon word containing most consecutive letters in the alphabet after letter p (7-t)—*extremely curious*

superstitiously—common word with highest letter sum for length 15 (248-t)

supranasal—length five linkade with an uncommon word [supra & upran & prana & ranas & anasa & nasal] (10)—*above the nose*

swashbuckling—common word with the most infrequently used letters for length 13 (573)

sweaterdresses—longest uncommon word with typewriter letters from left hand (14-t)—*knitted dresses*

sweeswee—longest uncommon tautonym beginning with letter s (8)—*North American bird*

sweeswees—longest uncommon word containing all letters restricted to primes (9)

swelled-headednesses—longest   hyphenated three-cadence (6)—*egotisms*

sweltering—longest common progressive transdeletion [sweltering → wrestling → wresting → winters → strewn → wrest → west → wet → we → w] (10-t)

swims—longest common uppercase upside-down word (5)

swinging—longest nontrivial internal tautonym for a common word (6-t)

swoop—see "dooms"

symbolization—common word containing most consecutive letters in order after letter y (3-t)

synchronization—common word containing most consecutive letters in order after letter y (3-t)

synchronous clocks—longest phrase without ETAI (17)—*clocks synchronized to power lines*

synchronous transmission—see "asynchronous transmission"—*transmission of information at a fixed rate*

synonymously—common word containing the most repeats of letter y (3-t)—common word with highest letter sum for length 12 (217)

synonymy—common word containing the most repeats of letter y (3-t)—common word with highest letter sum for length 8 (150)

syrup of ipecac—longest and shortest phrase containing each vowel (including y) once in reverse order (13)—*emetic syrup*

syssel—see "scissel"—*governmental unit of Iceland*

systematization—longest common roller-coaster (15-t)

systemization—common word containing most consecutive letters in order after letter y (3-t)

T

t—longest common head 'n' tail centered on letter t (1)

taels—see "atles"—*Asian units of weight*

tales—see "atles"

talk—example of a word that contains silent letter l

tamin—see "ketamines"—*type of fabric*

tamine—see "ketamines"—*variant of tamin*

tang—see "gnat"

tangantangan—longest tautonym for an uncommon word (12-t)—longest uncommon tautonym beginning with letter t (12)—*castor-oil plant*

tangier—example of a word pronounced differently when capitalized, beginning with letter t [more tangy, city in Morocco]

tangiers—see "angriest"—*from the city of Tangier, Morocco*

taniers—see "anestri"—*plants with edible roots*

tank—see "brief"

tap—see "pat"

tapered—longest length three linkage with common words [tap & ape & per & ere & red] (7-t)

taramasalata—uncommon word containing the most repeats of letter a (6-t)—*Greek fish dish*

tarantara—longest uncommon head 'n' tail centered on letter n (9-t)—*sound of a trumpet*

tartar—longest common word with Morse code that is entirely dash-dots (6)—longest common tautonym beginning with letter t (6-t)

tasering—see "angriest"—*shocking with an electronic gun*

tass—see "demitasse"—*Scottish for cup*

tat—example of a word that exists only in an idiom, beginning with letter t [tit for tat]—longest common head 'n' tail centered on letter a (3-t)—shortest common word that starts and ends with letter t (3-t)

tates—see "prestates"—*locks of hair*

tathagatagarbhas—longest uncommon word containing one type of vowel for vowel a (16)—*essences of Buddhahood*

tat-tat-tat—highest ratio length to letters for a hyphenated non-tautonym (4.5)—highest ratio length to letters for a hyphenated word (4.5)—longest hyphenated palindrome beginning with letter t (9)—longest hyphenated palindrome centered on letter a (9)—longest vertical catoptron for a hyphenated word (9)—*sound of repeated knocking*

tattoo—longest common word containing one type of consonant for consonant t (6)

tau—shortest common word with last letter next in alphabet after first for letter t (3)

tavering—longest uncommon fixed offset shift pair that are reversals [tavering] [shift of 13] (8)—longest uncommon rot-13 pair that are reversals [tavering] (8)—*wandering or raving*

tea—see "ate"

teaette—closest to one million letter product for an uncommon word (1000000-t)—*holder for tea leaves*

teaettes—uncommon word with the most frequently used letters for length 8 (773)

teals—see "atles"—*bluish greens*

tearings—see "angriest"—*waterings of the eyes*

tea rings—see "angriest"—*coffeecakes*

tedious—example of a word that sounds like letters, beginning with letter t sound [TDS]

tee—common word with the most frequently used letters for length 3 (327)—longest common word where each letter is one symbol in Morse code (3)

teen—common word with the most frequently used letters for length 4 (395)

teene—uncommon word with the most frequently used letters for length 5 (513)—*injury*

teentsiest—uncommon word with the most frequently used letters for length 10 (899)—*tiniest*

teetee—uncommon word with the most frequently used letters for length 6 (654)—longest uncommon word where each letter is one symbol in Morse code (6)—*South American monkey*

teetered—common word with the most frequently used letters for length 8 (748)

teetertotter—uncommon word with the most frequently used letters for length 12 (1125)— longest uncommon word with typewriter letters from top row (12)—*seesaw*

teeter-tottered—hyphenated word with the most frequently used letters for length 14 (1277)— longest hyphenated word with a letter sum divisible by each letter (14)—*seesawed*

teeter-tottering—hyphenated word with the most frequently used letters for length 15 (1285)

teeter-totters—hyphenated word with the most frequently used letters for length 13 (1191)— *seesaws*

teethy—closest to two million letter product for an uncommon word (2000000)—*irritable*

teetotalers—common word with the most frequently used letters for length 11 (953)

telephone—longest common word in which changing one letter radically changes the pronunciation [telephone → telephony] (9-t)

telephony—see "telephone"—*electronic voice transmission*

temper—example of a self-antonym, beginning with letter t [harden steel, soften justice]

temperamentally—longest common snowball [t & em & per & amen & tally] (15)

tend—example of a false antonym beginning with letter t [intend]

tenet—common word with the most frequently used letters for length 5 (486-t)—longest common palindrome beginning with letter t (5)— longest common palindrome centered on letter n (5-t)

tennesseean—uncommon word with the most frequently used letters for length 11 (979)— *from the state of Tennessee*

tents—longest common onalosi [bents & tints & teats & tends & tenth] (5-t)

tepa—example of an acronym that has become uncapitalized, beginning with letter t [Tri-Ethylene Phosphor-Amide]—*South American tree*

terra—see "green"

terret—longest uncommon palindrome beginning with letter t (6-t)—*part of a harness*

tertius gaudet—see "doppler effect"—*third party who benefits from a dispute between others*

tes—see "prestates"—*letter t's*

tesla—see "atles"

tesseradecades—longest uncommon word with typewriter letters from left hand (14-t)—*periods of forty years*

testament-testamentar—longest nontrivial internal tautonym for a hyphenated word (18)— longest repeated prefix for a hyphenated word (18)—*a will appointing an executor*

testes—longest common tautonym beginning with letter t (6-t)

testosterone—common word with the most frequently used letters for length 12 (1043)

tete—uncommon word with the most frequently used letters for length 4 (418)—*tall wig*

tete-à-tete—hyphenated word with the most frequently used letters for length 9 (916)—longest hyphenated word containing one type of consonant for consonant t (9)—*private conversation between two people*

tete-à-tetes—hyphenated word with the most frequently used letters for length 10 (982)

tetes-à-tetes—hyphenated word with the most frequently used letters for length 11 (1048)— longest hyphenated head 'n' tail centered on letter a (11)

tetraacetates—uncommon word with the most frequently used letters for length 13 (1118)— *oxidizing agents*

tetrahydrocannabinol—common word with the lowest ratio length to number of different letters for length 20 (1.53)

tetranitroanilines—see "internationalities"— *explosives*

Crashing Word Lists

Lewis Carroll invented a form of wordplay that he called "Doublets," but which is usually called "Ladders" today, in which the object is to pick two words of the same length that are antonyms or at least contrasting pairs, and to find a list of words that link these two words. Each word in the list is to differ from the previous word by only one letter. Thus each word "crashes" with the next word in all but one position.

Here are some examples:

love – hate: love hove have hate

soup – nuts: soup noup nous nots nuts

slow – fast: slow slot slit flit fait fast

small – large: small stall stale stage suage surge sarge large

chaos – order: chaos ciaos cipos sipos sipes sides sider aider arder order

The amusement value (aside from trying to pursue a lot of options at once and exercising one's vocabulary) lies in finding that although the meanings of these words are worlds apart, the spelling draws them together.

The shortest possible ladder between two words has one more rung than there are letters that differ between the two words. For example, "love" and "hate" differ in three letters (L → H, O → A, V → T), and therefore the four-rung ladder given above is the shortest possible. "Soup" and "nuts" differ in all four letters, so the five-rung ladder given above also is the shortest possible. The ultimate challenge is to find such shortest ladders for all antonyms with the same length. The other examples given above are not minimal, and the reader is challenged to improve them.

Sometimes it is not possible to find a ladder that connects one word with another; for example, there is no way to transform "good" into "evil," which I guess is a good thing.

But just before the chasm between two words becomes infinite and uncrossable, it becomes as long as possible. Many wordplay explorers have tried to find the longest possible ladder. This is quite a challenge, for three reasons. First, the requirement that the two words be antonyms or even contrasting pairs is incredibly difficult to maintain, and is usually dropped. Second, the number of parallel paths that must be searched increases dramatically as the length of the ladder increases. Third, there is always the risk that your lexicon omits a word that will shorten your ladder.

With that said, the longest ladder of which I am aware spans the chasm between "install" and "puranas" and is 64 rungs long. Here it is: instill instils instals instars enstars ensears enseals unseals unheals unheads unleads unloads unlords uncords uncorks uncocks unlocks unlucks untucks untacks unpacks unparks unbarks unbares unbared unbaged uncaged uncages encages enrages earages parages panages manages manases mantses manties masties pasties pastils pastels pasters passers possers dossers dossels dossils dessils desoils resoils recoils recools recooks recorks records rewords rewards retards petards petaras pitaras pitayas pirayas piranas puranas.

Can anyone shorten this list, or find a longer one?

Since wordplay lovers are always looking for a new challenge, they have generalized the idea of lists of words that crash only with the next word in the list to the idea of words that crash with every other word in the list. This multiplies the challenge many times. The ultimate pinnacle on this peak is a list of words that crash with each other on the list in exactly one place.

For example, consider the following list of six five-letter words: sanes swipe waist tense tweet weeps. In this list, "sanes" crashes with "swipe" in the first "s" only, with "waist" in the second "a" only, with "tense" in the third "n" only, with "tweet" in the fourth "e" only, and with "weeps" in the last "s" only. What is more, this same pattern is true of every other word in the list. "Swipe" crashes with "waist" in the third "i" only, with "tense" in the last "e" only, with "tweet" in the second "w" only, and with "weeps" in the fourth "p" only. Such lists exhibit a "fearful symmetry."

The longest known list is the following list of eight seven-letter words: sorties slickly concord ternery tritone pensile pronked closens.

tetrasters—longest uncommon progressive letter subtraction [tetrasters → erasers → eases → ass → a] (10-t)—*abnormal embryos*

tha—see "thanatopsides"—*thee*

thanatopsides—longest length three linkade with an uncommon word [tha & han & ana & nat & ato & top & ops & psi & sid & ide & des] (13)

thanklessly—see "buckishly"—*without gratitude*

thar—see "cantharidates"—*Himalayan goat*

theetsees—uncommon word with the most frequently used letters for length 9 (835)—*Burmese trees*

their—example of a word spelled with e before i, beginning with letter t

theocracies—example of a word spelled with i before e after c, beginning with letter t

there's no love lost between them—longest phrase containing two types of vowels (27)

thermophosphorescences—longest uncommon word containing two types of vowels (22-t)—*glow caused by heating*

thorough—example of a common word with the most variably pronounced suffix [see "Pronunciation Variants" article, page 135]

though—example of a common word with the most variably pronounced suffix [see "Pronunciation Variants" article, page 135]

thoughts—longest one-syllable word beginning with letter t (8)

thrashes—longest common progressive delete letter from any position to form another word [thrashes → trashes → rashes → ashes → shes → hes → es → s] (8-t)

thricecocks—longest uncommon word with consecutive letters adjacent on phone keypad beginning with letter t (11-t)—*European thrushes*

throatstraps—longest two-syllable word beginning with letter t (12)—*parts of a bridle*

through—example of a common word with the most variably pronounced suffix [see "Pronunciation Variants" article, page 135]

through-and-through coal—longest roller-coaster for a hyphenated phrase (21)—*coal straight from the mine*

thrush fungus—longest phrase containing one type of vowel for vowel u (12-t)

thumbnails—longest common word with consecutive letters adjacent on phone keypad beginning with letter t (10-t)

thumbscrewing—see "poldavy"—*torturing*

thymomata—longest uncommon word spelled with vertical symmetry letters (9-t)—*tumor of the thymus*

tippit—longest uncommon palindrome beginning with letter t (6-t)—longest uncommon palindrome centered on letter p (6)—*gambling game*

tin ears—see "anestri"—*lacks of musical appreciation*

tirelessnesses—see "irelessnesses"

tit—longest common palindrome centered on letter i (3-t)—shortest common word that starts and ends with letter t (3-t)

titbits—longest common progressive letter subtraction [titbits → ibis → bs] (7-t)

tittle-tattle—hyphenated word containing the most repeats of letter t (6)—*small talk*

tiv—example of a plural that ends with letter v—*people of Nigeria*

tizzy—common word with highest letter sum for length 5 (106)

to—see "two"

tone—example of a common word formed by borrowing or lending letters to frequent companions, beginning with letter t [thet on → the tone]

tontiners—see "internationalised"—*participants in a mutual insurance arrangement*

to order—see "stop order"—*customized*

toot—longest common palindrome centered on letter o (4-t)—longest vertical catoptron for a common word (4)

tootsy-wootsy—longest hyphenated word containing letters from last half of alphabet (12)—*sweetheart*

topsyturviness—uncommon word with highest letter sum for length 14 (242)—*confusion*

topsy-turvydoms—hyphenated word with highest letter sum for length 14 (252)—*confusions*

tortonis—see "coadministrations"—*ice cream*

torturous—common word with highest letter sum for length 9 (167)—longest common word containing letters from last half of alphabet (9)

tot—longest common head 'n' tail centered on letter o (3-t)—shortest common word that starts and ends with letter t (3-t)

tother—example of an uncommon word formed by borrowing or lending letters to frequent companions, beginning with letter t [thet other → the tother]—*the other*

tough—example of an antonym of two different words, beginning with letter t [soft, weak]—example of a common word with the most variably pronounced suffix [see "Pronunciation Variants" article, page 135]

tow—example of a word that ends with silent letter w

traditionalist—longest common word that starts and ends with letter t (14)

transceiver—example of a portmanteau, beginning with letter t [transmitter, receiver]

transcripts—longest common word containing two vowels (11-t)

transformists—longest uncommon word with a phonetic spelling identical to its regular spelling (13)—*believers in evolution*

transliterations—longest well-mixed common transubstitution [transliterations → gastrointestinal] (16)

transmission electron microscopes—see "transmission electron microscopies"—longest well-mixed phrase with same letter sum [nicotinamide adenine dinucleotide phosphate] (40)—*powerful microscopes using electron beams*

transmission electron microscopies—longest phrase that can nontrivially delete letter from any position to form another word [transmission electron microscopies → transmission electron microscopes] (32)

transplants—longest common word containing one type of vowel for vowel a (11-t)—longest common word containing two vowels (11-t)

transubstantiationalist—longest uncommon word that starts and ends with letter t (23)—*believer that wine changes to blood during Eucharist*

treatment—longest common four-cadence (3-t)

trentonians—see "internationalised"—*from Trenton, New Jersey*

trentons—see "internationalised"—*objects from a certain geological period*

trinitrin—longest uncommon head 'n' tail centered on letter i (9)—*nitroglycerin*

trio—longest common progressive sum pair [trio → lax → my → l] (4-t)

triple blocks—longest phrase with consecutive letters adjacent on phone keypad beginning with letter t (12)—*pulleys with three loops*

trivialists—longest uncommon word with consecutive letters adjacent on phone keypad beginning with letter t (11-t)—*experts in trivia*

triviality—longest common word with consecutive letters adjacent on phone keypad beginning with letter t (10-t)

trollied—longest uncommon word with letters in reverse alphabetical order when allowing repeats (8-t)—*rode on a cart*

troubadour—example of a common multisyllabic American word ending "our" but pronounced like "or"

trough—example of a common word with the most variably pronounced suffix [see "Pronunciation Variants" article, page 135]

truelove—common word containing most consecutive letters in order after letter t (3-t)

trustworthiness—common word with highest letter sum for length 15 (248-t)

trustworthy—common word with highest letter sum for length 11 (207)

trusty—common word with highest letter sum for length 6 (123)

tryouts—common word with highest letter sum for length 7 (138)

tsetse—longest common tautonym beginning with letter t (6-t)

tsine—example of a word that is a confusing code for letter t [sign]—*Malay ox*

tsktsks—longest uncommon word containing all consonants (7)—*sound of scolding*

tsunami—example of a word that begins with silent letter t

tuck—longest common word with no subsequence that is a word (4-t)

tuffet—see "steeds"

tumultuous—common word containing the most repeats of letter u (4-t)—common word with highest letter sum for length 10 (183)

tumultuously—uncommon word with highest letter sum for length 12 (220)

turnover—common word containing most consecutive letters in order after letter t (3-t)

turn up trumps—longest phrase containing one type of vowel for vowel u (12-t)—*be unexpectedly helpful*

tut—longest common palindrome centered on letter u (3-t)—shortest common word that starts and ends with letter t (3-t)

tuzz—uncommon word with highest letter sum for length 4 (93)—*tuft*

tuzzy-muzzies—hyphenated word with highest letter sum for length 12 (237)

tuzzy-muzzy—hyphenated word with highest letter sum for length 10 (229)—*garland of flowers*

twain—see "dough"

twitched—example of a word that contains silent letter e

two—example of homophones differing by letter w [to]—example of a word that contains silent letter w

tylenchulus—longest uncommon word with consecutive letters adjacent on phone keypad beginning with letter t (11-t)—*type of worm*

typewriter—longest common word with typewriter letters from top row (10-t)

typey—closest to one million letter product for an uncommon word (1000000-t)—*individual that defines a breed*

U

u—longest common palindrome beginning with letter u (1)—longest common word containing all vowels (1-t)

ua mau ke ea o ka aina i ka pono—highest vowels minus consonants for a phrase (9)—*Hawaiian motto "The life of the land is perpetuated in righteousness"*

uang—example of a word that is a confusing code for letter u [wang]—*rhinoceros beetle*

ugly—shortest stingy and hostile common word (4-t)

uku—shortest uncommon word that starts and ends with letter u (3-t)—*Hawaiian fish*

ulaula—longest uncommon tautonym beginning with letter u (6)—*type of fish*

ulu—shortest uncommon word that starts and ends with letter u (3-t)—*Eskimo knife*

ululu—longest uncommon palindrome beginning with letter u (5)—longest uncommon palindrome centered on letter u (5-t)—*wailing cry*

umbrage—example of a word that exists only in an idiom, beginning with letter u [take umbrage at]

umphs—longest one-syllable word beginning with letter u (5)—*enthusiasms*

umpire—example of a common word formed by borrowing or lending letters to frequent companions, beginning with letter u [a noumpere → an oumpere]

umpteen—example of a portmanteau, beginning with letter u [umpty, -teen]

unbending—example of a self-antonym, beginning with letter u [rigid, relaxing]

unchristian—longest common word with consecutive letters adjacent on phone keypad beginning with letter u (11)

unchristianlike—longest uncommon word with consecutive letters adjacent on phone keypad beginning with letter u (15)

uncomplementarinesses—longest uncommon homophones [uncomplementarinesses → uncomplimentarinesses] (21)

uncomplimentarinesses—see "uncomplementarinesses"

uncomplimentary—longest common word containing each vowel (including y) once (15)

uncompromisingly—longest common word without ETA (16)

unconscientiousnesses—longest uncommon word containing four types of consonants (21)

unconsciousness—longest common word containing three types of consonants (15-t)

unconventionally—longest common word with balanced letter sum (16-t)

uncopyrightable—longest uncommon isogram (15-t)—*not copyrightable*

underplay—see "plunder"

understudy—common word with most consecutive alphabetic letters in order consecutively (4-t)

ungossiping—longest uncommon well-mixed isotel pair [uninspiring] (11-t)

unimmigrating—longest uncommon double progressive beheadment [unimmigrating → immigrating → migrating → grating → ating → ing → g] (13-t)—*not moving from a foreign country*

uninspiring—see "ungossiping"

union—longest common word containing one type of consonant for consonant n (5-t)

universal—example of an antonym of two different words, beginning with letter u [parochial, particular]

unloosen—see "loosen"

unostentatiousnesses—longest uncommon word containing three types of consonants (20)

unprosperousnesses—longest uncommon polygram (18)

unravel—see "ravel"

unscientific—example of a word spelled with i before e after c, beginning with letter u

unscrupulous—common word containing the most repeats of letter u (4-t)

unscrupulously—common word with the most infrequently used letters for length 14 (624)—longest common word without ETAI (14)

unstretched—longest two-syllable word beginning with letter u (11)

unsuccessfully—most doubled letters for a common word (3-t)

unswerving—common word containing most consecutive letters in the alphabet after letter u (3-t)

untrustworthily—uncommon word with highest letter sum for length 15 (263)—*betraying trust*

untrustworthy—uncommon word with highest letter sum for length 13 (242)—*not worthy of trust*

untruthful—longest common word containing one type of vowel for vowel u (10-t)

upon—shortest common isolano (4-t)

upraiser—see "upraisers"—*something that lifts*

upraisers—longest uncommon alternating terminal elision [upraisers → upraiser → praiser → praise → raise → rais → ais → ai → i] (9-t)

upran—see "supranasal"—*up ran*

ur—see "aer"—*expression of hesitation*

ureic—example of a word spelled with e before i, beginning with letter u—*related to urea*

urgently—longest Morse code reversal pair with common words [maintenance] (11-t)

ursigram—example of an acronym that has become uncapitalized, beginning with letter u [Union Radiophonique Scientifique Internationale -GRAM]—*scientific data transmission*

us—see "as"

ushabtiu—longest uncommon word that starts and ends with letter u (8)—*Egyptian tomb figure*

ushers—shortest common word containing the most pronouns [us & she & he & her & hers] (5)

ushabtiu

utu—shortest uncommon word that starts and ends with letter u (3-t)—*Sumerian god*

V

v—longest common palindrome beginning with letter v (1)—longest common word with typewriter letters from bottom row (1-t)

vale—example of a word that exists only in an idiom, beginning with letter v [vale of tears]

valenciennes—example of a word spelled with i before e after c, beginning with letter v—*lace*

valuable—example of a false antonym beginning with letter v [invaluable]

valval—longest uncommon tautonym beginning with letter v (6-t)—*valve-like*

various—example of an antonym of two different words, beginning with letter v [uniform, many]

vasa—example of a plural that ends with letter a—*ducts*

vasoconstriction—longest common word with balanced letter sum (16-t)

vav—longest uncommon palindrome beginning with letter v (3)—longest uncommon word that starts and ends with letter v (3)—shortest uncommon word that starts and ends with letter v (3)—*sixth Hebrew letter*

veneer—example of a word that sounds like letters, beginning with letter v sound [VNER]

ventriculography—uncommon word with the lowest ratio length to number of different letters for length 16 (1.06-t)—*graph of heart activity*

ventriloquist—common word containing most consecutive letters in the alphabet after letter q (6)

verein—example of a word spelled with e before i, beginning with letter v—*social organization*

verisimilitude—longest alternating vowels and consonants for a common word (14-t)

vernacular—example of a self-antonym, beginning with letter v [nonstandard speech, standard speech]

versesmiths—longest two-syllable word beginning with letter v (11)—*poets*

verve—longest common head 'n' tail centered on letter r (5)

verver—longest uncommon tautonym beginning with letter v (6-t)—*voodoo sign*

victoria—longest common word spelled with two-letter U.S. postal codes (8-t)

vidicon—example of an acronym that has become uncapitalized, beginning with letter v [VIDeo + ICONoscope]—*camera tube*

view—common word containing most consecutive letters in order after letter v (2-t)

viewpoint—common word containing most consecutive letters in order after letter v (2-t)

virulently—longest common word with consecutive letters adjacent on phone keypad beginning with letter v (10-t)

viscount—example of a word that contains silent letter s—*son or younger brother of a count*

visibilities—longest common two-cadence (5-t)

visibility—longest common word with consecutive letters adjacent on phone keypad beginning with letter v (10-t)

vital—example of a word pronounced differently when capitalized, beginning with letter v [essential, Palestinian author]

viva—longest common word containing one type of consonant for consonant v (4)

volleyball—common word containing the most repeats of letter l (4-t)

volumeter—example of a portmanteau, beginning with letter v [volume, -meter]—*volume-measuring instrument*

vouched—longest one-syllable word beginning with letter v (7)—*guaranteed*

vow—shortest common word with last letter next in alphabet after first for letter v (3)

vozhds—see "qwerty"—*Russian leaders*

vrow—example of a word that is a confusing code for letter v [fro]—*Dutch or Afrikaner woman*

vugh—see "waqf"—*hole in rock lined with different material*

W

w—shortest three-syllable word (1)

waf—see "waff"—*woman in the air force*

waff—example of homophones differing by letter f [waf]—*wave*

wagger-pagger-bagger—hyphenated word containing the most repeats of letter g (6)—*trash can*

waive—example of homophones differing by letter i [wave]

waiwai—longest uncommon word containing one type of consonant for consonant w (6-t)—*natives of South America*

wallawalla—longest uncommon tautonym beginning with letter w (10)—*natives of the Pacific Northwest*

waqf—uncommon word that is part of a pangram using the fewest letters [jynx & speltz & vugh & mockbird]—*Islamic endowment*

wardencies—example of a word spelled with i before e after c, beginning with letter w—*powers of someone in charge*

warders—see "redrawn"

wattage—see "regatta"

wave—see "waive"

wax—shortest common word with last letter next in alphabet after first for letter w (3)

waxy—common word containing most consecutive letters in order after letter w (3)—common word containing most consecutive letters in the alphabet after letter w (3-t)—shortest common word that cannot have a letter added and transposed to form another word (4-t)

waxy maize—phrase containing most consecutive letters in order after letter w (4)—phrase containing most consecutive letters in the alphabet after letter w (5)—*Indian corn*

weather—example of a self-antonym, beginning with letter w [withstand a storm, wear away]

weave—example of a false antonym beginning with letter w [inweave]

wee—longest common word containing one type of consonant for consonant w (3-t)

weewee—longest uncommon word containing one type of consonant for consonant w (6-t)—*urine*

weigh—longest common word containing letters in order from typewriter (5-t)

weird—example of a word spelled with e before i, beginning with letter w

welkin—example of a word that exists only in an idiom, beginning with letter w [make the welkin ring]—*celestial sphere*

well—example of an antonym of two different words, beginning with letter w [ill, badly]

wer—see "blowers"—*value of a person in Medieval law*

wers—see "blowers"

western diamondback rattlesnake—see "eastern diamondback rattlesnake"

wettish—longest uncommon word containing letters in order from typewriter (7-t)—*moist*

western diamondback rattlesnake

wheelbarrow—longest common word that starts and ends with letter w (11)

wherethrough—longest two-syllable word beginning with letter w (12)—*through which*

whippersnapper—common word containing the most repeats of letter p (4)

who—see "ohm"

wibbly-wobbly—hyphenated word with the most infrequently used letters for length 12 (380)—*unsteady*

wids—see "oriel"—*variant of woods*

wiliwili—see "corocoro"—*Hawaiian tree*

willfully—common word containing the most repeats of letter l (4-t)

winter-fallow—longest hyphenated word that starts and ends with letter w (12)—*fallow in the winter*

wireless—example of a word that sounds like letters, beginning with letter y sound [YRLS]

wirelessnesses—see "irelessnesses"

wis—example of an uncommon word formed by borrowing or lending letters to frequent companions, beginning with letter w [iwis → i wis]—*know*

wistful—example of a portmanteau, beginning with letter w [wistly, wishful]

witchcraft—longest consonant string for a common word (5-t)

wizard—longest common equidistant word (6-t)

wob—see "dowts"—*variant of web*

woken—longest common word with consecutive letters adjacent on phone keypad beginning with letter w (5-t)

wolvishly—longest uncommon word with consecutive letters adjacent on phone keypad beginning with letter w (9)—*like a wolf*

woo—longest common word containing one type of consonant for consonant w (3-t)

woodwork—longest common word where each letter is three symbols in Morse code (8-t)

woodworks—longest uncommon word where each letter is three symbols in Morse code (9-t)

wordiness—see "worldliness"

worldliness—longest letter subtraction with common words [worldliness → wordiness] (11-t)

worms—example of a word pronounced differently when capitalized, beginning with letter w [invertebrates, German city]

worst of both worlds—longest phrase containing one type of vowel for vowel o (17)

worthwhile—longest consonant string for a common word (5-t)

would—longest common word with consecutive letters adjacent on phone keypad beginning with letter w (5-t)

wound—longest common word with consecutive letters adjacent on phone keypad beginning with letter w (5-t)

wow—longest common head 'n' tail centered on letter o (3-t)—longest common palindrome beginning with letter w (3)—longest common word containing one type of consonant for consonant w (3-t)—shortest common word that starts and ends with letter w (3)—see "mom"

wow-wow—longest hyphenated palindrome beginning with letter w (6)—hyphenated word containing the most repeats of letter w (4)—*Indonesian gibbon*

wrap—example of a word that is a confusing code for letter w [rap]

wreathed—longest one-syllable word beginning with letter w (8)

wreckless—see "reckless"—*without crashing*

write—example of a word that begins with silent letter w

wronged—longest common word with letters in reverse alphabetical order (7)—longest common word with letters in reverse alphabetical order when allowing repeats (7-t)

wry—common word with highest letter sum for length 3 (66)

wy—uncommon word with highest letter sum for length 2 (48)—*letter y*

wysiwyg—example of an acronym that has become uncapitalized, beginning with letter w [What You See Is What You Get]—longest acronym that has become an uncapitalized word for an uncommon word (7)—*looking like the final printed output*

X

x—example of an antonym of two different words, beginning with letter x [select, unselect]—example of a self-antonym, beginning with letter x [select, deselect]—longest common head 'n' tail centered on letter x (1)—longest common palindrome beginning with letter x (1)—longest common word with typewriter letters from bottom row (1-t)—longest common word with consecutive letters adjacent on phone keypad beginning with letter x (1)

xanthines—longest two-syllable word beginning with letter x (9)—*chemicals that oxidize to form uric acid*

xeriscape—example of a portmanteau, beginning with letter x [xeric, landscape]—*dry landscape*

xerography—shortest common word with last letter next in alphabet after first for letter x (10)

xerophagy—example of a word that sounds like letters, beginning with letter z sound [ZRFAG]—*Christian fast*

xerox—common word containing the most repeats of letter x (2)—longest and shortest common word that starts and ends with letter x (5)

xhosa—example of an uncommon word in which adding letters to beginning makes it plural [xhosa → amaxhosa]—*Bantu language*

xi—example of a word pronounced differently when capitalized, beginning with letter x [Greek letter, river in China]

xoana—longest uncommon word with consecutive letters adjacent on phone keypad beginning with letter x (5)—*wood carvings*

x-ray—shortest hyphenated word with last letter next in alphabet after first for letter x (4)—*high energy light*

xurel—example of a word that is a confusing code for letter x [jurel]—*tropical fish*

x virus—longest phrase with consecutive letters adjacent on phone keypad beginning with letter x (6)—*latent virus*

xylary—shortest uncommon word with last letter next in alphabet after first for letter x (6)—*woody*

xylindein—example of a word spelled with e before i, beginning with letter x—*yellow-brown dye*

xyloglyphy—uncommon word with the most infrequently used letters for length 10 (319)—*wood carving*

xylomancies—example of a word spelled with i before e after c, beginning with letter x—*divination with wood*

xysts—longest one-syllable word beginning with letter x (5)—*xystus*

xystus—uncommon word with highest letter sum for length 6 (128)—*Greek portico*

Y

y—longest common palindrome beginning with letter y (1)

yabber-yabber—longest hyphenated tautonym beginning with letter y (12)—*jabber*

yada-yada-yada—longest hyphenated word containing all letters restricted to squares (12)—*and so on*

yankeeism—example of a word spelled with e before i, beginning with letter y—*North Americanism*

yaray—longest uncommon palindrome beginning with letter y (5)—*Puerto Rican palm*

yariyari—longest uncommon tautonym beginning with letter y (8)—*lancewoods*

yay—shortest uncommon word that starts and ends with letter y (3)—*dialect of Tai*

ye—example of a word that is a confusing code for letter y [the]

yean—example of a word that begins with silent letter y—*bear young*

yearned—longest one-syllable word beginning with letter y (7)

yen—example of a word that exists only in an idiom, beginning with letter y [have a yen for]

yesterday—longest common word that starts and ends with letter y (9)

yez—shortest uncommon word with last letter next in alphabet after first for letter y (3)—*you*

yield—example of an antonym of two different words, beginning with letter y [keep, withstand]

yieldability—longest uncommon word that starts and ends with letter y (12)—*ability to yield*

Yinglish—example of a portmanteau, beginning with letter y [Yiddish, English]—*English with many Yiddish words*

yokelish—longest uncommon word with consecutive letters adjacent on phone keypad beginning with letter y (8)—*unrefined*

yokels—longest common word with consecutive letters adjacent on phone keypad beginning with letter y (6)

yourselves—longest two-syllable word beginning with letter y (10)

you scratch my back and I'll scratch yours—longest phrase without E (34)—*if you do something for me, I'll do something for you*

ys—see "as"

yuk—example of a self-antonym, beginning with letter y [express pleasant surprise, express unpleasant surprise]

yummy—shortest common word that starts and ends with letter y (5)

yuppie—example of an acronym that has become uncapitalized, beginning with letter y [Young Urban Professional + -PIE]

yurt—common word with highest letter sum for length 4 (84)

Z

z—longest common head 'n' tail centered on letter z (1)—longest common palindrome beginning with letter z (1)—longest common palindrome centered on letter z (1)—longest common word with typewriter letters from bottom row (1-t)

zabra—example of a word that is a confusing code for letter z [sabra]—*small Spanish frigate*

zamia—example of an uncommon word formed by borrowing or lending letters to frequent companions, beginning with letter z [azaniae → a zaniae]—*palmlike plant*

zea—shortest uncommon word with last letter next in alphabet after first for letter z (3-t)—*indian corn*

zeitgeist—example of a word spelled with e before i, beginning with letter z—*spirit of the times*

zeitgeists—longest two-syllable word beginning with letter z (10)

zemi—example of a word pronounced differently when capitalized, beginning with letter z [West Indian fetish, Naga people]

zero—example of an antonym of two different words, beginning with letter z [infinite, entity]

zero-zero—longest hyphenated tautonym beginning with letter z (8)—*weather with zero ceiling and zero visibility*

zeta—shortest common word with last letter next in alphabet after first for letter z (4)

zia—shortest uncommon word with last letter next in alphabet after first for letter z (3-t)—*native people of northern New Mexico*

zigzagging—common word containing the most repeats of letter g (4-t)—common word with the most infrequently used letters for length 10 (374-t)

zillionaire—example of a portmanteau, beginning with letter z [zillion, millionaire]—*multimillionaire*

zincier—example of a word spelled with i before e after c, beginning with letter z—*more zinc-like*

zing—example of a self-antonym, beginning with letter z [improve, criticize]

zip—example of an acronym that has become uncapitalized, beginning with letter z [Zone Improvement Plan]

ziz—longest uncommon palindrome beginning with letter z (3-t)—shortest uncommon word that starts and ends with letter z (3-t)—*sleep*

zizz—longest uncommon word that starts and ends with letter z (4)—*sleep*

zoa—shortest uncommon word with last letter next in alphabet after first for letter z (3-t)—*all offspring of one egg*

zooeae—longest uncommon word containing one type of consonant for consonant z (6-t)—*larvae of crabs and relatives*

zoot—example of a word that exists only in an idiom, beginning with letter z [zoot suit]—*suit with extreme tapering from padded shoulders to narrow cuffs*

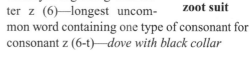

zoot suit

zoozoo—longest uncommon tautonym beginning with letter z (6)—longest uncommon word containing one type of consonant for consonant z (6-t)—*dove with black collar*

zorotypus—uncommon word with highest letter sum for length 9 (175)—*small wingless insects related to lice*

zouaves—longest one-syllable word beginning with letter z (7)—*French Algerian soldiers with colorful uniforms and special drills*

zs—common word with highest letter sum for length 2 (45)

zuz—uncommon word with highest letter sum for length 3 (73)—uncommon word with the most infrequently used letters for length 3 (33)—longest uncommon palindrome beginning with letter z (3-t)—shortest uncommon word that starts and ends with letter z (3-t)—*ancient Palestinian coin*

zu-zu—hyphenated word with highest letter sum for length 4 (94)—*member of regiment in U.S. Civil War that dressed and drilled like the Zouave unit of French Algerian soldiers*

zu-zus—hyphenated word with highest letter sum for length 5 (113)

zygophyllums—uncommon word with the most infrequently used letters for length 12 (421)—*bean capers*

zyzzyva—uncommon word with highest letter sum for length 7 (151)—uncommon word with the most infrequently used letters for length 7 (134)—*tropical American weevil*

zyzzyvas—uncommon word with highest letter sum for length 8 (170)

INDEX

ABOUT THE AUTHOR

Chris Cole has been a lifelong fan of puzzles, collecting puzzle books from a young age. As an early user of the Internet in the 1970s, Cole actively participated in the puzzles newsgroup and eventually became the editor of its archive. It was here that he met other puzzlers and became a reader of and later a contributor to *Word Ways, The Journal of Recreational Linguistics* (www.wordways.com) and a member of the National Puzzlers' League (www.puzzlers.org), the world's oldest wordplay organization.

Cole studied physics and philosophy at Harvard University and did graduate work at Caltech in particle physics with Richard Feynman. Afterward, he became a software entrepreneur, and was involved in the creation of the symbolic algebra system *Mathematica* (www.mathematica.com), the network management company Peregrine Systems (www.peregrine.com), and the Internet virtual reality company Worlds, Inc. (www.worlds.net).

Cole is a researcher into artificial intelligence and natural language processing. As part of this research, Cole has been accumulating a large linguistic database. One of the ways to test the completeness of this database is to see if the best known word records can be derived from it. Hence, this book was born.

Cole has been able to indulge his twin passions for reference books and Disney by helping *Encyclopedia Britannica* (www.eb.com) and the Walt Disney Company (www.disney.com) to "go online." He also created both the CD-ROM and online versions of the Merriam-Webster dictionaries (www.m-w.com). Most recently, he has started up four companies in the emerging field of online communities and entertainment. They don't have Web pages yet.

Cole makes his home in Newport Beach, California, and has been married for over 20 years to Joan. Their two children, Wyatt (age 10) and Chloe (age 7), enjoy bragging that their father works for Disney. Their hobbies include anything that a family can do together, especially sports and traveling. And, of course, puzzles. Correspondence concerning this book is welcome at wordplay@questrel.com.